9,26

9 7

Essay Index

SIX FAMOUS LIVING POETS

Photo
Elliott & Fry

SIX FAMOUS LIVING POETS

POETS

Introductory Studies, illustrated by
Quotation and Comment

BY

COULSON KERNAHAN

Essay Index Reprint Series

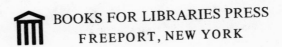

BOOKS FOR LIBRARIES PRESS
FREEPORT, NEW YORK

First Published 1922
Reprinted 1968

LIBRARY OF CONGRESS CATALOG CARD NUMBER:
68-8475

PRINTED IN THE UNITED STATES OF AMERICA

Contents

To
FLORA KLICKMANN

(A DEDICATION, A FOREWORD, AND AN ACKNOWLEDGMENT.)

DEAR MISS KLICKMANN,

You bade me pen these appreciations, and you read each as written. When you thought I had done well, you said so more than generously, thereby heartening me, in later chapters, to do my best. When you thought I had done less well, or ill, you said so as frankly, thereby inducing me to strike out what was worst. As to you I owe not only the book's inception, but much invaluable criticism, will you accept the Dedication? If any chapter, or section of a chapter gave you, in the reading, half as much pleasure as I found in " The Flower-Patch among the Hills," " Between the Larch Woods and the Weir," and " The Trail of the Ragged Robin," I am content.

As you can confirm what I say, may I add—though for other eyes than yours—that " criticism," in any scholarly or academic sense, these articles never set out to be. They are no more than Introductory Studies for the general reader, and penned, admittedly, from a personal standpoint. Rambling, discursive and gossipy as they are, my hope is that they are not altogether without freshness of outlook and illustration ; for though I confess to taking pleasure only in appreciation, and none in depreciation, I have not for that reason refrained from indicating what seems to me—wrongly perhaps, but at least sincerely and outspokenly—an occasional defect or weakness in the poems under consideration. But the intention of the book is to set the work of each poet in so attractive a light as to send my readers to study for themselves all that he has written.

Were it not so, I should not have ventured to ask permission to quote so widely. As one of the publishers concerned (unknown to me personally) wrote, at the time, after reading the appreciation,

9

" We have every reason to give you permission, for your quotations stimulate interest, without detracting from the book, and so we have cause for satisfaction, rather than complaint."

In gratefully acknowledging, first to the six poets, permission to quote what is printed in this volume, I ought to add that the order in which their names appear was chosen only for sake of contrast. Taking those names as they appear in the book, I have to express to Messrs. Sidgwick & Jackson, and to Mr. Sidney Pawling, of Messrs. Heinemann, as publishers of Mr. Masefield; to Messrs. Macmillan & Co., as publishers of Mr. Kipling; to Mr. John Murray, as publisher of Sir Henry Newbolt; to Mr. Martin Secker, Mr. B. H. Blackwell, of Oxford, and Mr. John Lane, as publishers of the Hon. Maurice Baring; to Messrs. William Blackwood & Sons, as publishers of Mr. Noyes; and again to Messrs. Sidgwick & Jackson, as publishers of Mr. Drinkwater, the heartiest possible thanks for their kindness, courtesy, and generosity in so readily according the necessary permission.

With one poet, at least, I am conscious I have dealt inadequately. When these articles were planned, the length of each was to be about 3,000 words. That on Sir Henry Newbolt was the first to be written and published in serial form. It brought so many appreciative letters to the Editor that I was asked to make the succeeding articles longer—was in fact given a free hand. Perhaps I ought to have rewritten the article on Sir Henry Newbolt. But, penned as it was when my mind was full of the subject, I feared that any freshness which the appreciation may chance to have, would be lost in rewriting. There remains only to add that my title does not imply that I have written of the six most famous living poets—there are of course others as famous—but only of six representative men whose work I happen to know well.

Sincerely yours,

COULSON KERNAHAN.

" Frognal,"
Fairlight, Hastings.

John Masefield

John Masefield

IN one of his sonnets, Mr. Masefield writes of

"Eternal beauty's everlasting rose
Which casts this world as shadow as it goes,"

and in another he likens roses to

"Those blood drops from the burning heart of June."

I wish that, in that flowering and lovely colour-poem, *The Daffodil Fields*, he had spared us blood-drips from the colder, if kindling heart of March. As a sun which rises in dawn's own daffodil-gold, to set in crimson over a corpse-strewn battlefield, so a poem which opens with the promise of young love, ends in a welter of murder. To kill off all three of his characters—two by a ghastly double-murder which leaves his loved daffodils bedraggled in gore, and causes the death of the third character —is somewhat cruelly to wring the heart of his reader. If I may use a word coined by a girl-friend of mine who runs a magazine in manuscript, I should say that the end of *The Daffodil Fields* is unduly "tragerous," and all the more so for the fact that it has passages of tranquil beauty.

In lines with such picture-making adjectives as (he is writing of an old woman)—

"The tears ran down
Her worn, *blood-threaded* cheeks and splashed upon her gown,"

or—

"When the *peaked* lawyer entered like a gnome,"

Mr. Masefield may do no more than silhouette a

13

character or a type ; but when he writes of " the *birded* dawn," or of " When the light *gentles*," he uses, first an adjective and then a verb, freshly and finely.   In imagery, *The Daffodil Fields* abounds, as for instance :

> " Then a vast breathing silence took the plain,
> The moon was like a soul within the brain
> Of the great sleeping world,"

or—

> " Smoke, like the house's breathing, floated, sighed ;
> Among the trembling firs strange ways it took,"

and—

> " June's very breast was bare this night of nights."

Though he is a poet and a beauty-worshipper, not Apollo nor Venus stands most often at John Masefield's side, to guide his pen, but Fate.   His *dramatis personæ* are many, but in every play which he stages, Fate is cast for a controlling, if unseen, part.   Had Fate, in whom Mr. Masefield's faith is so steadfast, ordained that he should be born a proseman, he might have taken place with the great descriptive writers.   Genius he has as a poet, but I am not sure that his genius is not sometimes more nearly allied to that of great journalism.

" It has been given to Mr. Masefield," writes Miss Sturgeon in the new and enlarged edition of her *Studies of Contemporary Poets* (Harrap) " to lure the multitudinous reader of magazines—that wary host which is usually stampeded by the sight of a page of verse."

Miss Sturgeon presumably refers to the fact that Mr. Masefield's four most popular poems, *The Everlasting Mercy*, *The Widow in the Bye Street*, *The Daffodil Fields*, and *Dauber*, appeared first in the pages of the *English Review*.   Their popularity I attribute in no small measure to the fact that each of the four has the story to tell so beloved of magazine readers.   Were the narratives in prose, and were they judged by the plot, one would have to admit that they are not without the sensational element associated with "Shockers." The hero of *Dauber* comes to a tragic and violent end. In *The Daffodil Fields* the two lovers of the same woman kill each other, and she falls dead on the body of the man of her choice. In *The Widow in the Bye Street* the story of an illicit love, a murder, a trial, and an execution is told with realism and dramatic power. Nor is *The Everlasting Mercy* lacking in sensation. It begins with a prize fight. Then comes a drunken debauch, a false alarm of fire, raised in a semi-alcoholic semi-religious mania, under the influence of which he has stripped himself naked, by a man called Saul Kane, of whose conversion to Christianity the poem thereafter tells.

Had the four poems in question been classical in subject, as, for instance, Mr. Maurice Baring's *Proserpine*, or historical, as in the case of Mr. Noyes's *Drake*, instead of being in a sense up-to-date novelettes in verse more nearly resembling great narrative poems than great poetry, I question whether they would have thus caught the public ear.

Whyte Melville, or even Nat Gould, if endowed with genius akin to that of John Masefield, might have written *Reynard the Fox* or *Right Royal*, the one a racing, the other a sporting novelette transfigured into a poem, and with such skill, strength and beauty as to make of *Reynard the Fox* a little Odyssey of fox hunting, of *Right Royal* a brief Iliad of the race-course.

The Widow in the Bye Street

Of Mr. Masefield's plays I am not here writing, but only of his poems, of which twelve volumes stand upon my shelf. I begin with *The Widow in the Bye Street*.

This story of " the only son of his mother and she was a widow " is a great achievement in tragic art, a masterpiece of compression.   Within less than a hundred pages, the story, not of one, but of four tragic souls—of the widow, of her son, of the woman whose harlot-wiles wrought his ruin, and of that woman's paramour, whom, in a moment of mad passion, the boy killed—is told without the omission of a single essential detail.

Pitifully poor, the widow had, for her boy's sake, starved, toiled (she was a seamstress) till her eyes were red and bleared, and nothing of womanly comeliness remained.   Mother and son were, however, all in all to each other, and she was happy, though haunted ever by the thought of the time—

" When the new wife would break up the old home."

Mr. Masefield holds that all is decreed by Fate. The fatalistic note is struck so early in the poem as page 4 :

" And all the time fate had his end prepared."

Fate, in the person of the woman, Anna, soon comes upon the scene :

" Lovely to look on when the wits were drowned.

.   .   .   .   .   .

Her smile, her voice, her face, were all temptation,
All subtle flies to trouble man, the trout ;
Man to entice, entrap, entangle, flout, . . .
To take and spoil, and then to cast aside :
Gain without giving was the craft she plied."

For her own base ends, Anna sets herself (an easy task to a beautiful woman, whose dupe is an ignorant boy, inflammable of passion, and to whom the world has thus far held only one woman, his mother) to win his love away from that mother and to herself.   Section I of the poem ends on the fatalistic note :

> " So the four souls are ranged, the chess-board set,
> The dark, invisible hand of secret Fate
> Brought it to come to being that they met
> After so many years of lying in wait.
> While we least think it, he prepares his Mate."

Then the boy's mother makes a false move in the
tragedy which Mr. Masefield likens to a game of
chess :

> " Life can be bitter to the very bone
> When one is poor, and woman, and alone."

One week-end her son brings home no money, having
spent his wages in buying jewellery for Anna, dis-
covering which, and seeing the two together, the
mother denounces the object of his infatuation to
the boy, and by the most degrading of all names
which can be applied to a woman. It is, as I say, a
false move, for all that there is of chivalry in the
lad awakens in defence of Anna, whom he champions
against his mother. From denunciation the mother
passes into an hysterical and pitiful appeal, described
by Mr. Masefield in a stanza the last line of which
must surely wring every reader's heart :

> "' Jimmy, I won't say more. I know you think
> That I don't know, being just a withered old
> With chaps all fallen in and eyes that blink,
> And hands that tremble so they cannot hold,
> A bag of bones to put in churchyard mould,
> A red-eyed hag beside your evening star.'
> And Jimmy gulped, and thought, ' By God, you are.' "

To many readers that last line will seem the most
tragic in the book, not only because one has infinite
pity for the mother and none for Anna or for her
paramour Ern, but because the tragedy is of the
soul, not of outward happenings. Thus, even the
mad killing of Ern by the boy, and the expiation
of the crime on the scaffold, seem less terrible than
the mother's heartbreak.

B

Mr. Masefield's Psychology

Only on one point do I question Mr. Masefield's psychology. The poem would, I think, be even more greatly tragic and more greatly human had he drawn Anna as less heartless and inhuman. She had had a child of her own of whom, as the phrase goes, she had " got rid." Mr. Masefield shows her as communing with herself and saying :

> " I only turned the blanket with my hand.
> It didn't hurt, he died, as I had planned—
> A little skinny creature, weak and red ;
> It looked so peaceful after it was dead."

The brutality of this seems to me unnecessary, not only because the poem would in no way be weakened were Anna shown with some redeeming feature, but because, even of so abandoned a woman, one finds it hard to believe that she could so speak and feel about the poor little child, done to death by her own hand.

One evening—

> " Bells came in swoons, for it was Sunday night "—

the boy meets Anna with Ern, and is instantly insanely jealous. He spies on them ; discovers the relations on which they are ; there is a " scene " ; and Ern, egged on by Anna, strikes him :

> " Jimmy went down and out : ' The kid,' said Ern.
> ' A kid, a sucking puppy ; hold the light.'
> And Anna smiled : ' It gave me such a turn,
> You look so splendid, Ernie, when you fight.'
> She looked at Jim with : ' Ern, is he all right ? '
> ' He's coming to.' She shuddered, ' Pah, the brute,
> What things he said ' ; she stirred him with her foot.'

Mr. Masefield—no " minor " poet—seems to me the most Shakespearean of his contemporaries. I am not, of course, comparing the one with the other, but that Shakespeare is the master upon whom he

has modelled himself, and something of whose robust-
ness, as well of whose tenderness, he shares, is evident.
His sonnets are very Shakespearean, and just as,
into the last line of a sonnet, Shakespeare, as it
were, threw all his weight, so not seldom John
Masefield reserves his strength for the last line of
one of his seven-line stanzas. Often his last line
stains the printed page as if with his own heart's
blood. I have already instanced the terrible last
line :

> " And Jimmy gulped and thought, ' By God, you are ; ' "

and the last line of the stanza just quoted, in which
we see Anna thrust with contemptuous foot at the
unconscious form of the lad who had loved her too
well, not only bites into the paper like acid, but
burns itself upon the reader's memory. None the
less, I say again that Anna would be truer to life
were she shown as not altogether without some spark
of womanhood, among the ashes of a dead soul.

The Tragedy

The next scene in the drama is that of Ern and
Anna as lovers in the latter's cottage :

> " And in the dim the lovers went upstairs,
>   Her eyes fast closed, the shepherd's burning stark,
>   His lips entangled in her straying hairs,
>   Breath coming short as in a convert's prayers,
>   Her stealthy face all drowsy in the dim
>   And full of shudders as she yearned to him."

All this and more the jealousy-maddened boy, in
his imagination, sees.

> " ' And now I'll drink,' he said.
>   ' I'll drink and drink—I never did before—
>   I'll drink and drink until I'm mad or dead.'
>   .   .   .   .   .
>   His wits were working like a brewer's wort
>   Until among them came the vision gleaming
>   Of Ern with bloody nose and Anna screaming.

> " ' That's what I'll do,' he muttered ; ' knock him out,
> And kick his face in with a running jump.
> I'll not have dazzled eyes this second bout,
> And she can wash the fragments under pump.'
> It was his ace, but Death had played a trump.
> Death, the blind beggar, chuckled, nodding dumb,
> ' My game, the shroud is ready, Jimmy—come.' ".

Murder, be it remembered, was not the boy's intention, but only savagely and revengefully to maul the rival who had mocked him before Anna, and—an older, bigger and heavier man than he—had taken advantage of the fact of the light being in the lad's eyes to strike a cowardly blow. But the boy drinks recklessly ; he does not return home that night ; he has no work to which to go in the morning, for his love-sick listlessness and inattention have lost him his job. Inevitably his steps tend towards Anna's cottage :

> " Ern had just brought her in a wired hare,
> She stood beside him stroking down the fur.
> ' Oh, Ern, poor thing, look how its eyes do stare,'
> ' It isn't it,' he answered, ' It's a her.'
> She stroked the breast and plucked away a bur,
> She kissed the pads, and leapt back with a shout,
> ' My God, he's got the spudder. Ern, look out.' "

But she is too late. The boy had stolen on the two unaware. " Kid " and " sucking pup," as Ern had taunted him with being, Jimmy is no weakling. The blow, savagely delivered, with a heavy weapon, fractures Ern's skull, and the lad is tried, convicted and sentenced.

> " Guilty. Thumbs down. No hope. The Judge passed sen-
>   tence ;
> ' A frantic passionate youth, unfit for life,
> A fitting time afforded for repentance,
> Then certain justice with a pitiless knife.
> For her, his wretched victim's widowed wife,
> Pity. For her who bore him, pity.' (Cheers.)
> The jury were exempt for seven years."

I wish that Mr. Masefield (was it to find a rhyme for " years " ?) had not introduced that bracketed " Cheers." Cheers, even if instantly suppressed, may perhaps be heard in a court of justice, on the return of a " popular verdict," and low murmurs of pitying assent when sympathy has been expressed with sorrowing relatives, but the " cheers " in connexion with pity, I question. For other reasons, the word jars—as possibly this critical word of mine concerning so tragic a scene may jar upon a reader. Then comes one of those greatly-original and unexpected interpolations so characteristic of Mr. Masefield.

Genius and Mediocrity

Again and again he startles the reader by some vivid supplementary picture, some pregnant " aside " of psychological insight. With the conviction and sentencing of the prisoner, one would expect Section VI, in which the trial scene is described, to end. Fear of losing something of tragic tenseness by an addition, in the nature of a post-climax, would prevent a less consummate artist from prolonging the section. Art, as well as religion, has its personal devil who bears the artist aloft to some pinnacle of the temple to show him how easily this world and its kingdoms may be his, if only he will bow the knee to the false gods of accepted traditions. Mediocrity may be wise in yielding. Genius rejects the offer and makes answer that it will possess no world which is not of its own creating and moulding. Again and again such a devil must have whispered to John Masefield that here, ready to hand, was the very " curtain " to his drama, the ringing down of which would set the " house " in a roar of applause ; and again and again the poet has resolutely turned away, to close upon a quiet, even a pastoral note, which is like the indistinguishable dying away of distant music.

Instead of closing the description of the boy's trial with the verdict and sentence, we pass with Mr. Masefield into the robing-room, where the judge is on his knees :

> " ' O God, who made us out of dust, and laid
> Thee in us bright, to lead us to the truth,
> O God, have pity upon this poor youth.
> Show him Thy grace, O God, before he die ;
> Shine in his heart ; have mercy upon me,
> Who deal the laws men make to travel by
> Under the sun upon the path to Thee.
>
>   .   .   .   .
>
> Thy pity, and Thy mercy, God did save,
> Thy bounteous gifts, not any grace of mine,
> From all the pitfalls leading to the grave,
> From all the death-feasts with the husks and swine.
> God, who has given me all things, now make shine
> Bright in this sinner's heart that he may see,
> God, take this poor boy's spirit back to Thee.' "

And that the God Who (to use the words of the broken-hearted mother)—

> " Warms His hands at man's heart when he prays,"

and makes of the end of such a life as her son's—

> " A rest for broken things too broke to mend,"

does hear the boy's and his mother's prayers, the reader is convinced.

Of the happenings between the trial and the execution, and of the exquisitely beautiful close of the poem, I will not here write. The effect upon the reader is tumultuous. He is swept and submerged by a tidal wave of emotion. In my own case, I do not know which emotion—heartbreak for the widowed mother ; hatred of the wanton creature who deliberately wrought the boy's ruin ; or horror of the so-called law which hanged him—is uppermost. As an indictment of the system by which capital punishment is inflicted upon such transgressors as

the son of *The Widow in the Bye Street*, the effect
of the poem is overwhelming.

Sea Poems

And now I have something to say of *The Widow
in the Bye Street* as well as of *The Everlasting Mercy*,
Mr. Masefield's two most extolled poems, which will
cause the Masefield enthusiast to hold me heretic,
and no true Masefieldian. It is that, having read
them two or three times, I am conscious of no insistent
impulse to re-read either. That is not so when Mr.
Masefield writes of Ships and of the Sea. Then the
poet in him turns pirate. Then he boards us, as
pirates or press-gang men board a captured craft.
Go with him, sail under him, we must, be it as
pressed men, as his prisoners, or as eagerly volun-
teering our services as one of his crew ; and none the
less because he warns us that—

" Not the ruler for me, but the ranker, the tramp of the road
The slave with the sack on his shoulders pricked on with the
     goad,
The man with too weighty a burden, too weary a load.
The sailor, the stoker of steamers, the man with the clout,
The chantyman bent at the halliards putting a tune to the
     shout,
The drowsy man at the wheel and the tired look-out."

In both *Salt Water Ballads*, from which this is taken,
and *Ballads and Poems*, are poems in which, for the
reader—

" A star will glow like a note God strikes on a silver bell."

In the former volume, I instance *Sea Fever*, *A Wan-
derer's Song*, and *On Eastnor Knoll ;* in the latter,
Cargoes, *Roadways*, *Twilight*, *Invocation*, *The West
Wind*, C. L. M. (in memory of his mother), *The Wild
Duck*, and *Imagination*.

The one and only word which can be urged against
Masefield's sea poems, has, rather unkindly if with
some measure of truth, been said by Miss Geraldine

Hodgson in her very able volume, *Criticism at a Venture*. She is of opinion that his sea poems are not even " new in kind," inasmuch as " England possessed their analogue for the Army, one more inspired too by originality and energetic vitality, in Rudyard Kipling's *Soldier Ballads*."

Of course Masefield's early work is derivative, as early work almost invariably is, and his poem *Consecration* no doubt owes something to Kipling :

" The men of the tattered battalion which fights till it dies,
Dazed with the dust of the battle, the din and the cries,
The men with the broken heads and the blood runn ng into
    their eyes.
.   .   .   .
Theirs be the music, the colour, the glory, the gold ;
Mine be a handful of ashes, a mouthful of mould.
Of the maimed, of the halt, and the blind, in the rain and the
    cold—
Of these shall my songs be fashioned, my tales be told.
                                        Amen."

But Masefield is no servile imitator of Kipling, and though *Barrack-Room Ballads* is greater work than *Salt Sea Ballads*—I am not aware that anyone has said otherwise—was it necessary, when criticizing one kind of poem, to declare that some one else has written more memorably on quite another subject ? The question, surely, is, " Has better work, on its own lines, been done by any contemporary poet than is to be found in Masefield's sea poems ? " and to that question the answer is " No."

Dauber

Some of his narrative work has passages which seem to me metrical and rhymed prose, rather than poetry. But in *Dauber*, at least, he reaches a height of sustained splendour which should give it permanent place among sea-poetry.

Of all Mr. Masefield's penetrative and powerful studies in psychology, I place *Dauber* first. This

may be because it strikes one as more or less auto-
biographical, and that in *Dauber*, Mr. Masefield's
passion for ships and for the sea, as well as his hunger
for Beauty and his devotion to his art, are most
finely expressed.

The poem tells not only of the makings of an artist,
but of a Man. Dauber, when we first meet him, is
feverish of soul and somewhat sickly of body. His
passion is twofold—for Art and for the Sea. His
life's dream is to be the sea's greatest interpreter,
to show her as she is in all her moods, the most
terrible as well as the tenderest, not as remembered
or imagined in the studio, but as actually seen on
board a ship. Dauber's life-dream was in fact to
accomplish in one art—Painting—what Mr. Masefield has achieved in another—Poetry. For Masefield as for Dauber, a ship is one of the most beautiful
things in the world :

> " Beauty in hardest action, beauty indeed
>
> Thou art untouched by softness, all that line
> Drawn ringing hard to stand the test of brine."

Of the beauty of line of ships, in calm or in storm,
of the grandeur of great seas in anger, other artists
than Dauber have painted pictures, other singers
than Masefield have penned poems. But to Dauber,
as to Masefield, there was as yet unrecorded poetry
even in the sight of—

> " sleeping seamen tired to the soul ;
> The space below the bunks as black as coal,
> Gleams upon chests, upon the unlit lamp,
> The ranging door-hook, and the locker-clamp.
>
> This he would paint, and that, and all these scenes,
> And proud ships carrying on, and men, their minds,
> And blues of rollers toppling into greens,
> And shattering into white that bursts and blinds,
> And scattering ships running erect like hinds,
> And men in oilskins beating down a sail
> High on the yellow yard, in snow, in hail."

Dauber saw, as Masefield sees—

> "That this, and so much like it, of man's toil,
> Compassed by naked manhood in strange places,
> Was all heroic, but outside the coil
> Within which modern art gleams or grimaces ;
> That if he drew that line of sailors' faces
> Sweating the sail, their passionate play and change,
> It would be new, and wonderful, and strange.
>
> That this was what his work meant ; it would be
> A training in new vision."

Here may I interpolate a word ?   Of what I hold to be defects in art, and errors in taste in the work of John Masefield, I shall, later in this article, plainly speak.   But against anything that may be thus said, Mr. Masefield has, as it were in anticipation, even if unconsciously so, entered—in the lines I have just quoted—his weightiest protest. He, no less than Dauber, has sought and striven to give us work which shall be—

> "new and wonderful, and strange.
>   .   .   .   .
> A training in new vision."

In many of his poems he has achieved this noble aim, and even when he has failed, or when his work is, in my opinion, marred by defects in art, or errors in taste, I believe with all my heart that his purpose as a poet is high.

How Dauber, already an artist, " won through " —ill-treated as he was by his fellow-seamen because of the artist soul in him which, not understanding, they despised—to become not only a sailor but a man, I must not in detail relate.   In all literature one would find it hard to find anything finer than the passage descriptive of the rounding of Cape Horn, and of the long agony and martyrdom (endured with cheerful heroism, comparable only to that of our soldiers in the trenches) of the seamen on board the clipper in which the unfortunate Dauber sailed.

Perhaps the finest touch is that in which we see Dauber—his natural timidity now beaten down and disciplined—as, in death, both artist and man—

> " He had had revelation of the lies
> Cloaking the truth men never choose to know ;
> He could bear witness now and cleanse their eyes.
> He had beheld in suffering ; he was wise."

And so, even in the laying down of his life, Dauber cries out triumphantly of his Art—these were his last words—" It shall go on."   Not only of the dead Dauber, but also of the living John Masefield, his creator, one says as one lays down the book, " Here is a Man."

In Dauber Mr. Masefield has " found himself " as he never found himself in early work reminiscent of Mr. Kipling nor in early work so reminiscent of Mr. Yeats as—

> " Would I could win some quiet and rest, and a little ease,
> In the cool grey hush of the dusk, in the dim green place of
>   the trees,
> Where the birds are singing, singing, singing, crying aloud
> The song of the red, red rose that blossoms beyond the seas."

The writer of this seems to me to be a make-believe Masefield—a dreamy-eyed young gentleman " got up " (long hair and a loosely-tied butterfly bow) to look as much as possible like Mr. W. B. Yeats.   The real Masefield is a sportsman and an athlete.   Some one said to me towards the end of 1911, " I hear that John Masefield has slipped a white surplice over his seaman's rig and is coming out strong on religion in the new number of the *English Review*." Had that been true, there would have been a pair of running shorts under Mr. Masefield's surplice, to say nothing of a pair of boxing gloves under his surplice sleeve.

The Everlasting Mercy touches on other matters

than conversion.   Even Saul Kane speaks contemptuously—

> " of men who'd never been
> Merry or true or live and clean ;
> Who'd never felt the boxer's trim
> Of brain divinely knit to limb,
> Nor felt the whole live body go
> One tingling health from top to toe,
>
> .   .   .   .   .   .
>
> The men who don't know to the root
> The joy of being swift of foot,
> Have never known, divine and fresh,
> The glory of the gift of flesh,
> Nor felt the feet exult, nor gone
> Along a dim road, on and on,
> Knowing again the bursting glows,
> The mating hare in April knows,
> Who tingles to the pads with mirth
> At being the swiftest thing on earth."

Reynard the Fox

The swiftest things on earth, in the shape of poetry, are John Masefield's *Reynard the Fox* (a classic of the chase) and *Right Royal* (almost a classic of the race-course).   Speed, speed strained to the breaking point, awakens in him such wild zest of delirious joy that we, as well as he, are carried off our feet when he writes about it.   Him it so intoxicates that, though he ride with a sure seat and a firm rein, the pace of it so goes to his head that he can persuade himself into believing (I cannot) that even the hunted creature finds fun in the chase.   Of the fox we read on page 96 :

> " Till the terror of death, though there indeed,
>   Was lulled for a while by his pride of speed ; "

and, on the opposite page, of the fox's

> " pride in the speed, his joy in the race."

There is no " joy " for the fox in being hunted, Mr.

Masefield. Of that I am as sure as that your Saul Kane and I are—each in his own way—sinners.

I had meant to write more of *Reynard the Fox,* in which, apart from the ebullient high spirits (Mr. Harold Munro tells us that a sportsman of his acquaintance spoke of it as " a damned good run, but a Bank Holiday Field "), is a whole gallery of character-sketches each different, and each drawn with a touch that recalls Dickens. But, chancing to take up *Authors and I* by Mr. Lewis Hind, I lighted upon a passage which so exactly expresses what one feels about the book that, instead of writing more, I quote Mr. Hind's words :

" With *Reynard the Fox* he reaches the height of his achievement. I have read it four times, and each time I have kindled. It goes on my bookshelves against Chaucer's *Canterbury Tales.* It sings the England we all love, the wholesome out-of-doors England, the types, the cries, the sights, the sounds. It gallops into our hearts, and it is John Masefield's best poem because he loved the doing of it—every line."

Of another and very different poem—this time short and a lyric—one suspects that Mr. Masefield " loved the doing of it—every line." I refer to *The Wild Duck*, which is equally sure in touch, and has such quiet beauty that, unlike some of Mr. Masefield's breathless and spasmodic work, it seems almost " to have written itself " :

> " Twilight. Red in the west.
> Dimness. A glow on the wood.
> The teams plod home to rest.
> The wild duck come to gleam.
> O souls not understood,
> What a wild cry in the pool ;
> What things have the farm ducks seen
> That they cry so—huddle and cry ?

Only the soul that goes
Eager. Eager. Flying,
Over the globe of the moon,
Over the wood that glows,
Wings linked. Necks a-strain,
A rush and a wild crying.

.   .   .   .   .

A cry of the long pain
In the reeds of a steel lagoon,
In a land that no man knows."

The poem which gives the volume *Philip the King*
its title, being a play, I pass by. But three poems
in the book, *August, 1914* (Mr. Masefield's one and
only but very noble war poem), *Biography* (actually
a biography, if spiritually so, in verse) and *Ships*,
no reader should miss. The two lengthy narrative
poems, *Enslaved* and *Rosas*, are disappointing, but
included in the volume *Enslaved* is a shorter narrative poem (it recalls Francis Thompson only by its
title) *The Hounds of Hell*, which has a touch of the
diablerie in which Stevenson excelled.

Mr. Masefield's Rhyming

Tribute must be paid to Mr. Masefield's skill in
finding new rhymes—always refreshing to the ear
of a reader wearied by the monotonous ringing of
the changes on the same words. Such rhymes,
however, as " boy or " and " blubber for," " rid-
dance " and " kittens," " reskied " and " weskit,"
" took firm " and " book worm," which may serve
to turn a rhyme in comic verse, sound a little
strangely in a poem so serious in subject as *The
Everlasting Mercy*.

Mr. Masefield's eye seems surer than his ear.
Within the space of a single short poem (*Lollingdon
Downs, XXII*), he rhymes " suffer " and " brother,"
" folk " and " wold " and even " sister " and
" liquor." Though " know " and " no " (*The Widow*

in the Bye Street, page 17) do not look the same to
the eye—to the ear they are exactly alike, and so
are not rhymes. Here both eye and ear have failed
him. He seems incapable of self-criticism, and of
knowing what is best and what is worst in his work.
In *Lollingdon Downs*, published as late as 1917, we
read :

> " ' Stop beating sister,
>   Or by God I'll kill you ! '
>   Kyrle was full of liquor—
>   Old Kyrle said : ' Will you ? '
>
>   .   .   .   .   .
>
>   Young Will, the son,
>   Heard his sister shriek ;
>   He took his gun
>   Quick as a streak,

which might well have been composed while Mr.
Masefield was undergoing a course of the physical
training known in the Army as " Jerks." Yet,
shoved away among what printers call the " odd-
ments " of his play on Pompey, and printed, not as
an Epilogue, but elbowed out even by the Notes,
at the tail of which it comes, we find such a lyric as
this :

> " And all their passionate hearts are dust,
>   And dust the great idea that burned
>   In various flames of love and lust
>   Till the world's brain was turned.
>
> ' God, moving darkly in men's brains,
>   Using their passions as His tool,
>   Brings freedom with a tyrant's chains
>   And wisdom with the fool.
>
>   Blindly and bloodily we drift,
>   Our interests clog our hearts with dreams.
>   God make my brooding mind a rift
>   Through which a meaning gleams."

In another poem Masefield writes :

> " Out of the mist a little barque slipped by,
>   Spilling the mist with changing gleams of red,"

followed a little lower down by—

> " The night alone near water when I heard
> All the sea's spirit spoken by a bird,"

and one's comment on both passages is, " This is poetry." Yet a few lines later, and on the same page, we read :

> " And when I count those gifts, I think them such
> As no man's bounty could have bettered much,"

as well as such an appalling couplet, three pages on, in the same poem, as—

> " Wearing the last of night out in still streets
> Trodden by us and policemen on their beats."

Love Poems

Mr. Masefield's Love Poems are not many, but are often beautiful :

> " I have seen dawn and sunset on moors and windy hills
> Coming in solemn beauty like slow old tunes of Spain :
> I have seen the lady April bringing the daffodils,
> Bringing the springing grass and the soft warm April rain.
>
> I have heard the song of the blossoms and the old chant of the
> sea,
> And seen strange lands from under the arched white sails of
> ships ;
> But the loveliest things of beauty God ever has showed to me,
> Are her voice, and her hair, and eyes, and the dear red
> curve of her lips."

Another and scarcely less beautiful love poem is *The Word*, in which the poet prays that, when he and the loved one are old—

> " May love be sweeter for the vanished days,
> And your most perfect beauty still as dear
> As when your troubled singer stood at gaze
> In the dear March of a most sacred year."

Imagination is less a love poem to one woman than an offering of incense—the worshipper humbly

kneeling as before an altar shrine—to the Womanhood of which she is, to him, the supreme and eternal
type. Other love poems which I commend to the
reader are *Born for Nought Else, Ignorance, Being
Her Friend*, and *Her Heart*. That Mr. Masefield
should so often, in imagination, see the loved one
in her coffin or in her grave, as in *Waste, The Watch
in the Wood*, and *When Bony Death*—

" When bony Death has chilled her gentle blood,
    And dimmed the brightness of her wistful eyes,
And changed her glorious beauty into mud
    By his old skill in hateful wizardries,"

may be attributable to no more than a poet's many-
changing moods. Not because of this touch of
morbidity in one whose work is generally aflush with
the joy of living, but because of certain other—shall
I say " symptoms " ?—in poems of his writing, I am
minded to ask a question. His poems are, for the
most part, as I have said, aflush with the joy of
life. Is it possible that the flush is sometimes a
trifle hectic, reminding one just a little of the con-
sumptive who is feverishly eager, then and there, to
cram all he can into life ? Masefield's writings
convey, perhaps are intended to convey, the impression of one who is robust alike in body and mind.

Over-emphasis

I do not question his physical health, but some of
his poems seem to me to indicate a too self-conscious
" nerviness," of which the violence which he mistakes
for power, and the over-anxiety to emphasize seem
to me to be signs. Not thus is power in poetry
attained, any more than an ambitious pianist, too
eager to seem a Paderewski, can, by the keeping
down of the loud pedal, achieve the effect which
comes only of a born and trained musician's brilliancy
of " touch." Or, to use another musical simile, one

c

might say that Masefield marks his score " *Fortis-
simo*," when the passage is really " *Staccato* " :

> " By God, he's stripped down to his buff."
> " By God, we'll make him warm enough."
> " After him."   " Catch him."   " Out him."   " Scrob him."
> " We'll give him hell."   " By God, we'll mob him."
> " We'll duck him, scrout him, flog him, fratch him."
> " All right," I said, " but first you'll catch him."

Not thus do the athletes of the poetical arena, whose
nerves are under, not out of control, convince us of
their skill and strength.   Of effort, of " wrestling
for a throw," Mr. Masefield may have been conscious
when writing these lines, but they are not for that
reason Herculean.   Not when effort is most evident
is the greatest effect produced, but often with
seeming ease ; and when the athlete, be he poet or
wrestler, seems least to have made call upon his
strength.

Lollingdon Downs

In the narrative poems one sometimes finds a
certain wild grandeur, but beauty more rarely.   In
the sonnets of *Lollingdon Downs*, Mr. Masefield has
written out for us the narrative—not of other men's
lives, but of his own life's quest for beauty.   Here
we see beauty as mirrored in his own heart, not as a
reflection of the light which he casts upon the souls
of others.   At the theatre I am more interested in
the actors and actresses as real and living women
and men—in a word, as *themselves*—than as repre-
senting this or that make-believe character.   That
may be the wrong attitude in which to see a play,
and mine may be the wrong attitude of mind towards
poetry.   None the less, not until I had read *Lollingdon Downs* could I rightly apprehend Mr. Masefield's
own attitude towards the spiritual matters on which
he writes with power and insight :

" There is no God, as I was taught in youth,
    Though each, according to his stature, builds
    Some covered shrine for what he thinks the truth,
    Which day by day his reddest heart-blood gilds.
    There is no God but death, the clasping sea,
    In which we move like fish, deep over deep,
    Made of men's souls that bodies have set free,
    Floods to a Justice though it seems asleep.
    There is no God ; but still behind the veil,
    The hurt thing works, out of its agony.
    Still like the given cruse that did not fail
    Return the pennies given to passers by.
    There is no God ; but we, who breathe the air,
    Are God ourselves, and touch God everywhere."

I knew from the poem *A Creed* that Mr. Masefield
is a believer in reincarnation :

" I hold that when a person dies
    His soul returns again to earth ;
    Arrayed in some new flesh-disguise
    Another mother gives him birth.
    With sturdier limbs and brighter brain
    The old soul takes the roads again."

Equally, the sonnet just quoted indicates Mr. Masefield's leaning towards Pantheism—sublimest, if
semi-pagan, of conceptions, outside revealed religion
—the goal to which such intellects as his so often
tend.   And just as he holds that we—

" Are God ourselves, and touch God everywhere,"

so he holds that the poet's quest for Beauty should
be, not without us, but within :

" Here in the self is all that man can know
    Of Beauty, all the wonder, all the power,
    All the unearthly colour, all the glow,
    Here in the self which withers like a flower.

        .   .   .   .   .   .

    Here in the flesh, within the flesh, behind,
    Swift in the blood and throbbing on the bone,
    Beauty herself, the universal mind,
    Eternal April wandering alone ;
    The God, the Holy Ghost, the atoning Lord,
    Here in the flesh, the never yet explored."

Except to say that I do not share Mr. Masefield's
views on reincarnation, on pantheism, or in thinking
—unless in the sense that beauty is said to be in the
eye of the beholder—that beauty is to be found only
within ourselves, I do not propose to discuss these
highly controversial questions. Some knowledge
of a poet's standpoint or beliefs may assist readers
the better to understand his work. These stand-
points and beliefs I do but indicate and pass on.

In *Lollingdon Downs* Mr. Masefield asks himself
why it is that—

> " No mortal knows
> From what immortal granary comes the grain,
> Nor how the earth conspires to make the rose ? "

He asks, too, why—

> " that little thing the seed
> Has, all alone in earth, to plan the tree ? "

He ponders on the beauty of—

> " Those women who were summer in men's hearts
> Before the smile upon the Sphinx was cold."

But when all is said, he has no solution of Life's
problems to offer except philosophically to say :

> " Let that which is to come be as it may,
> Darkness, extinction, justice, life intense,
> The flies are happy in the summer day,
> Flies will be happy many summers hence."

This, from the final poem in the volume, takes us
no farther than old Khayyám, of whom it is an echo ;
but rightly to know the beauty-haunted soul of
John Masefield, one must read and many times, the
remarkable sonnet-sequence in *Lollingdon Downs*.

The Everlasting Mercy

The Everlasting Mercy is the so-called story of a
conversion. I say so-called, not because I do not

believe in conversion, nor because I am unable to
visualize Saul Kane—for the creatures begotten of
Mr. Masefield's brain are as real to us as the men
and women begotten of the body—but for another
reason. That reason is that what Mr. Masefield has
done is to transform Saul Kane into John Masefield,
—and that neither conversion nor John Masefield can
accomplish. Saul tells the story himself, and as is
not uncommon among converts of his type, he holds
that his past record is the weightiest testimony, as
no doubt it is, of what Christianity has done for him.
Christianity can work miracles. It can so change
the whole nature, that a sinner, even a criminal,
may become a saint, but it does not transform a Saul
Kane into a John Masefield. At a conjuring per-
formance I once saw a cloak thrown over a man,
and when the cloak was withdrawn, another and a
different man stood in his place, but Mr. Masefield
claims to be telling the story of a conversion, not
to be performing a conjuror's trick.

Now we will let Saul Kane speak for himself and
of himself as he was before conversion.

> " I drunk, I fought, I poached, I whored,
> I did despite unto the Lord,
> I cursed, 'twould make a man look pale,
> And nineteen times I went to jail.
> > Now, friends, observe and look upon me,
> > Mark how the Lord took pity on me."

Then Saul tells of a quarrel—in which he was in the
wrong—with " Billy Myers, a friend of mine " :

> " This field is mine," he says, " by right ;
> If you poach here, there'll be a fight.
> Out now," he says, " and leave your wire ;
> It's mine."
> > " It ain't."
> > > " You put."
> > > > " You liar."

" You closhy put."
          " You bloody liar."
" This is my field."
          " This is my wire."
" I'm ruler here."
          " You ain't."
                    " I am."
" I'll fight you for it."
          " Right, by dam."

A fight is arranged,

> " ' And Silas Jones, that bookie wide,
> Will make a purse five pounds a side.'
> These were the words, that was the place
> By which God brought me into grace."

The first evidence of this " grace " is when Saul thinks :

> " ' I'll go and take Bill's hand.
> I'll up and say the fault was mine,
> He shan't make play for these here swine.'
> And then I thought that that was silly,
> They'd think I was afraid of Billy :
> They'd think (I thought it, God forgive me)
> I funked the hiding Bill could give me."

" Forgive me " and " give me " are not a rhyme, but it is the fight not the rhyme which matters, and neither George Borrow nor Sir Arthur Conan Doyle could better Mr. Masefield's description. The fight at first goes against Saul, who would have lost had not his opponent sprained his thumb. Saul is adjudged the winner, and the party adjourns to a public-house. On the way thither, that half-hearted sinner, if whole-hearted seducer—a curious blend of sensuality and sentimentality, not uncommon in men of his type—thus meditates concerning Christmastide :

> " When Christ's own star comes over the wood,
> Lamb of the sky come out of fold
> Wandering windy heavens cold.
> So they shone and sang till twelve
> When all the bells ring out of theirselve ;
> Rang a peal for Christmas morn,
> Glory, men, for Christ is born."

**Realism in
Poetry**

Next we read of the foul talk and unclean stories told during the drunken debauch at the inn, with the interpolation of certain later views of Saul on religion and immorality.   They strike one queerly in a setting almost Zolaesque in its realism :

> " Jim Gurvil said his smutty say
> About a girl down Bye Street way.
> And how the girl from Froggatt's circus
> Died giving birth in Newent work'us.
> And Dick told how the Dymock wench
> Bore twins, poor thing, on Dog Hill bench ;
> And how he'd owned to one in court,
> And how Judge made him sorry for't.
>
> .   .   .   .
>
> For three long hours of gin and smokes,
> And two girls' breath and fifteen blokes',
> A warmish night, and windows shut,
> The room stank like a fox's gut."

But Zola wrote only in prose, and in poetry such realism as this should have no place.   I do not speak as a puritan, nor as one who would emasculate Art. The Art which is virile, mates with Imagination, and the children of the union are virile and comely. When Art forsakes the lovely bride, Imagination, for unlovely Realism, the offspring of that mating are often grotesque and ill-shaped.   Not of such a union are the children, in art, of Shakespeare, Milton, Keats, Wordsworth and Tennyson.   Coarseness of speech there is in Shakespeare's poetry, but little realism.   In the immense bulk of his work, as compared with Mr. Masefield's, the coarse passages, remembering the times in which he wrote, are few. Nor, in such matters, can Shakespeare's time be held to set a standard for our own.   Are we to discard our habits of greater personal cleanliness because,

in Shakespeare's time, there was less facility for a
bath, and for men and women to be verminous was
not uncommon ? By poets, a certain reticence
must be observed, not to taboo this or that subject,
but only in regard to treatment. All human life is
within the province of poetry, preferably that which
is beautiful, but not to the exclusion of that which
is evil or ugly, so long as the treatment be noble,
imaginative, and symbolic. Poetry interprets life
by means of symbols of deep spiritual significance.
When it ceases to deal with life symbolically, calling
in instead the aid of realism, it ceases to be poetry.
Poetry, moreover, seems to me the consecrated place
of all literature's wide domains. Perhaps because
we personify Poetry as a woman, and of womanhood
so pure and rare as not to be far from angelhood—
as bodying, in lovely woman-form, a spirit so lovely
as to be half-divine ; as both of earth and of heaven ;
of Time and of Eternity—perhaps, because of this,
we are conscious, in poetry, of rising into a purer
atmosphere and of standing, as it were, in a pure and
radiant Presence. Or to use less imaginative imagery
—imagery of the world which is known to us all—
shall I say that prose is to poetry as is our everyday
speech to the language of courts ? At court, as elsewhere, we are aware that life has its disagreeable
facts, but the subject is not by choice introduced.
If mention of these facts has to be made, a certain
reticence, not incompatible with sincerity, is observed. This reticence means no more than that
a right distinction between time and place has been
made. In the market-place, buying and selling are
spoken of in terms of commerce. In the office of a
sanitary inspector the subject of drains, in relation
to hygienics, is discussed. In the dissecting-room
the various organs of the body, their functions and
the purposes they serve, are, without thought of
offence, explained, and in the presence of both sexes.

But unless unavoidably so, we do not introduce the
subject of drains, or the dissecting-room, into
general conversation, to say nothing of such subjects
being out of place at court. If in an inn or in the
street we hear foul language, there is no necessity—
unless as evidence in a police court—to repeat in
detail what was said. In literature, even in poetry,
to convey an atmosphere of corruption and to
indicate moral corruption, is possible without explicitly describing the corrupt act or recording the
exact unclean word. If we cannot do so, our place
is with the police-court reporters and we have no
business in literature, still less in poetry. Even in
a well-conducted tavern, if anyone used such language
as we find in *The Everlasting Mercy*, he would be
requested by the landlord to desist. To me, no
puritan, no Bowdlerizer, it does not seem fitting that,
in a poem, language should be recorded to which
objection would be taken if spoken in a respectably
conducted public-house, as, for instance, the following
couplet from *The Everlasting Mercy* :

> " I'll bloody him a bloody fix,
> I'll bloody burn his bloody ricks."

" Strong meat is not for delicate stomachs," I was
told by an admirer of Mr. Masefield, who defended
the passage. I replied that though I had no objection
to strong meat, I did not like meat so strong, not to
say so " high," as to be nasty. Moreover meat un-
cooked, almost as it comes from the shambles, finds
place in my kitchen not on my library table. By
all means let Mr. Masefield depict his characters as
of flesh and blood, but to do so it is not necessary
in a poem to sprinkle the pages with an offensive
adjective formed from the latter noun. In reading
poetry one does not wish to be reminded of Billings-
gate Market or a butcher's shop.

Mr. Edmund Gosse on
The Everlasting Mercy

In presenting the Edmond de Polignac Prize of £100 to Mr. Masefield on behalf of the Royal Society of Literature, Mr. Edmund Gosse, one of the most accomplished and distinguished of living Men of Letters, spoke of *The Everlasting Mercy* as " A narrative of conversion, a story of the Light of God breaking into a dark soul."

On the subject of conversion, I had not hitherto thought of Mr. Gosse as an authority. Nor am I. But I recall a passage from *Margaret Ogilvy*, in which Sir James Barrie writes : " For when you looked into my mother's eyes you knew, as if He had told you, why God sent her into the world—it was to open the mind, of all who looked, to beautiful thoughts, and that is the beginning and end of literature."

This is of course no more than generalizing on the aim of literature. It means only that Sir J. M. Barrie ranges himself with those who would keep the white shield of Art and Letters unspotted, and whose quest is beauty. So does John Masefield. Read in *Lollingdon Downs* his sonnet-sequence on Beauty—not physical beauty only, but the beauty which is spiritual—and you will ask yourself, as I did, where in the work of living poet is more passionate love for beauty, as his life's ideal, revealed ? To Masefield as to Barrie, beauty is, I doubt not, the beginning and end of literature, but perhaps because his muse is the more feminine, the more tender, fanciful and graceful, Barrie picks his way daintily. Masefield's muse is masculine, and if an apprenticeship a muse can be said to have served, the first apprenticeship of Masefield's muse was not to Song, but to the Sea, where strange words are heard and a rude language is spoken. Elbow her way into most

of men's occupations woman may, but the fo'c'sle
is as yet woman-free. And in the fo'c'sle the speech
is not always pretty. The muse who frequents
social circles accustoms herself to changing fashions
in catch word and phrase, but in the fo'c'sle the
fashion and figures of speech are unchanging and
are all the fo'c'sle's own. And though, for the
Golden Isles of Beauty, Mr. Masefield may and does
set his sail, the course which he takes is sometimes
through turgid and muddy waters. Beautiful
thoughts there are in *The Everlasting Mercy*, but to
any glowing tribute which so great a critic as Mr.
Gosse accords, some of us small critics are over-
ready, insincerely, to act as chorus. One plays for
safety in doing so, for if the great critics are in agreement with us, or rather if we are in agreement with
the great critics, our judgment is not likely to be
questioned. But cant is cant, whether talked of
religion or of poetry. Were I to pretend that I
think the passages I have quoted to be poetry, or,
as part of a poem to be other than repellent, I should
be guilty of cant as well as of cowardice. Regret
I must that so true a poet as Mr. Masefield should
disfigure a poem, sometimes of great beauty, and
making in intention for righteousness and purity,
by descending to realism, which to greater, and so to
truer art would be unnecessary. And, to make an
end of carping, I regret too that he should think it
necessary, in *The Widow in the Bye Street*, to put
into the mouth of his characters such words as—

" By Jesus, chaps, I never meant to kill 'un,"

or, in *The Everlasting Mercy*, to associate even as
rhymes two such words as those at the end of the
following lines :

" They went, and some cried, ' Good old sod.
She put it to him straight, by God.' "

Saul Kane's
"Conversion"

Returning to the narrative at the point where I broke off, we read (the passage is perhaps intended to prepare us for Saul's coming conversion) :

" I opened window wide and leaned
Out of that pigstye of the fiend
And felt a cool wind go like grace
About the sleeping market-place.
The clock struck three, and sweetly, slowly,
The bells chimed Holy, Holy, Holy ;
And in a second's pause there fell
The cold note of. the chapel bell,
And then a cock crew, flapping wings,
And summat made me think of things,
How long those ticking clocks had gone
From church and chapel, on and on,
Ticking the time out, ticking slow
To men and girls who'd come and go.

.   .   .   .

And how that night was Lambert's Feast,
The night I'd fought and been a beast.
And how a change had come. And then
I thought, ' You tick to different men.'
What with the fight and what with drinking
And being awake along there thinking,
My mind began to carp and tetter,
' If this life's all, the beasts are better.'

.   .   .   .

I wondered, then, why life should be,
And what would be the end of me
When youth and health and strength were gone
And cold old age came creeping on ?
A keeper's gun ?   The Union ward ?
Or that new quod at Hereford ?
And looking round I felt disgust
At all the nights of drink and lust,
And all the looks of all the swine
Who'd said that they were friends of mine ;
And yet I knew when morning came,
The morning would be just the same,

> For I'd have drinks, and Jane would meet me,
> And drunken Silas Jones would greet me,
> And I'd risk quod and keeper's gun
> Till all the silly game was done."

Soon after this, Saul goes on to say :

> " A madness took me then. I felt
> I'd like to hit the world a belt.
> I felt that I could fly through air,
> A screaming star with blazing hair,
> A rushing comet, crackling, numbing
> The folk with fear of judgment coming,
> A 'Lijah in a fiery car
> Coming to tell folk what they are."

Tearing off his clothes, and smashing the bottles and tumblers, he rushes out into the street—

> " A naked madman waving grand
> A blazing lamp in either hand.
> I yelled like twenty drunken sailors,
> ' The devil's come among the tailors.'
> A blaze of flame behind me streamed,
> And then I clashed the lamps and screamed
> ' I'm Satan, newly come from hell,'
> And then I spied the fire bell."

He rings it frantically and rushes on to run amuck at the property of " parson, lawyer, squire." Then comes one of those strange and lucid intervals in what seems to me to be less a narrative of conversion, in the true sense of the word, than of a mania, which fear of hell causes to assume a religious form.

> " At all three doors I threshed and slammed
> And yelled aloud that they were damned.
> I clodded squire's glass with turves
> Because he spring-gunned his preserves.
> Through parson's glass my nozzle swishes
> Because he stood for loaves and fishes,
> But parson's glass I spared a tittle,
> He give me an orange once when little,
> And he who gives a child a treat
> Makes joy-bells ring in Heaven's street,

And he who gives a child a home
Builds palaces in Kingdom come,
And she who gives a baby birth
Brings Saviour Christ again to earth."

These fourteen lines are, to me, illusion-destroying. One may believe with Mr. Gosse that it is " the Light of God " which converts Saul Kane, or one may have an uneasy feeling that it is John Masefield who —on paper—converts Saul Kane, and for the reason that, to do so, Mr. Masefield from the first intended. Take whichever view we may, these fourteen lines seem to throw light upon Mr. Masefield's methods of work in writing *The Everlasting Mercy*. The story is supposed to be told by Saul himself, and is so told, except when for Mr. Masefield's purpose, Saul must be shown as under process of conversion. Then, as if even Mr. Masefield is uncertain of the reality of Saul's conversion, and cannot trust Saul to speak for himself, Mr. Masefield, disguised as Saul, comes upon the scene to take up the story. If the reader will look again at the lines just quoted, he will see that the first eight are Saul's, the last six are Masefield's. Saul's last spoken line is,

" He give me an orange once when little,"

and one would expect Saul to say " give " instead of " gave." That being so, how comes it that, in the very next line and twice in the lines which follow, Saul uses the very same verb, " to give," correctly, and as Mr. Masefield himself would use it ? The last six lines are beautiful, but illusion is as I say destroyed, for the reason that the man who speaks them is not Saul Kane but John Masefield. Reading these and similar lines, one seems to hear Mr. Masefield say : " Here I must again interpolate a passage of Christian sentiment, to indicate the change which is coming over Saul. Otherwise, when I finally convert my sinner—as of course I shall—the reader may think the conversion too sudden to be convincing."

Quite so, but if Mr. Masefield would have us to believe that it is Saul who is speaking, he should at least make Saul express himself in the language which, even if now beautiful in spirit and Christian in sentiment, is still such speech as would rise naturally to the lips of such a man. Saul is fast coming to see the error of his ways, but he would not for that reason be aware of and correct the errors in his English. He would cease from pouring out oaths and filth, but his manner of speech and his figures of speech even if chastened would still be so crude and so rude as to remind us of Saul Kane the ex-poacher. As recorded in *The Everlasting Mercy* they remind us only of John Masefield the poet.

I am of the same opinion concerning many later and beautiful passages in this very powerful and remarkable poem. The story I need not further outline, except to say that the final factors in Saul's conversion are three. First we have—what fitter in the leading of a broken-hearted sinner to Christ? —the lovely episode of the intervention of a little child. By that child's trust in him and, later, by words spoken by the child's mother, the soul of Saul is profoundly stirred. Then in a public-house, for Mr. Masefield knows human nature and its weakness too well not to show Saul as lapsing, and more than once, into the " old Adam " (the words are his, not mine), Saul finds his way to the Cross. God's angel to the sinner comes in the person of a Quaker lady of holy life. She it is who makes the appeal which brings the man to his knees :

> " ' Saul Kane,' she said, ' when next you drink,
> Do me the gentleness to think
> That every drop of drink accurst
> Makes Christ within you die of thirst,

That every dirty word you say
Is one more flint upon His way,
Another thorn about His head
Another mock by where He tread,
Another nail, another cross.
All that you are is that Christ's loss.'
The clock run down and struck a chime
And Mrs. Si said, ' Closing time.'

The wet was pelting on the pane,
And something broke inside my brain,
I heard the rain drip from the gutters
And Silas putting up the shutters,
While one by one the drinkers went ;
I got a glimpse of what it meant.

.   .   .   .

I know the very words I said,
They bayed like bloodhounds in my head.
' The water's going out to sea
And there's a great moon calling me ;
But there's a great sun calls the moon,
And all God's bells will carol soon
For joy and glory and delight
Of some one coming home to-night.' "

Passages of
Supreme Loveliness

Thereafter is many a passage of supreme loveliness which, as poetry, is the noblest that Mr. Masefield has written :

" O Christ who holds the open gate,
O Christ who drives the furrows straight,
O Christ, the plough, O Christ, the laughter
Of holy white birds flying after,
Lo, all my heart's field red and torn,
And Thou wilt bring the young green corn,
The young green corn divinely springing ;
The young green corn for ever singing ;
And when the field is fresh and fair
Thy blessèd feet shall glitter there.
And we will walk the weeded field,
And tell the golden harvest's yield,

> The corn that makes the holy bread
> By which the soul of man is fed,
> The holy bread, the food unpriced,
> Thy everlasting mercy, Christ."

Reading these and other lines in *The Everlasting Mercy*, I asked myself for a moment, " Ought I not to feel rebuked that, thus far, in my reading I have doubted the reality of the sinner's conversion. Repelled as I may have been by the language sometimes put into the mouth of Saul, ought I not to remember that, in taking us among Life's outcasts, Life's fallen, among the drunkards and the foul-mouthed, Mr. Masefield follows great Precedent ? "

The next moment I knew that the appeal that had been made to me was all emotional. God's miracle the conversion of the man may have been, but conversion, while changing the heart and the life, does not change the intellect. Saul Kane, even after conversion, would never so have thought and spoken. He might in all sincerity have preached such sermons as those of " Billy Sunday." He might have been what I have heard called " a means of grace " at meetings held at street corners or in mission rooms by the Salvation Army, but of feelings so wholly those of a poet, of thoughts so manifestly those of high intellect and so divinely expressed, Saul was incapable. They are the thoughts, feelings and expressions not of Saul Kane the converted poacher, but of John Masefield the poet. And so, deeply moved, but all unconvinced, I take leave of this marvellous *tours de force*, which Mr. Gosse commends to us as " A poem which would make memorable any year in recent literary history."

When Mr. Gosse, speaking as a poet and a critic, thus addresses an audience of students of poetry, I, as a member of that audience say, " Hear, hear ! " But when Mr. Gosse stands, as it were, white-robed in the pulpit, or on the chancel-steps, to

D

pronounce with uplifted hands a pious benediction on *The Everlasting Mercy* as " a narrative of conversion, a story of the Light of God breaking into a dark soul "—one member of his congregation at least is unable sincerely to join in the " Amen."

Rudyard Kipling

Rudyard Kipling

NOT even in the organ roll of Handel's *Largo*, one of the most majestic works of musical genius, is a more spacious or a more stately note sounded than in Kipling's *Recessional*, yet how superbly simple, alike in thought and expression !

Whenever a supreme word is spoken, you shall know it for what it is by the fact that though it were spoken but a moment ago, you seemed to have known it all your life. You feel that it *was* before you *were*—that it *was*, even before the brains which conceived it had been called into being. It seems at once strangely new, yet strangely old— new as the sunset which last night you saw ebb and fade away in the west ; old as the dreaming sunsets of our lost childhood ; old even as the sunset which ended the first day in the very morning of the world.

So also the poem, if it be a poem, seems *ours* no less than *his* who wrote it. In it our own recognized, inarticulate, and often discarded thoughts come back to us, as Emerson says, " with a certain alienated majesty."

In *Recessional* Mr. Kipling speaks for all of us. He has made articulate and noble the unuttered thoughts of England and the Empire.

In his *Song of the English* he says :

" Now must ye speak to your kinsmen and they must speak
 to you,
 After the use of the English, in straight-flung words and few.'

It is because Rudyard Kipling uses English in which words are straight-flung and few, because he is a master of the speech understanded of the people, that he is so " universal "—addressing himself as he does to a race which leaves no part of this globe of ours unexplored. Scots, the wide world over, read and love their Burns ; Britons, their Kipling, for the reason that these two poets have dared to be themselves, to say what they actually think, and to say it naturally, if nobly, in their own and their readers' every-day words.

Lesser men do not so dare. They strain after fine words and phrases. They aim at a " style," shrink from saying what they really think and as they think it, lest they be accounted undignified, unoriginal, forgetting that only by being natural can one attain dignity, only by being oneself can one be original.

A great Englishman, great alike in heart, intellect, and humanity, penned *Recessional* ; but I doubt whether anyone who heard the hymn sung at the Victory Thanksgiving (and none who ever heard it will ever forget) was humbler or more reverent of heart than the writer.

I do not imply that Mr. Kipling is unaware of or underrates his powers. Possibly no one knows better than he how greatly and rarely God has gifted him ; but he is not for that reason puffed up with pride or self-sufficiency. On the contrary, he is perhaps ashamed, rather than otherwise, to feel that so much has been made of what he feels is, comparatively, so little ; and that the written and spoken words of one so conscious of his own human weaknesses and shortcomings should have so potent a power to sway the souls of his fellows.

The Rubáiyát
of Belief

That he realizes his gifts, and realizes, too, how heavy are the responsibilities of one so gifted, seems clear from a poem now included in *Songs from Books*, part of which I quote:

" If there be good in that I wrought,
    Thy Hand compelled it, Master, Thine—
Where I have failed to meet Thy Thought
    I know, through Thee, the blame was mine.

One instant's toil to Thee denied,
    Stands all Eternity's offence.
Of that I did with Thee to guide
    To Thee, through Thee, be excellence.

The depth and dream of my desire,
    The bitter paths wherein I stray—
Thou knowest, Who hast made the Fire,
    Thou knowest, Who hast made the Clay.

   .   .   .   .

One stone the more swings into place
    In that dread Temple of Thy worth.
It is enough that, through Thy Grace,
    I saw nought common on Thy Earth."

This seems to me one of the noblest and certainly the most challenging poem that Mr. Kipling has written. He has staked his all on one throw; he has risked everything which his reputation as a poet means to him on a single work. To have dared and to have claimed thus greatly—and to have failed—would be in a word, Disaster.

Unless supremely done, the thing would be naught. It would indeed be worse than naught, for the higher one essays to climb, the farther must one fall in the case of failure. But Mr. Kipling has not failed. He has fulfilled the conditions, and succeeded supremely.

The poem seems to me the very Rubáiyát of the Faithful., The Rubáiyát of Omar Khayyám, for all the grandeur of FitzGerald's translation, is but a beautiful Epic of Unbelief. " That large Infidel, your Omar," as Tennyson calls the old Persian poet in the dedication of *Tiresias* to FitzGerald, would have us to hold with him that " nothing matters." His is the gospel of eat, drink, and be merry, and " sport with Amaryllis in the shade " while you may, for to-morrow you die. Kipling, on the contrary, claims that everything matters, and infinitely :

> " One instant's toil to Thee denied,
> Stands all Eternity's offence."

The condemnation is scarcely less terrible than the hurled judgment of some old Hebrew prophet.

Not only for God must we spare ourselves in nothing. What of our duty to our country in war ?

> " No easy hope or lies
>   Shall bring us to our goal,
> But iron sacrifice
>   Of body, will, and soul.
> There is but one task for all—
>   One life for each to give.
> Who stands if Freedom fall ?
> Who dies if England live ? "

Again, of our little human craftsmanship, if truly done, done as in sight of the Master Craftsman, he says :

> " One stone the more swings into place
> In that dread Temple of Thy worth."

The superb self-confidence of genius ! Pharisees of old might have taken up stones to cast at one who

Photo
Elliott & Fry

had thus written. " Whom makest thou thyself ? " they would have demanded.

Even here in England to-day I was asked : " Is not the claim made somewhat arrogantly and presumptuously ? "

" On the contrary," I replied. " I believe it to be made in a spirit of profound humility and dependence upon God."

So far from resenting that Mr. Kipling should look directly to God as the Source of all high poetry ; should humbly and reverently hope and believe that what is best in his own human work is divine of origin, I rejoice that our most representative national poet is a man of such great faith.

Barrack-Room Ballads

Departmental Ditties was published in India in 1886. Since then it has been reprinted here, and has been in continual demand ; but it is by *Barrack-Room Ballads*, issued in 1892, that Mr. Kipling established his reputation as a poet.

George Herbert, in a poem *The Elixir*, which might be a voice calling to Mr. Kipling from the seventeenth century to " carry on " in the nineteenth and twentieth, with the message that nothing is to be accounted common or unclean, speaks of making " drudgery divine." Of some of the contents of *Barrack-Room Ballads* one may say that the writer has made, what some critics would have called doggerel, " divine." These critics would not have disallowed some poetical licence, some eccentricity of poetical dress ; but here was the native, naked, almost aboriginal poetry of the " natural man." Here was the nugget gold of poetry, whereas they were accustomed only to the finished article, wrought into vase or trinket, carven or chased. Some of them were a little alarmed. They admitted that Mr. Kipling could on occasion write sublimely; could write high poetry, which appealed, both in conception and in art, to the idealist, the critic and the student; but none the less they entered their protest.

Even Stevenson, himself a defier of the conventions, wrote of Kipling to Henry James: "I look on, I admire, I rejoice for myself; but in a kind of ambition we all have for our tongue, and literature, I am wounded."

Charles Kingsley once remarked that when you say or do anything to take a man's breath away, the first thing he does when he gets his breath back is to fall to abusing you.

Barrack-Room Ballads not only took our breath away, but took the reading world by storm. It interpreted "Tommy" as "Tommy" had never been interpreted before—the "Tommy" who is neither a "blackguard" nor one of a "thin red line of 'eroes," but a very ordinary human being, "most remarkable like you." It showed us *the makings of a soldier,* and the makings of the soldier's soul, just as *The Five Nations,* published, as it was, soon after conclusion of peace with the Boers, did more to bring home to us the horrors and the heroisms of war than all the official "histories."

The British public took both "Tommy" and Mr. Kipling to its heart with *Barrack-Room Ballads,* and there both have remained firmly established ever since. The book is dedicated to the memory of Mrs. Kipling's brother, and those of us who, as I did, knew Wolcott Balestier, feel that in Mr. Kipling's picture of such men as he there is small exaggeration:

> "Gods, for they knew the hearts of men—
> Men, for they stooped to Fame,
> Borne on the breath that men call Death,
> My brother's spirit came."

Of Mr. Kipling himself, indeed, are not the same words true ?

**The Power of
the Dog**

How truly he knows the hearts of some men and women, the poem *The Power of the Dog* sufficiently shows :

> " Buy a pup, and your money will buy
> Love unflinching that cannot lie—
> Perfect passion and worship fed
> By a kick in the ribs or a pat on the head.
> *Nevertheless it is hardly fair*
> *To risk your heart for a dog to tear.*
>
> When the fourteen years which Nature permits
> Are closing in asthma, or tumour, or fits,
> And the vet's unspoken prescription runs,
> To lethal chambers or loaded guns,
> *Then you will find—it's your own affair,*
> *But . . . you've given your heart to a dog to tear.*
>
> When the body that lived at your single will,
> When the whimper of welcome is stilled (how still !),
> When the spirit that answered your every mood
> Is gone—wherever it goes—for good,
> *You will discover how much you care,*
> *And will give your heart to a dog to tear.*"

I have heard Mr. Kipling called " brutal," and the lines :

> " Perfect passion and worship fed
> By a kick in the ribs or a pat on the head,"

have been instanced in proof.

" The whole poem is spoilt for me," said a woman of my acquaintance, " by the brutal dragging in, as if he wished deliberately to outrage one's feelings, wantonly to insult his fellows, of the hateful allusion to ' a kick in the ribs.' It is like a sudden blow in the face, coming when one's head is bowed in silent sympathy, one's eyes blinded with pitiful tears."

I replied that it is true that Mr. Kipling scorns evasions, half-truths (which make generally for doctored lies), and the dressing up of painful facts, lest one offend a reader. He writes fearlessly and with Shakespearean outspokenness. He is incapable of twisting or faking the facts of life, of picturing anyone or anything other than that one or that thing is. He is not one who, in Shakespeare's words,

> " Capers nimbly in a lady's chamber
> To the lascivious pleasing of a lute."

His are the banjo tunes,

> " that bring the laugh that brings the groan.
> I can rip your very heartstrings out with those,"

and he does rip our very heartstrings out, as when he reminds us (alas, that we need reminding) that there are, among those to whom has been given speech and a soul, who have only a kick in the ribs for the dumb creature, with no speech, and to whom they would deny a soul. But since such brutality there is among human beings—are honest and humane men to hush it up ? or so to deal with it that even a callous and cruel man, chancing to read what has been written, may feel himself condemned for what he is, may even squirm under the wielded lash ?

" You call," I went on to say to my woman friend, " that momentary side-picture of a hobnailed boot, thrust out to kick at the dumb creature's ribs, ' brutal.' How brutal, had it not been shown as brutal ! And how much (I had almost said) more Godlike, more Christlike, but let us phrase it ' how unmanlike,' is the love of the dumb creature, who, even for the human brute who kicks him, has only ' perfect passion and worship,' ' love unflinching that cannot die.' "

Just as in *The Power of the Dog* we find an underlying meaning in words which at first may pain or
repel a sensitive reader, so, as we see more deeply
into the author's intention, we realize that, even
while showing us human nature nakedly as it is,
that intention is to make us slow to judgment,
swift in sympathy, large-hearted, large-visioned
and loving, for all the creatures, mortal or immortal,
of God's making.

Read what Mr. Kipling says of the so-called
" Heathen," and remember that we are not entirely
without heathen of our own, even in Christian
England ; and that it is for them, too, that he pleads
in this great-hearted prayer for sympathy, fellowship,
and understanding :

> " ' My brother kneels,' so saith Kabir,
>   ' To stone and brass in heathen-wise,
> But in my brother's voice I hear
>   My own unanswered agonies.
> His God is as his fates assign.
> His prayer is all the world's—and mine.' "

The Poet shows Sin as
Horrible and Hateful

In *The Power of the Dog* it is Mr. Kipling himself
who is speaking. But because in some of his other
poems he makes his characters speak and act as
in real life—what those characters say or do has no
more to do with Mr. Kipling, than what Bill Sikes
said or did had to do with Charles Dickens. It is
for neither the novelist nor the poet to picture men
and women merely as he wishes them to be. He
may—perhaps more indirectly than didactically,
for the very folk who most need help are apt to fight
shy of a sermon, and to resent being " preached at "—
seek to inspire in them, if only by contrast, the desire
for what is high, instead of what is low. But to

effect his contrast he can no more leave sin out of
his picture than an artist can put upon canvas a
painting in which there are no shadows.　Mr. Kipling paints life as he sees it, shadows and all.　He
writes in two lines of—

> " The feasting, and the folly and the fun—
> And the lying, and the lusting and the drink,"

but in the next following lines he warns us of—

> " The merry play that drops you, when you're done,
> To the thoughts that burn like irons if you think."

The note recurs again and again in his work.　He—

> " Gives you eyes to see your sin
> And the heavier repentance at the last."

" There is no punishment equal to the punishment
of being base," said Robertson of Brighton.　That
was in a sermon to civilians.

Mr. Kipling, though no preacher, is writing of a
dissolute soldier under arrest, and puts the same
terrible truth in his own way :

> "When the drunken comrade mutters and the great guard
> lantern gutters,
> And the horror of our fall is written plain,
> Every secret, self-revealing on the aching white-washed ceiling,
> Do you wonder that we drug ourselves from pain ? "

If Mr. Kipling writes of sin, he shows it not as
pleasure-affording, attractive, and alluring, but as
the hateful, revenge-wreaking, hell-bringing thing it
is :

> " An' the end of it's sittin' and thinkin',
> An' dreamin' Hell fires to see."

It has been said of him that he has made poetry
out of the refuse of language, and it is true that he has
taken the slang, even the oaths that are sometimes

to be heard in barrack-yard or street, and has wrought them into rude poetry.

But though he will not picture these men or women as other than they are ; though he put into their mouths the words they actually use, he shows us also—under the coarseness and grossness of speech, which may repel a sensitive reader—human hearts more like our own than we could otherwise have thought possible.

Turn to the poem *That Day* in *The Seven Seas*, in which he shows us—a terrible object lesson—that even British soldiers who are undisciplined (as well call a man with no belief in God " religious," as call undisciplined troops " soldiers "—for undiscipline is the atheism of the army)—even they can, on occasion, become a mutinous, morale-less, and runaway mob :

" I 'eard the knives be'ind me, but I dursn't face my man,
    Nor I don't know where I went to, 'cause I didn't 'alt to see,
Till I 'eard a beggar squealin' out for quarter as 'e ran,
    An' I thought I knew the voice an'—it was me !
We was 'iding under bedsteads more than 'arf a march away,
    We was lying up like rabbits all about the country-side,
An' the Major cursed 'is Maker 'cause 'e lived to see that day
    An' the Colonel broke 'is sword acrost an' cried.

            .   .   .   .

An' there ain't no chorus 'ere to give,
    Nor there ain't no band to play ;
But I wish I was dead 'fore I done what I did
    Or seen what I seed that day ! "

Just as in the two lines :

" Till I 'eard a beggar squealin' out for quarter as 'e ran,
    An' I thought I knew the voice an'—it was me,"

Mr. Kipling puts you, who read, and me, who write, into that soldier's place ; just as he makes us realize that, undisciplined and mutinous as the men of that regiment were—you, who read, and I, who

write, might, in like case, and in like lack of discipline
(more even than lack of courage) have lost our morale,
have done what they did, and have run away—so,
writing of the men and women who have sinned,
Mr. Kipling makes the reader feel that the reader
and the sinner are one.

His Meaning for
You and Me

" A convict or a man who drinks," says the author
of *The Story of an African Farm*, " seems something
so far-off and horrible when we see him ; but to
himself he seems quite near to us, and like us. We
wonder what kind of a creature he is, but he is just
we ourselves."

Some of us do not like this composite-portrait
making of Mr. Kipling's. We do not care to see the
negative of our own portrait thus " imposed," as
photographers say, upon the negatives of folk whom
we should perhaps describe as " common."

That is where we are wrong and Mr. Kipling is
right. He has learned the lesson divinely taught
in a vision to St. Peter :

> " It is enough that through Thy Grace
> I saw nought common on Thy Earth."

To him " the Colonel's lady an' Judy O'Grady "
are sisters under their skins, each with her small
vanities, each with her noble virtues ; each unreason-
ably, perhaps fretfully exacting and capricious at
times, each capable, and uncomplainingly, of endurance and self-sacrifice so great as to call for wonder,
almost for worship ; each half-angelic, half-human ;
and each all, and all the time, a woman.

Not every " Colonel's Lady " may approve the
comparison, or care to see an unpalatable truth thus
nakedly presented. When she can say with Mr.
Kipling, " I saw nought common on Thy Earth,"

her resentment will pass, and she will marvel that to one man it has been given thus to see into the hearts alike of women and men.

He can Read the Hearts of
Women and Men

I say " women and men " advisedly, for though men-novelists and poets have written understandingly of their own sex, not many have the insight into the complex soul of womanhood, wifehood, motherhood, which Mr. Kipling has.

He understands, too, the hearts of women of other races. We all remember the exquisite scene of the young Indian mother, Ameera, with her baby, Tota, on the housetop.

    " ' What shall we call him among ourselves ? ' ":

she asks the child's father, who has the little fellow in his arms.

    " ' Look ! Art thou ever tired of looking ? He carries thy very eyes. But the mouth——'

    ' Is thine, most dear. Who should know better than I.'

    'Tis such a feeble mouth. Oh, so small ! And yet it holds my heart between its lips. Give him to me now. He has been too long away.'

    ' Nay, let him lie ; he has not yet begun to cry.'

    ' When he cries thou wilt give him back—eh ? What a man of mankind thou art ! If he cried he were only the dearer to me.' "

In *The Song of the Women*, written for Lady Dufferin's Fund for Medical Aid to the women of India, he is the wise interpreter who finds words whereby the women of the East make known their gratitude to their sister-women of the West :

" Say that we be a feeble folk who greet her,
　　But old in grief, and very wise in tears ;
Say that we, being desolate, entreat her
　　That she forget us not in after years ;
　　For we have seen the light and it were grievous
　　To dim that dawning if our Lady leave us.

　　　　　.　　.　　.　　.　　.　　.　　.

By hands uplifted to the Gods that heard not,
　　By gifts that found no favour in their sight,
By faces bent above the babe that stirred not,
　　By nameless horrors of the stifling night ;
　　By ills fordone, by peace her toils discover,
　　Bid Earth be good beneath and Heaven above her !

If she have sent her servants in our pain,
　　If she have fought with Death and dulled his sword ;
If she have given back our sick again,
　　And to the breast the weakling lips restored,
　　Is it a little thing that she has wrought ?
　　Then Life and Death and Motherhood be nought."

Mr. Kipling has told us in *Barrack-Room Ballads* :

" Oh, East is East, and West is West, and never the twain shall
　　meet."

Shall the twain never meet ?　It seems to me
that in these lines, and in the poem beginning :

" The dead child lay in the shroud,"

he at least has made East and West one in heart
and in motherhood :

" ' O feet I have held in my hand,
　　O hands at my heart to catch,
　How should they know the road to go
　　And how should they lift the latch ? '

　　　　　.　　.　　.　　.　　.　　.

　' Lie still, dear lamb, lie still ;
　　The child is passed from harm,
　'Tis the ache in your breast that broke your rest,
　　And the feel of an empty arm.' ' "

Mr. Kipling has drawn a terrible picture of evil womanhood in the lines, *The Vampire*. They were written for his relative Sir Phillip Burne Jones' picture of that name, and were first printed, if I remember rightly, in the Catalogue of the New Gallery Summer Exhibition, 1897.

But true and noble women no one reverences more than he. His reverence for women, most of all for motherhood, is too deep to find frequent or easy expression. One feels that to him it is sacred and apart from all else in life ; sacred perhaps as the memory of his own mother, some pulse of whose mother-heart—so marvellously does this man understand the mystery and the miracle of motherhood—still seems to beat in the heart of her son.

Mr. Kipling and the Children

Perhaps that is why he is instantly at home with children and they with him. The *Jungle Books* and *Just So Stories* are the joy of the nursery, for Mr. Kipling makes his little folk readers free of the jungle, and lets them into the secret of the jungle folks' lives, thought, and speech. I know children by the score who are never weary of hearing of the doings of Mowgli and Rikki-Tikki-Tavi ; of how the Camel got his hump, the Rhinoceros his skin, the Leopard his spots, or of the Elephant's Child, the Cat that walked by Himself, or the Crab that played with the Sea.

Boy Scouts and Girl Guides

At the moment it is Mr. Kipling's poems for children that we are considering. He writes a song for Boy Scouts, and the Chief Scout himself could not show greater knowledge of what scouts should or should not do, nor more entirely understand and express the true scout spirit. Here are some stanzas from *A Patrol Song*.

" Look out for the birds of the air,
    Look out for the beasts of the field ;
They'll tell you how and where
    The other side's concealed.
When the blackbird bolts from the copse,
    And the cattle are stirring about,
The wise commander stops
    And (*chorus*) All patrols look out !

Look out when your front is clear,
    And you feel you are bound to win.
Look out for your flank and your rear—
    For that's where surprises begin.
For the rustle that isn't a rat,
    For the splash that isn't a trout,
For the boulder that may be a hat,
    (*Chorus*) All patrols look out.

Look out when your temper goes
    At the end of a losing game ;
And your boots are too tight for your toes,
    And you answer and argue and blame.
It's the hardest part of the law,
    But it has to be learnt by the Scout—
For whining and shirking and ' jaw '
    (*Chorus*) All patrols look out ! "

The Glory of the Garden

At another time Mr. Kipling takes up his pen to sing *The Glory of the Garden*, and shows that the spirit of the gardener is, or should be, very like that of the boy scout and the girl guide.

Of the eight stanzas I quote the last four :

" Our England is a garden, and such gardens are not made
    By singing : ' Oh, how beautiful ! ' and sitting in the shade,
While better men than we go out and start their working lives
    At grubbing weeds from gravel paths with broken dinner-knives.

There's not a pair of legs so thin, there's not a head so thick,
There's not a hand so weak and white, nor yet a heart so sick,
But it can find some needful job that's crying to be done,
For the Glory of the Garden glorifieth every one.

Then seek your job with thankfulness and work till further
    orders ;
If it's only netting strawberries or killing slugs on borders ;
And when your back stops aching and your hands begin to
    harden,
You will find yourself a partner in the Glory of the Garden.

Oh, Adam was a gardener, and God who made him sees
That half a proper gardener's work is done upon his knees,
So when your work is finished, you can wash your hands and
    pray
For the Glory of the Garden that it may not pass away ;
And the Glory of the Garden it shall never pass away ! "

In *Big Steamers* the writer sets the Kipling system
of wireless telegraphy at work between the great
steamers, thousands of miles away at sea, and the
nursery—compelling the steamers to yield up their
secrets to the children, and to answer questions as
easily as the Elephant Trainer in a circus compels
the huge creature to reply to a question, by picking
out lettered cards to spell the word he wants.

Can Animals Speak ?

Turn to *Twenty Poems*, if you wish to make the
acquaintance of yet another Mr. Kipling.

One often hears the phrase that this or that dog-
friend can " do everything but speak." It is a
phrase which " places " those who so use it. They
are dog-likers, a class distinct from, and a whole
world of understanding away from, dog-lovers, to
whom dog-language is as understandable, often more
delightful and interesting, than much human speech.

One does not need to be a linguist to learn
dog-language. English itself is unnecessary. The

language with the tiniest vocabulary in the world is
the language of love. Even human lovers have
few words. The dog who loves you has fewer, but
each word carries infinite meaning to him or her
who can understand. Some of my human friends
are busy learning Esperanto. My dog and I do not
need to do this—we speak it already. Love is the
Esperanto which makes all God's creatures, even
His dumb creatures, of one tongue.

Mr. Kipling knows that Esperanto by heart—
the only way in which you can know it. Without
heart, even though you have " brains " and eloquence,
you are as one born deaf and dumb to it—at least,
if not deaf, as one listening to some unintelligible
foreign tongue.

Mr. Kipling and the Machines

Mr. Kipling has by his heart-knowledge of this
language interpreted for us the utterances of the
live creatures not only of our fireside, but also of
field, forest and jungle. Nor is that all. He has
so endowed *unalive* things—ships, engines, machines
of every sort—with personality, human personality,
that to him as he writes, and to us as we read, these
things are no longer inanimate machines, but living
creatures with a soul of their own, and yet without
speech.

Then Mr. Kipling comes along. " This won't
do," he says, " the poor things can't speak. What a
lot they could teach us if they did ! I'm a bit of
a word conjurer, among other things, as well as a
bit of an inventor. Wonder whether I could invent
or discover an Esperanto for them ? "

Then, hey presto ! the thing is done. These
dumb things—one refuses any more to think of
them as dead things—lift up their voices and speak—
the Wireless Installation, the Marine Engines, the

Locomotives, Pumps, and Mining Tools, each separately, and finally all together, in a slightly Indian accent—of *The Secret of the Machines.*

The poem so named will appeal alike to young and old, which reminds me to ask whether there is a child, be that child eight years old or eighty years young, girl or woman, boy or man—who can read the very wisest, and certainly one of the most wonderful (if only for its simplicity) poem that ever was written—*If*—without the stirring within him or her of all that makes for girlhood or boyhood, womanhood or manhood, herohood, hardihood, nationhood. To say more of *If* is to waste time. The best criticism is to quote some stanzas and be silent :

" If you can keep your head when all about you
　　Are losing theirs and blaming it on you ;
　If you can trust yourself when all men doubt you,
　　But make allowance for their doubting too;
　If you can wait and not be tired by waiting,
　　Or being lied about, don't deal in lies,
　Or being hated, don't give way to hating,
　　And yet don't look too good, nor talk too wise **:**

　　　　•　　•　　•　　•　　•　　•　　•

　If you can bear to hear the truth you've spoken
　　Twisted by knaves to make a trap for fools,
　Or watch the things you gave your life to, broken,
　　And stoop to build 'em up with worn-out tools. . . .

　If you can talk with crowds and keep your virtue,
　　Or walk with Kings—nor lose the common touch,
　If neither foes nor loving friends can hurt you,
　　If all men count with you, but none too much ;
　If you can fill the unforgiving minute
　　With sixty seconds' worth of distance run,
　Yours is the Earth and everything that's in it,
　　And—which is more—you'll be a Man, my son ! "

" The Children "

The Children must be read as it was written—and I have copied here only two out of the five stanzas.

I say " as written," but it does not seem to me like a poem set down in words. It is as if a sublime Funeral March for all our young and noble dead had found utterance through the medium of one human and still-speaking voice. *The Children*, not merely *Our Sons*, those who have fallen will always be in the memory of their fathers and mothers, and in this poem the mother-heart and the father-heart seem (as in others of Mr. Kipling's poems) strangely to blend and to meet.

In low undertones, in which is no word of hate, nor raised voice of revenge, *The Children* thunders the most terrible retribution against Germany. It is more than a poem, a dirge ; it is the blood of murdered children crying out to God from the ground, the heart-break of mothers and fathers made audible :

" These were our children who died for our lands : they were
        dear in our sight.
    We have only the memory left of their home-treasured sayings
        and laughter.
    The price of our loss shall be paid to our hands, not another's
        hereafter.
    Neither the Alien nor Priest shall decide on it. That is our
        right.
    But who shall return us the children ?

    At the hour the Barbarian chose to disclose his pretences,
    And raged against Man, they engaged, on the breasts that
        they bared for us,
    The first felon-stroke of the sword he had longtime prepared
        for us,
    Their bodies were all our defence while we wrought our defences.

    But who shall return us our children ? "

A Poet and a Patriot

From this memorial to those who fell in the war I pass on to speak of the writer's part in warning us of the coming of war. Only in an article devoted

entirely to the subject could one hope to deal ade-
quately with Mr. Kipling's patriotic work. His
pre-war patriotic poems were for the most part a
warning, an appeal, almost a command, pointing
directly to the coming of the day of ordeal and to
the duty of preparation.

The purpose of the poems he wrote after the coming of war, when the ordeal he had foretold was upon
us, was the achievement of national unity, national
endurance, national self-sacrifice and national humiliation before, and dependence upon, God.

Long before the war Mr. Kipling had written
National Hymns—if one may differentiate a national
hymn from a patriotic poem—which had a similar
aim and sounded a similar note to that sounded
in what he has since written. By these National
Hymns, as for instance *Recessional*, whether penned
before or after August, 1914, the name of Rudyard
Kipling will, I believe, be for all time remembered.
They have the qualities by which our great religious
hymns endure, and are already accorded a place
beside those hymns.

Nor should posterity forget the poems written
directly for our own day and generation. The man
who penned *The Islanders*, who—ridiculed as an
alarmist, and aware that he jeopardized his own
prestige and popularity by the advocacy of a lost
cause—continued year in and year out, with all
his energies and abilities, and by every means at his
command, to warn his country of what was coming,
will not be forgotten. Roberts and Kipling are
names which Englishmen, generations hence, will
revere and honour.

Open your *Five Nations* and turn to the poem
The Islanders :

" Given to strong delusion, wholly believing a lie,
  Ye saw that the land lay fenceless, and ye let the months go
    by

Waiting some easy wonder : hoping some saving sign—
Idle—openly idle—in the lee of the forespent Line.

. . . . . .

But ye say, ' It will mar our comfort.'
    Ye say, ' It will 'minish our trade.'
Do ye wait for the spattered shrapnel
    Ere ye learn how a gun is laid ?

. . . . . .

(Light ye shall have on that lesson, but little time to learn.)"

" You're a queer lot, you English ! " said a distinguished American soldier at the beginning of the war. " You go to war, and you lose every battle—*except the last.*"

Exactly ! The English do, if only by virtue oɪ certain national characteristics, " hold on " and win—if only by the last battle. But at what a cost !

It is true that since then, " light we have had on the lesson," even if, as foretold, " little time to learn," but whether we have learned the lesson is a question I will not here attempt to answer. Instead, may I remind the reader that just as in *The Islanders* and other poems Mr. Kipling foretold the coming of Armageddon, so he foretold the loyalty of our Overseas Dominions—on the disloyalty and the breaking away in open revolution of which, the fatuous Kaiser relied as a factor in a German victory. In *England's Answer* to the Song of the cities of India, Canada, Australia, New Zealand, and South Africa, you read :

**His
Prophecy—**

"So long as The Blood endures,
I shall know that your good is mine : ye shall feel that my strength is yours :
In the day of Armageddon, at the last great fight of all,
That Our House stand together, and the pillars do not fall."

The prophecy has been more than fulfilled, for Mr. Kipling knew the *real* India, Canada, Australia, New Zealand, and South Africa, just as he knew the *real* England, the England of our dreams :

> " If England was what England seems,
> An' not the England of our dreams,
> But only putty, brass, an' paint,
> 'Ow quick we'd chuck 'er ! *But she ain't !* "

He knew the real England's Sea Power. Not while our glorious Royal Navy, our scarcely less glorious Mercantile Marine, fly, the one the White, the other the Red Ensign, will *The English Flag* cease to be read with wonder and pride. I have space only for a few lines :

> " The South Wind sighed . .
> ' Strayed amid lonely islets, mazed amid outer keys,
> I waked the palms to laughter—I tossed the scud in the breeze—
> Never was isle so little, never was sea so lone,
> But over the scud and the palm trees an English flag was flown.
>
> I have wrenched it free from the halliard to hang for a wisp on the Horn ;
> I have chased it north to the Lizard—ribboned and rolled and torn ;
> I have spread its fold o'er the dying, adrift in a hopeless sea ;
> I have hurled it swift on the slaver, and seen the slave set free.' "

Then the East Wind speaks :

> " Never the lotos closes, never the wild-fowl wake,
> But a soul goes out on the East Wind that died for England's sake."

And the West Wind :

> " First of the scattered legions, under a shrieking sky,
> Dipping between the rollers, the English Flag goes by."

Even Mr. le Gallienne, for all his gifts as poet and critic, the very last man alive competently to write of Mr. Kipling, is in a book as unworthy of the

writer as of the subject, compelled reluctantly to
admit of Mr. Kipling : " His work nobly enforces
those old-fashioned virtues of man which it is to
be hoped will never go out of fashion—to do one's
duty, to live stoically, to live cleanly, to live cheerfully."

The Makings of a
Soldier

" Warcraft " (he warns us) is—

" not to be mastered in haste,
But after trial and labour, by temperance, living chaste.

. . . .

So at the haggard trumpets, instant your soul shall leap
Forthright, accoutred, accepting—alert from the wells of
sleep.
So at the threat ye shall summon—so at the need ye shall
send
Men, not children or servants, tempered and taught to the end ;
Cleansed of servile panic, slow to dread or despise,
Humble because of knowledge, mighty by sacrifice."

Has a cleaner, manlier, more soldierly standard
ever been set the lads who were training to defend
the country in her hour of peril ? The last two
lines might well stand as the epitaph of our fallen
Old Contemptibles—in morale, manhood, and soldier-
hood the most magnificent force of trained men
that ever took the field.

In another poem *The 'Eathen* we are given a
picture of the young recruit as he is when he joins
up, and as he is when he has come under discipline
and training.

" The young recruit is 'ammered—'e takes it very 'ard ;
'E 'angs 'is 'ead an' mutters—'e sulks about the yard ;
'E talks o' ' cruel tyrants ' 'e'll swing for by an' by,
An' the others 'ears and mocks 'im, and the boy goes orf to
cry.

The young recruit is silly—'e thinks o' suicide ;
'E's lost 'is gutter-devil ; 'e 'asn't got 'is pride.

                    .   .   .   .   .   .

The cruel-tyrant-sergeants they watch 'im 'arf a year ;
They watch 'im with 'is comrades, they watch 'im with 'is beer ;
They watch 'im with the women at the regimental dance,
And the cruel-tyrant-sergeants send 'is name along for " Lance."

                    .   .   .   .   .   .

An' last, a Colour Sergeant, as such to be obeyed,
'E schools 'is men at cricket, he tells 'em on parade."

Then we are taken from the barrack-yard to the
battle-field. The mutinous young recruit is a
trained and disciplined soldier, and in command of
a " section." Mark the change in the man.

" 'E sees the blue-white faces all tryin' 'ard to grin,
  An' 'e stands an' waits an' suffers till it's time to cap 'em in.

An' now the hugly bullets come peckin' through the dust,
An' no one wants to face 'em, but every beggar must ;
So, like a man in irons which isn't glad to go,
They moves 'em off by companies uncommon stiff an' slow.

Of all 'is five years' schoolin' they don't remember much
Excep' the not retreatin', the step, an' keepin' touch.
It looks like teachin' wasted when they duck an' spread an' 'op,
But if 'e 'adn't learned 'em they'd be all about the shop !

An' now it's ' Oo goes backward ? ' an' now it's ' Oo comes
  on ? '
An' now it's ' Get the doolies,' an' now the captain's gone ;
An' now it's bloody murder, but all the while they 'ear
'Is voice, the same as barrick drill, a-shepherdin' the rear.

'E's just as sick as they are, 'is 'eart is like to split,
But 'e works 'em, works 'em, works 'em, till 'e feels 'em take
  the bit ;
The rest is 'oldin' steady till the watchful bugles play,
An' 'e lifts 'em, lifts 'em, lifts 'em through the charge that wins
  the day."

This poem—I have not quoted the half of it here
—was once recited to a number of girls. I was not

the reciter, but I watched their eager faces as they heard of the sulky young recruit being hammered into shape, taught discipline, cleanliness, self-respect, and taught to " drop the ' bloodies ' from every word 'e slings," then of his coming to non-commission rank, and in battle, steadying, holding— " the same as barrick drill "—and shepherding the men under his command, and finally of his lifting them to " the charge that wins the day."

At this point, to the reciter's surprise, for the poem does not end there, the bevy of girls—it was in wartime—broke out into such proud and exultant cheers at the battlescene-picture, finely rendered as it was, of what British pluck, training, and discipline will do that the reciter could not go on.

Yes, Rudyard Kipling has " made poetry out of the refuse of language," and it is because he writes with—

" . . . the faith of men that ha' brothered men
    By more than easy breath,
 And the eyes o' men that ha' read wi' men
    In the open books of death."

His Flower
Poems

Yet this man, who has drawn such stern and terrible pictures of battle and death (as in *Cholera Camp*, *The 'Eathen*, and *Danny Deever*), can, when he chooses, write of *The Dawn Wind*, of love, of fairies (he does not so call them) and of flowers with the exquisite sensitiveness, the delicacy, and the tenderness of a woman. I have already exceeded my quotations limits, and *The Dawn Wind* is too perfect a thing to print other than in full ; but by way of illustrating Mr. Kipling's gifts as a word-musician, I filch a snatch or two from *The Flowers*. It has the lyric " lilt " and " lift " of the Elizabethans :

" Buy my English posies !
 Kent and Surrey may—
Violets of the Undercliff
 Wet with Channel spray ;
Cowslips from a Devon combe—
 Midland furze afire—
Buy my English posies
 And I'll sell your heart's desire !

Buy my English posies !
 You that scorn the May,
Won't you greet a friend from home
 Half the world away ?
Green against the draggled drift
 Faint and frail and first—
Buy my Northern bloodroot
 And I'll know where you were nursed :

Robin down the logging-road whistles ' Come to me ! '
 Spring has found the maple grove, the sap is running free ;
All the winds of Canada call the ploughing rain,
 Take the flower and turn the hour, and kiss your love again.

. . . .

Buy my English posies !
 Ye that have your own,
Buy them for a brother's sake,
 Overseas, alone :
Weed ye trample underfoot
 Floods his heart abrim—
Bird ye never heeded,
 Oh, she calls his dead to him ! "

The Kipling Gallery

Whether Mr. Kipling's mastery of word-music be
or be not inherited, I do not know ; but as regards
the power by which he makes of his pen a brush, of
his inkpot a painter's palette of many colours, one
remembers that he was not only born into Art, but
came of a family which married into Art. His
father, the late Mr. John Lockwood Kipling, whom
I remember meeting many years ago, was a gifted

artist. One sister of Rudyard Kipling's mother married Sir E. Burne-Jones, another, Sir E. Poynter, P.R.A. That being so, I was not surprised to hear from the father that his son is no indifferent draughtsman. That son's pictures, in another realm of Art, are in all our homes; there is a gallery of them in every liner that leaves port; they bring England and home to the squatter's hut in some far outpost of the Empire, and the gallant explorers, groping their way through icefloes, and the Northern dark towards the Pole :

> " Hear the hansoms slurring
> Once more through London mud."

True, as we read in that poem of sheer magic :

> " There ain't no 'busses runnin'
> From the Bank to Mandalay,"

but 'busses are slow and out of date. You now need to do no more than seat yourself on a magic carpet of Mr. Kipling's weaving, and—again one must say, " Hey ! Presto ! "—he wafts you out and away, and sets you down :

> " By the old Moulmein Pagoda, lookin' eastward to the sea
> .   .   .   .   .   .
> An' the sunshine an' the palm-trees an' the tinkly temple bells ;
> On the road to Mandalay."

Where other artists paint laboriously with the brush, he but dips a pen into the ink, flicks it once or twice on paper, and your picture is drawn—sometimes grim and grotesque, almost alarming, as when Adam-zad the Bear rears upon you out of the printed page, as the genie of the *Arabian Nights* spiralled upwards from a bottle's mouth :

> " Horrible, hairy, human, with paws like hands in prayer,
> Making his supplication rose Adam-zad the Bear !

I looked at the swaying shoulders, at the paunch's swag and
    swing,
And my heart was touched with pity for the monstrous, pleading
    thing."

Sometimes the picture is comical, as when Mr.
Kipling shows us the commissariat camel :

" With 'is silly neck a-bobbin' like a basket full o' snakes."

There are roomsfull of large canvases on exhibition in the Kipling Art Gallery, but these time and
space compel me to leave unnoticed. My readers
must inspect them in detail for themselves. But
let me for five minutes direct attention to a very
few little works of art in the Miniature Room.
First a couple of Sea Impressions from *The Five
Nations* :

" Who hath desired the Sea ?—the sight of salt water unbounded—
The heave and the halt and the hurl and the crash of the comber
    windhounded ?
The sleek-barrelled swell before storm, grey, foamless, enormous,
    and growing.
            .   .   .   .
The shudder, the stumble, the swerve, as the star-stabbing
    bowsprit emerges."

Again from *The Five Nations* :

            " . . . the ocean-meadows
        All purple to the stars."

A Khyber Pass Impression from *Barrack-Room
Ballads* :

        " Voices of jackals calling
            And, loud in the hush between,
        A morsel of dry earth falling
            From the flanks of the scarred ravine."

The Veldt :

" Violet peaks uplifted through the crystal evening air."

Or, coming back to England, who (I ask) has
pictured for us as Mr. Kipling has :

F

" Our blunt, bow-headed, whale-backed Downs—

.   .   .   .   .   .

Bare slopes where chasing shadows skim,
    And through the gaps revealed
Belt upon belt, the wooded, dim
    Blue goodness of the Weald " ?

Who can so call up for us the Downland scent of :

" Close-bit thyme that smells
    Like dawn in Paradise " ?

In the Portrait Room hangs a picture of John Bunyan. It is entitled *The Holy War*, but I have only space for the first eight lines :

" A Tinker out of Bedford,
    A vagrant oft in quod,
A private under Fairfax,
    A minister of God—
Two hundred years and thirty
    Ere Armageddon came,
His single hand portrayed it,
    And Bunyan was his name."

And one of Lord Roberts. There are several noble verses. Here are the last three :

" Clean, simple, valiant, well-beloved,
    Flawless in faith and fame,
Whom neither ease nor honours moved
    An hair's-breadth from his aim.

Never again the war-wise face,
    The weighed and urgent word
That pleaded in the market place—
    Pleaded, and was not heard.

Yet from his life a new life springs
    Through all the hosts to come,
And Glory is the least of things
    That follow this man home."

As an artist, Mr. Kipling may owe a little to the Coleridge of *The Ancient Mariner*, and, many years ago, may have come under the spell and glamour

of Edgar Allen Poe. His Anglo-Saxon forbears—
something of their rude, glad, aboriginal love of and
gladness in life lives and leaps in his veins to-day—
have undoubtedly, in some strange way, set their
mark upon him ; but for the rest he owes all to
himself, and his many imitators owe everything to
him.

The Poet's Humour

Though I have not thus far spoken of Mr. Kipling's
humour, the fact that he is a humorist is implied
in everything that has been written. It is because
his sense of humour is so keen, that he is so self-sure,
and yet has so little self-pride. Neither mock-
modesty nor self-sufficiency can for long make head-
way against a sense of humour.

Because he is a humorist, Mr. Kipling sees not
only human life and his fellow-mortals, but also
himself, and his gifts, great as they are, truly, and
in perspective :

" Hear now a song—a song of broken interludes—
A song of little cunning ; of a singer nothing worth.
Through the naked words and mean
May ye see the truth between
As the singer knew and touched it in the ends of all the Earth ! "

Genius, which is balanced, is first cousin to sublim-
ated Common Sense. It is Common Sense to which
has been given the great gift of Vision—far, clear
and true.

The mischief of a certain kind of genius (half
genius really) is that though it have great brains,
they are lop-sided, and so are of small worth to
the race. The higher and rarer the genius, the more
perfect the equipoise, and as it is humour, more
than any other quality, which strikes life's balances
finely, I am not sure that without a sense of humour

true justice, true judgment, or true humanity there can be. The ex-Kaiser's megalomania, Germany's monstrous crimes, are partly due to the fact that Germans are colossally and notoriously without humour. Even in the trenches, Tommy's sense of humour, crude or Cockney as it might be, carried him, grinning, if growsing, through the terrors and the horrors under which the solemn-faced German, hymning his ridiculous howl of hate, collapsed.

Perhaps it was because Tommy knew his India— units of the Regular Army being stationed there for a time—that Mr. Kipling attained such instant popularity in the Service. His humour is sometimes strangely Indian and Eastern. It is no grin on the face of things. He does not angle for the cheap guffaw or invite the ready and self-conscious titter. You must seek his humour if you would find it, for it is often locked up and hidden away in what is seemingly sad. But if you are minded to seek, Mr. Kipling will not withhold the key. In his Dedication (*Departmental Ditties*) to the " dear hearts across the seas " in far India, he lets us into the secret :

" I have eaten your bread and salt,
    I have drunk your water and wine,
The deaths ye died I have watched beside,
    And the lives ye led were mine.

Was there aught that I did not share
    In vigil or toil or ease—
One joy or woe that I did not know,
    Dear hearts across the seas ?

I have written the tale of our life
    For a sheltered people's mirth,
In jesting guise—but ye are wise,
    And ye know what the jest is worth."

He has indeed written the lives of those who, in risk, exile, sadness, and temptations of which we wot not, serve our England in strange lands—and what we owe to those who thus sacrifice the happiness of home life and home friendships at the call of duty and in the interests of their country, few of us here in England realize.

He has indeed, too, written for " a sheltered people's mirth " and " in jesting guise." But those who read their Kipling aright—sheltered women, safeguarded by a home life, and the love of parents, from the temptations which assail the unsheltered; men living, snugly and securely in England, unexposed to the privations and the dangers, material or moral, which await the soldier, the " single man in barricks " who does not grow into a " plaster saint "—must give heed to the warning which underlies Mr. Kipling's humour, for though he jest, it is for them to reckon the jest at its true worth.

Whether he be, as some account him, " a man's poet," and that man something of what is called " a man of the world," he is (I must say it again) a very woman in understanding, and in the tenderness, sympathy and pity which underlie his strange " understanding." The living spirit of womanhood is surely service and self-sacrifice, and in that spirit Rudyard Kipling has written his poems :

> " Not as a ladder from Earth to Heaven,
>   Not as a witness to any creed ;
>   But simple service, simply given
>   To his own kind in their common need."

In his humorous as in his serious work that spirit prevails. We may say of him :

> " Thou art the Voice to kingly boys
>   To lift them through the fight."

To say, as some do, that he writes cynically of men and women and lightly of sin is entirely to misread him. The cynic sneers, and " doesn't care " : Kipling cares infinitely that his country, his fellows,

and himself shall be the best that is in them. No
one has written less " lightly " of what is false,
base, treacherous, in a word evil, and so of the
devil ; though it is equally true that he forbears
lightly and self-righteously to sit in judgment on
the errors, stumblings, sinnings—again in a word
on what is human—of us frail mortals of the dust.
Even under Mr. Kipling's slang, one catches the
throb in the throat which the slang is intended
—Englishman that he is—to conceal.   In many
of the South African and Indian poems he writes
sometimes humorously, sometimes ironically, but his
humour is half-sister to pathos, and the likeness
is not to be hidden.

Who can forget the picture of our one-time Boer
enemy, *Piet*, now—

" Dressed in stolen uniform with badge o' rank complete "

to snipe the British soldier unsuspected ; now making the British taxpayer " rebuild " his " country
seat " ; now—

" Ah, there, Piet ! whose time 'as come to die,
'Is carcase past rebellion, but his eyes inquirin' why " ?

Or the picture of *The Married Man* (Reservist of
the Line) and the Bachelor, night-camped on the
veldt :

" The bachelor 'e fights 'is fight
    An' stretches out an' snores ;
But the married man sits up all night—
    For 'e don't like out o' doors ;
'E'll strain an' listen an' peer
    An' give the first alarm—
For the sake o' the breathin' 'e's used to 'ear
And the 'ead on the thick of 'is arm."

Again, who can forget Chant-Pagan, or the wonderful poem *The Return* (" Peace is declared, an' I
return ") with its terrible picture of—

" . . . the pore dead that look so old
An' was so young an hour ago,
An' legs tied down before they're cold—
These are the things which make you know " ?

These *are* the things in very truth which make you know. Kipling has seen them for himself, and makes those who have not seen them to " know "— and in four lines—as no one else can.

Hitherto I have written only with gratitude of Rudyard Kipling. Now for a growse !

He appears to know something of everything, and to forget nothing—except the fact that the rest of the world is less wise than—not to say so omniscient as—he is.

When I was a very young man, I was foolish enough to hope that I knew a little of geography. Now that I am elderly, I am sure that my geography is all to learn. In those days, however, I was mighty proud (horrid young bounder) to tack the letters F.R.G.S. after my name on my (first) visiting-card, as well as after my signature to certain early effusions. But my attendances at the Royal Geographical Society's meetings convinced me that if I knew no geography, my fellow-members did—in spite of which latter statement I take leave to doubt whether half of them could pass an examination concerning the whereabouts of all the places mentioned by Mr. Kipling.

The touch of his pen-tip on paper establishes a sort of electric contact, by means of which names of places, of which most of us have never heard, tap out more quickly than one can work a typewriter. It is not done to parade knowledge. It is done unintentionally, unconsciously, and out of the fullness of his super-knowledge, his semi-omniscience.

Sydney Smith said that Jeffrey would " speak disrespectfully of the Equator." Mr. Kipling speaks,

not disrespectfully, but with next-door-neighbour
familiarity of the remotest spot on the earth.

If it were only in geography that he were so cock-
sure, so Kipling-confident, we should be less dismayed
by his omniscience and our own dismal ignorance.
But he appears equally encyclopædically-informed
on everything.

His Knowledge of
Machinery

Of machinery—of which I know less than nothing—I am told by experts that he seems to know
everything.   Pagett, M.P., was not more " dear "
to mosquitoes than every sort of machinery, the
more so for being complicated, is dear and known
to Rudyard Kipling.

Take him (so my expert friends tell me) to inspect,
if you can find such a thing, some newly invented
and complicated engine or machine, the " parts " of
which might well be known only to the inventor—and
Kipling will name these same " parts " for you, and
correctly, as readily as Adam named the animals at
the Creation.   So with folk-lore, so with science, so
with history, local as well as Imperial, Mr. Kipling
seems to have been born with the knowledge which
the rest of us have laboriously to acquire, and to
remember when acquired.

Heine, who could never master his Latin grammar,
said that if the Romans had not drawn in some
knowledge of Latin with their mothers' milk; if
they had had to learn their Latin grammar as he
had, he was quite sure they would never have had
time to conquer the world.

Similarly, if Mr. Kipling had not been born with a
brain which seems to be a cerebral magnet, automatically attracting all information to itself, but had
had to acquire the half of it, he would never have
had the leisure to write the half of his books.

That one single head should contain so much information is not merely curious ; it is uncanny. There is no keeping pace—still less competing with it—and that brings me to my solitary Kipling grievance.

It is not that he includes in *Songs from Books* (one wonders why) a nine-page prose play, *Gow's Watch*, in which there is not a single " song," but that in the whole three hundred odd pages there is only one footnote. Why should not Mr. Kipling take pity on our ignorance, and either, all together, at the book's end, or separately, append notes, explaining the historical, geographical, or local facts necessary for the right understanding of certain poems ? Turn, for instance, to the verse-heading to *The Looking Glass* in *Songs from Books* (page 193), and you read :

" Queen Bess was Harry's daughter.   Stand forward, partners all !
  In ruff and stomacher and gown
  She danced King Philip down-a-down,
  And left her shoe to show 'twas true—
  (The very tune I'm playing you)
In Norgem at Brickwall ! "

What meaning has the last line, noteless as it is to most readers ? None, I wager. Nor would it for me but for the fact that it has been my privilege on more than one occasion to be a guest at " Brickwall," which, in *Highways and Byways in Sussex*, Mr. E. V. Lucas describes as " The neighbouring seat of the Frewens, the great family of Northiam, for many generations, a noble old country mansion, partly Elizabethan and partly Stuart."

In a glass case in the hall at Brickwall the silk shoes which Queen Elizabeth left behind her at Norgem (now Northiam) are carefully preserved. Without this special knowledge which I chance to have, and lacking any explanatory note, Mr.

Kipling's references to " Norgem," Brickwall, and Queen Bess's shoe, carry no meaning.

In a botanical garden known to me, each tree and shrub is labelled with its name, for the information of visitors. When I asked, in visiting another botanical garden, why that course was not followed, the director replied : " Because I don't encourage laziness. Because what folk find out for themselves they remember ; what you tell them they forget."

It is not because Mr. Kipling shares this opinion, or is a disbeliever in the value of Notes, that *Songs from Books* is thus shorn of explanatory aids, for in *Barrack-Room Ballads* there are at least half a dozen footnotes. I venture to suggest that to the next edition of *Songs from Books* he append such notes as are needed—whether relating to folk-lore, Indian legend, or local history, for the better understanding and enjoyment of his innumerable readers.

The Children's Song

As this rambling and discursive paper is a personal appreciation, not a criticism in any academic sense, may I close by quoting a poem which is always associated in my mind with the circumstances in which I first heard it ?

Some years before the war, the Lady Principal (I did not know her personally) of a College for Girls wrote asking me to say a few words to her pupils about patriotism—as Service and Self-sacrifice. The occasion was Empire Day, which at that time was not, as now, widely celebrated.

As soon as I had taken my place on the school platform, the programme opened with the singing of a hymn. How it came about that I did not know the hymn, I cannot to this day explain, but it was *The Children's Song* from *Puck of Pook's Hill*, and

the Lady Principal had had it specially reproduced,
by some manifolding process, upon a cardboard
sheet, one of which was handed to every one in the
room—mine being still in my possession.

I shall never forget thus for the first time coming
to the knowledge of that lovely and noble poem—
not as something printed in a book, but hearing it
through the medium of those sweet girl voices, and
in sight of those fresh and glad young faces.

But so convinced was I, fresh as I was from a long
and serious talk with Lord Roberts, that England
was soon to be faced by a terrible war, in which only
the bodies of their fathers and brothers would stand
between the homes, the safety, possibly the lives of
these happy English girls, that when I began to
speak I found myself so faltering and uncertain of
utterance, that I feared, for the first time in my
life, I should be unable to go on. For it was of
what I *saw*, not of what I was *saying*, that I was
thinking. Listening to the children's song of England, I saw, as in a vision :

> " On the horizon's rim
> Great Armies gather, and the dim
> Grey mists of Armageddon's bloody dawn."

I saw the broken and bleeding bodies of England's
sons cast ruthlessly, and by the hundred thousand,
into War's furnace.

The College is an important one, and very many
girls heard me that day. Possibly some, who so
heard, may read these lines and remember. If the
Principal should do so she will understand why a
man accustomed to addressing audiences should
have been so faltering and nervous (I remember her looking in astonishment at the perspiration
on my forehead) when speaking a few words to an
audience of schoolgirls.

But remembering how I first heard that hymn,

remembering the fresh and innocent faces, the sweet
and innocent voices of the girl-singers, and remembering what ache there is to-day for a father, or a
brother, fallen, in many of their hearts, I can never
hear *The Children's Song* entirely unmoved.

And so I close this appreciation of a poet and a
patriot whom, it seems to me, every Englishwoman
and Englishman, every English girl and English boy
must hold in gratitude, affection and honour, not
with any unworthy words of mine, but in the words
of Mr. Kipling himself :

> " Land of our Birth, we pledge to thee
> Our love and toil in the years to be ;
> When we are grown and take our place,
> As men and women with our race.
>
> Father in Heaven, Who lovest all,
> Oh, help Thy children when they call ;
> That they may build from age to age,
> An undefilèd heritage.
>
> Teach us to bear the yoke in youth,
> With steadfastness and careful truth ;
> That, in our time, Thy Grace may give
> The truth whereby the Nations live.
>
> Teach us to rule ourselves alway,
> Controlled and cleanly night and day ;
> That we may bring, if need arise,
> No maimed or worthless sacrifice.
>
> Teach us to look in all our ends,
> On Thee for judge, and not our friends ;
> That we, with Thee, may walk uncowed
> By fear or favour of the crowd.
>
> Teach us the strength that cannot seek,
> By deed or thought, to hurt the weak ;
> That, under Thee, we may possess
> Man's strength to comfort man's distress.

Teach us delight in simple things,
And Mirth that has no bitter springs ;
Forgiveness free of evil done,
And love to all men 'neath the sun !

Land of our Birth, our faith, our pride,
For whose dear sake our fathers died ;
O Motherland, we pledge to thee,
Head, heart, and hand through the years to be."

Henry Newbolt

Henry Newbolt

"Crowned with the glitter of steel and the glimmer of tears."

WHERE shall one find in contemporary poetry a more unforgettable line than this, in which Sir Henry Newbolt acclaims a hero ?

We live to-day, it seems to me, in the heroic age, and it is well that we have among us a poet who can thus greatly acclaim and commemorate what is noble.

The poem from which the line is taken tells how in 1864, at Mobile Bay, a British sailor, Captain Craven—not calling gods and men to witness his deed, but taking it as a matter of course, as all in a sailor's day's work ; and making choice between life and death in commonplace, everyday words—gave his life that another might live :

"Over the manhole, up in the iron-clad tower,
  Pilot and Captain met as they turned to fly ;
The hundredth part of a moment seemed an hour,
  For one could pass to be saved, and one must die.

They stood like men in a dream : Craven spoke,
  Spoke as he lived and fought, with a Captain's pride,
'After you, Pilot ' : the pilot woke,
  Down the ladder he went, and Craven died.

      .   .   .   .   .   .

"Sidney thirsting a humbler need to slake,
  Nelson waiting his turn for the surgeon's hand,
Lucas crushed with chains for a comrade's sake,
  Outram coveting right before command.

These were paladins, these were Craven's peers,
   These with him shall be crowned in story and song.
Crowned with the glitter of steel and the glimmer of tears,
   Princes of courtesy, merciful, proud, and strong."

This with its fine restraint, amounting almost to austerity, and with no word of rhetoric, seems to me a masterpiece of poetic art. The superb simplicity with which Sir Henry tells the story reminds us strangely of the simplicity, yet the grandeur of Craven's words and deed. And if, next in our gratitude to him who has uttered a great word, comes—as we have been told on high authority—the man or woman who is first to quote that word—if that be so, then to be the first, nobly to commemorate a noble deed, is if not actually a title to nobility, at least a claim upon our gratitude and admiration.

I am not sure that what is heroic, chivalrous, self-sacrificing, *can* fitly be commemorated and interpreted by one who, in like circumstances, is not capable of like courage, chivalry and sacrifice. The spirit, which nerved and prompted the hero to the deed, inspired the poet to the song. Mr. Kipling, Sir Henry Newbolt, Mr. Alfred Noyes—there are others, but I mention only the three names which first come to mind—had, in 1914, passed the eligible age for carrying a rifle, commanding a company or battery in action, or training a battleship gun upon the enemy. I have spoken of Sir Henry Newbolt as "interpreting" the hero spirit to his fellows. Possibly he did more. Possibly it was his spirit, as uttered in his verse, which moulded the soul of many a fighting man to patriotism, and so, as I have said, inspired the hero to his deed. One feels, in reading or in listening to his words, not only that the heart, but also the manhood of the poet is pulsing behind the lines in which he writes of heroism. And you take up no book of his without lighting on the story of some deathless deed which he has so bravely commemorated, that I believe him to be already assured of immortality.

I do not mean that all his work will endure. I do not even mean that I count him as standing in the very highest places of poetry. It is not for a reason which is often adduced that I say this. Just as some musical critics call no composer " great " until his name appears on the score of an oratorio, so one hears certain critics of poetry say, " Can your poet point to such a *magnum opus* as Tennyson's *Beckett*, Browning's *Sordello*, Matthew Arnold's *Sohrab and Rustum* ? Has he written anything which, even in a small way, can be considered an epic ? Has he proved his ability to ' build the lofty rhyme ' upon a great scale ? If not—slight, even if excellent, as his poems are—he must be numbered with the minor poets."

Even a Tennyson was either not sufficiently sure of himself, or else was too ready to defer to, not to defy the conventions, and must need spend his splendid powers, wasting the national asset of his genius, in writing lengthy plays which now, I believe, remain unacted, and for the most part unread.

As if that only is an " epic " which is bulky ; as if one single miniature portrait, one tiny " interior," by painters who might be named, were not worth a round dozen of, say, Dore's vast canvases !

It is not because Sir Henry Newbolt's poems are in length comparatively slight, not because he has produced no huge masterpiece, that I do not hold him as in the very highest rank, but because I do not find in his work the evidence of great imaginative gifts. He is before all things, as becomes a poet, a man of the noblest ideals, of intense spirituality, of exquisite refinement. Again, as becomes a poet, he can love purely and can love passionately. Never did poet consecrate—I say " consecrate " in preference to " dedicate," which does not carry the same high meaning—a loftier, lovelier word to the woman of his choice, than in Sir Henry Newbolt's poem *The Presentation*. Loverhood, wifehood, motherhood, fatherhood—the weaknesses and the wonder of our nature, the human dearness and the holiness of wedded love, the symbolism and the sacredness of the tie, most of all the unfathomable underlying mystery of life—are all interwoven in this almost sacramental poem of no more than three stanzas.

Imagination and Invention

Yet, with all this, Sir Henry Newbolt does not seem to me to possess, on a great scale, the gift or quality of high vision.   I do not mean (to use homely imagery) that the maidservant, Invention, serves in the house of Poetry, where the queen and mistress, Imagination, should rule.   Imagination Sir Henry Newbolt undoubtedly has (he were no poet without it), but he invests that which is, or was, within his own experience, or has come within his knowledge, with the glamour and the glow of his imagination ; he rarely throws his imagination forward on that which is to be, that which is outside his own reading or experience—in a word, he is not primarily creative. There is always imagination in his poems, but his poems, for the most part, are not *greatly imagined*. They are chiefly memories, sometimes meditations, of culminating moments, of varying moods in the poet's own life ; more often they are the crowning, the sacramental commemoration, even the immortalization, of some superb deed, some supreme act of heroic self-sacrifice.

In the matter of technique—a false rhyme, an error in accent or the like—one remembers in this connexion that Newbolt is an accomplished classical scholar—he gives no opening for criticism. And if it be true that the form in which he clothes his thought is generally as stately as it is perfect, it is equally true that the soul of poetry, which he has thus beautifully bodied, is fairer even than the form. Dignity, distinction, reticence, restraint, unerring judgment, and faultlessly exquisite taste, mark all his work. His military ballads make their own battle-march music ; his songs of our unconquerable Navy, our incomparable Mercantile Marine, have the burst, the hurtle and the boom of great breakers. Some are shrill with the rage of the hurricane ; others, hoarse with the roar of the central seas. His songs of Devon, of England, and of rural joys, ring alike with sincerity and with sweetness. One misses sometimes the sensuous beauty of which Keats was so consummate a master ; and once or twice, a poem by Sir Henry Newbolt may soar, but to my ear fails to sing. As if the poet had suddenly tired, and his strength and his ear as suddenly failed him—the wings which had been upbearing him as noiselessly and as joyously as a lark's, flag and weaken. Now and then they even flap, rookwise, rather than soar larkwise, and—as when a low flying rook labours by us heavily—we hear the pinions creak. Turn for instance to *Minora Sidera*, the third verse of which runs :

"Such as were those, dogs of an elder day,
  Who sacked the golden ports,
And those later who dared grapple their prey
  Beneath the harbour forts."

Poetic licence possibly permits "who dared grapple" instead of "who dared to grapple," but since I was first instructed that—to quote my earliest book of grammar—"the word ' to ' is the sign of the infinitive mood "—to omit the ' to,' seems to me to make the verb of no mood at all. But it is the music, the

cadence, the lilt, not the construction of the line to
which I take exception :

"And those later who dared grapple their prey."

Our lark, surely, has become a rook, and a tired
rook, lumbering heavily home at that—so heavily,
so creakingly, that if some one could assure me that
our rook had alighted, and folded his wings to walk,
I should not gainsay him.

A Hundred
Years Hence

But enough of niggling criticism (it is little more)
of noble work ! Could readers, writers, and critics
of to-day be " told-off " into companies, and the
word be given by some angelic sergeant-major, some
marshalling Saint Michael, Saint Gabriel, or Saint
George :   " One pace a hundred years forward into
the future—march ! " then, and not till then, we
might see our little world of to-day in true perspective.   Could we thus step forward a hundred years,
I question whether we should find that as much
even as the very name of more than half a dozen
living poets would be remembered.   Those half-
dozen names would survive not on a tablet in West-
minster Abbey, but in that true Valhalla of song,
the anthologies which enshrine for all time our
noblest national verse.   Henry Newbolt's name will
be there.   It will not, in my opinion, be numbered
with our imaginative and creative poets, with Milton,
Blake, Shelley, Coleridge, but (a truer poet and
better craftsman than most of those I am about to
name) with James Thomson, Campbell, Drayton, and
Scott.

Rightly or wrongly on my part, it will, I think, be
by his patriotic poems and his Clifton songs that
Sir Henry Newbolt will be remembered.   Among
work which will live, I should name *Craven, Drake's*

Drum, Admirals All, Messmates, The Death of Admiral Blake, Gillespie, Seringapatam, A Ballad of John Nicholson, He Fell among Thieves (which holds a place of honour in Sir Arthur Quiller-Couch's *Oxford Book of English Verse*), *Clifton Chapel, Vitaï Lampada, The Vigil, The Only Son, The Schoolfellow, The School at War, The Best School of All ;* perhaps *The Youth's Awakening*, in the poem *The Fourth of August*, and *Devon* (which is included in Mr. William Robertson's *Golden Book of English Sonnets*).

For obvious reasons I am prevented from quoting these poems here, and must refer the reader to *Poems New and Old*, now published by Mr. John Murray at a popular price. But one lovely lyric, *Ireland, Ireland*, is so short that I give it in full. That it is melancholy, I agree. In writing of that Bride of the Sea whom, as Sir William Watson sings :

"We have wedded, but have never won,"

it is difficult to be other than melancholy, and Sir Henry Newbolt's poem, though penned years ago, previsions strangely the disorder and disaffection which to-day rend my unhappy country :

"Down thy valleys, Ireland, Ireland,
  Down thy valleys green and sad,
Still thy spirit wanders wailing,
  Wanders wailing, wanders mad.

Long ago that anguish took thee,
  Ireland, Ireland, green and fair,
Spoilers strong in darkness took thee,
  Broke thy heart and left thee there.

Down thy valleys, Ireland, Ireland,
  Still thy spirit wanders mad ;
All too late they love that wronged thee,
  Ireland, Ireland, green and sad."

Honour and patriotism :

" . . . love of country, that high passionate pride
In the old visions of a generous race,
Not yet fulfilled, but never yet forsaken "—

these are the inspiration of Sir Henry Newbolt's songs.

In *Sacramentum Supremum* he writes :

> " Life is no life to him that dares not die,
>   And death no death to him that dares to live."

And in *Clifton Chapel*, a poem which, though entirely unlike, to me recalls, possibly only because of the title, the *Rugby Chapel* of Matthew Arnold, a poet with whom Sir Henry has some poetic kinship, we read :

> " To set the cause above renown,
>   To love the game beyond the prize,
>   To honour, while you strike him down,
>   The foe that comes with fearless eyes."

Devon

Mr. Kipling has told us, in his *Sussex by the Sea*, that—

> " God gives all men all earth to love,
>   But since man's heart is small,
>   Ordains for each one spot shall prove
>   Beloved over all "—

and to Henry Newbolt it is Devon earth which is " beloved over all," as witness his sonnet *Devon* :

> " Deep-wooded combes, clear-mounded hills of morn,
>   Red sunset tides against a red sea wall,
>   High lonely barrows where the curlews call,
>   Far moors that echo to the ringing horn,—
>   Devon ! thou spirit of all these beauties born,
>   All these are thine, but thou art more than all :
>   Speech can but tell thy name, praise can but fall
> Beneath the cold white sea-mist of thy scorn.
>
> Yet, yet, O noble land, forbid us not
>   Even now to join our faint memorial chime
> To the fierce chant wherewith their hearts were hot
>   Who took the tide in thy Imperial prime ;
> Whose glory's thine till Glory sleeps forgot
>   With her ancestral phantoms, Pride and Time."

Henry Newbolt

This perfect sonnet is the work of a Devon lover, and of a Nature lover. How truly Sir Henry loves, not only Nature, but child life, flower life, animal life, bird life, there are many charming fancies or songs in *Poems New and Old* to prove. Read, for instance, *The Return of Summer*, or the enchanting *Dream Market*. The *Epistle* to Colonel Francis Younghusband will appeal more to men than to women, and most of all to old Cliftonians, though I cannot imagine a reader with public-school memories who will not delight in the picture of Sports Day :

> " The guarded course, the barriers and the rope ;
> The runners, stripped of all but shivering hope,"

as well as in the picture of the public-school boy, who, thereafter, as a Nation Builder in some outpost of the Empire :

> " . . . Links all nations while he serves his own."

For a lighter touch—for poems of graceful humour, raillery, and fancy—turn to *Rilloby Rill*, and it will set you dancing in spite of yourself by the magic of its fairy music. Of another side of this many-sided poet, one may say that *The Building of the Temple*, with its organ obligato to the alternate voices of men and boys, strikes a note of impressive and austere solemnity. The *Hymn* written to be sung in the Time of War and Tumults, breathes that very spirit of faith, dependence and humiliation by which—not as in " such boastings as the Gentiles use "—a nation is most exalted before God ; and with Mr. Kipling's *Recessional*, should have a place in all collections of National Hymns.

Clifton

One wonders that so enthusiastic a public school-man as Sir Henry Newbolt has so little to say of the 'Varsity where his record was distinguished. " The

thoughts of youth are long, long thoughts," says
Longfellow. A boy's heroes are often his heroes to
the end, and a boy's first love is sometimes his
purest and deepest passion. Clifton was Henry
Newbolt's first love. He passed out of her gates
(never thereafter out of her affection, her pride, her
history, and her life), but Clifton was, as it were,
his maiden love, and it is Clifton, not Oxford, his
Alma Mater, the city of the dreaming spires, which
appears most to have moulded his soul and to have
impassioned his poems.

Many years ago, speaking of a young woman who
just then was, somewhat brazenly, advertising herself
by attacks upon much that older folks held sacred
in the life of the family and the nation, Lady Henry
Somerset observed to me : " The worst of such women
is that they can never be gentlemen." I assented,
but added : " I know her personally and her history.
It is her upbringing which is at fault. We shall
change all that now that we are changing our system
of the education of girls. The worst of being a girl
to-day is that she can never be a public-school boy."

We *have* changed all that, which is one reason,
among others, why Sir Henry Newbolt's poems are
read and treasured as much by girls and women as
by boys and men. His love for his old school is
half a dreaming boy's first romantic love for a
maiden ; half a man's devotion to the worshipped
mother who rears her sons in one fear only—the
fear of God ; who teaches them not only to kneel
in prayer, but also to kneel that they may learn
to shoot straight, lest the call come to defend their
country in an hour of need ; who bids them not
only in all things to play the man, but in life's battle-
field, whether a battle-field only figuratively, or a
battle-field in reality, to " play the game." Space
I must find for Sir Henry Newbolt's noblest Clifton
song, *Vitaï Lampada* :

" There's a breathless hush in the Close to-night—
Ten to make and the match to win—
A bumping pitch and a blinding light,
An hour to play and the last man in.
And it's not for the sake of a ribboned coat,
Or the selfish hope of a season's fame
But his Captain's hand on his shoulder smote—
' Play up! play up! and play the game!'

The sand of the desert is sodden red,—
Red with the wreck of a square that broke ;—
The Gatling's jammed and the Colonel dead,
And the regiment blind with dust and smoke.
The river of death has brimmed his banks,
And England's far, and Honour a name ;
But the voice of a schoolboy rallies the ranks ;
' Play up! play up! and play the game!'

This is the word that year by year,
While in her place the School is set,
Every one of her sons must hear,
And none that hears it dare forget.
This they all, with a joyful mind,
Bear through life like a torch in flame,
And falling, fling to the host behind—
' Play up! play up! and play the game!' "

Is there anything, I ask, in the work of our younger
poets which more fires one, more inspires one, and
sets the youth of our England a more glorious
standard than this ? Whether as a poem or a call
to patriotism, one may speak of it as " direct " as
a sword-thrust.

That is why I have chosen the lines I have quoted
with which to conclude a brief, and, I fear, unworthy
appreciation of a poet of whom we can say, not only
in Tennyson's words of another poet, that he has
" uttered nothing base," but that the purpose of all
that he writes with serious intent is knightly, chivalrous, and noble.

Maurice   Baring

Maurice Baring

" I LEARNED more at my mother's knee than
he has learned in travelling five continents
in bad company."

So one well-known author is reported to have said
of another not less well known. I chance to have
some acquaintance with both men, and so take the
saying for what it is worth—or, rather, for what it
is not worth. Probably no two men have greater
respect, the one for the other, than the man who said
this and the man of whom it was said ; and I have
long ago written the remark off, as a specimen of
those literary " amenities " which co-exist with
excellent understanding and good-fellowship, and as
one of the clever half-truths to which the caustic of
tongue occasionally give utterance.

Though he has travelled all the continents there
are to travel, the remark was not made of Maurice
Baring. So far from ever being chargeable with
keeping bad company, that which he keeps is of the
best. And that he has learned much and observed
closely wherever he went, his books, *What I saw in
Russia*, now included in the Nelson Popular Library
of Notable Books, *With the Russians in Manchuria*,
Letters from the Near East, *Round the World in any
Number of Days*, and other travel books, sufficiently
prove.

As a writer, Maurice Baring has three different and
distinct publics. To the Man in the Street he is
well known as a traveller, and particularly as an

authority on things Russian. The general reader, when you name Maurice Baring, will reply, " Oh, yes, he wrote *Dead Letters, Orpheus in Mayfair, Lost Diaries.*" But if you wish for eagerness and enthusiasm, you must speak of Maurice Baring to the student and lover of poetry.

Poems: 1914-1917 (London : Martin Secker) is already in a fifth edition. Few memorial poems to those fallen in the Great War have been so widely quoted as *In Memoriam : A. H.* and *Julian Grenfell.* Both A. H. (Auberon Herbert, Captain Lord Lucas) and Julian Grenfell were intimate friends of the poet, and in France Lord Lucas was killed as a Flying Officer in the R.F.C., and Major Baring was on the staff of the same arm. Hence the noble threnody of the one to the memory of the other comes to us with greater and graver association, and surely with the greater poignancy !

> " You had died fighting, fighting against odds,
> Such as in war the gods
> Æthereal dared when all the world was young;
> Such fighting as blind Homer never sung,
> Nor Hector nor Achilles ever knew ;
> High in the empty blue,
> High, high, above the clouds, against the setting sun,
> The fight was fought and your great task was done.
>
> .   .   .   .
>
> A soaring death, and near to Heaven's gate ;
> Beneath the very walls of Paradise.
> Surely with soul elate,
> You heard the destined bullet as you flew,
> And surely your prophetic spirit knew
> That you had well deserved the shining fate.
>
> .   .   .   .
>
> God, Who had made you valiant, strong and swift,
> And maimed you with a bullet long ago,
> And cleft your riotous ardour with a rift,
> And checked your youth's tumultuous overflow,

Gave back your youth to you,
And packed in moments rare and few
Achievements manifold,
And happiness untold,
And bade you spring to Death as to a bride,
In manhood's ripeness, power and pride,
And on your sandals the strong wings of youth.

   .   .   .   .   .   .

Surely you found companions meet for you
In that high place ;
You met there face to face
Those you had never known, but whom you knew ;
Knights of the Table Round,
And all the very brave, the very true,
With chivalry crowned ;
The Captains rare,
Courteous and brave beyond our human air.

   .   .   .   .   .   .

And in the portals of the sacred hall
You hear the trumpets call
At dawn upon the silvery battlement,
Re-echo through the deep
And bid the sons of God to rise from sleep,
And with a shout to hail
The sunrise on the city of the Grail.

   .   .   .   .   .   .

And then you know that somewhere in the world,
That shines far off beneath you like a gem,
They think of you, and when you think of them
You know that they will wipe away their tears,
And cast aside their fears ;
That they will have it so,
And in no otherwise ;
That it is well with them because they know,
With faithful eyes,
Fixed forward and turned upwards to the skies,
That it is well with you,
Among the chosen few,
Among the very brave, the very true."

Even if with dimming eyes, the reader will, I am
persuaded, echo the sure, strong, almost glad note of
faith,

     " That it is well with you,"

H

with which the tribute closes. For me, here to come forward with further word of criticism or even appreciation, would be as unseemly as to break in upon the long and breathing silence which follows after Benediction.

"To Julian Grenfell"

In the sonnet to the memory of Julian Grenfell, a soldier's pride of service ; and readiness, if need be, to follow the dead hero's glorious leadership, and so to—

> " Hail the advent of each dangerous day,
>   And meet the last adventure with a song,"

again ring out triumphantly. Again, too, we hear the note of belief and hope ; and as I said when writing of Rudyard Kipling, I rejoice that the poet is a man of serene religious faith. Here is no place for tears, no gloomy brooding over a grave, or questioning as to what lies beyond the dark portal. No :

> " You led the way and leapt the golden stile . . .
>   And wave beyond the stars that all is well."

But let me quote the sonnet :

> " Because of you we will be glad and gay,
>   Remembering you, we will be brave and strong ;
> And hail the advent of each dangerous day,
>   And meet the last adventure with a song.
> And as you proudly gave your jewelled gift,
>   We'll give our lesser offerings with a smile,
> Nor falter on that path, where, all too swift,
>   You led the way and leapt the golden stile.
>
> Whether new paths, new heights to climb you find,
>   Or gallop through the unfooted asphodel,
> We know you know we shall not lag behind,
>   Nor halt to waste a moment on a fear ;
> And you will speed us onward with a cheer,
>   And wave beyond the stars that all is well."

Poems dealing
with the War

The first section of *Poems :* 1914-1917 contains work written and dealing with the war, and closes with lines which must strangely stir the heart of every soldier :

> " To meet a nobler fate :
> To serve in fellowship, O fortunate :
> To die in battle with your regiment."

Possibly only a soldier can entirely realize what this means to a soldier. Others may think they understand, but only from inside the army, only by serving, is the true service spirit born within a man. It is the spirit which annihilates self ; it is the strangest blending of what is lowly, and also what is lofty of mind.

A soldier with the service spirit has perhaps more of emulation within him than other men. He will spare himself nothing in the making of a good soldier, but his emulation is not for himself, but for the honour of his platoon, company, battalion, regiment, and of the army of which he is proud to be an unknown unit. He forgets himself, and gladly, in the glory of his regiment. And though it is his duty, as a soldier, not lightly or recklessly to throw away his life—placed as that life is at the service of his country, and so no longer his, a life of which his country has dire need—was there ever true soldier who did not dream of a day, when it might be his, and proudly, " to die in battle " with his regiment ?

Poems written in
Times of Peace

The second part of *Poems :* 1914-1917 contains only what was penned in times of peace. Of these the love poems are the most beautiful. With the exception of a certain langour, as of many poppies, which pervades the dramatic poem *Proserpine* (of which I shall presently speak), one may say of all Maurice Baring's love poems that the heavy-odoured, hot-house atmosphere, of which one is instantly sensible in the work of some poets, is entirely absent from his.   There is no single poem in which one is aware of the hot breath of the voluptuary upon one's cheek.   His love poems are human, whole-natured and passionate.   To him love is the mystic meeting and blending of spirit and sense in a union more sacramental, more symbolic, and more beautiful than aught else on earth.

The love of which he sings is not of Time but Eternity.   In the very portal of his House of Love, the first poem in the second section, we find a conception of love as both immortal and divine, of a love, in comparison with which, Death dwindles into insignificance as " a little thing " :

> " I watched you in the distance, tall and pale,
> Like a swift swallow in a pearly sky ;
> Your eyelids drooped like petals wearily,
> Your face was like a lily of the vale.
> You had the softness of all Summer days,
> The lovely radiance of the twilight hour,
> The mystery of bluebell-haunted ways,
> The passion of the white syringa flower.
>
> I watched you and I knew that I had found
> The long-delaying, long-expected Spring ;
> I knew my heart had found a tune to sing ;
> That strength to soar was in my spirit's wing ;
> That life was full of a triumphant sound,
> That death could only be a little thing."

Is this not a true picture, a perfect conception, of dear and happy human love ?

But into our human love, misunderstandings may come.   Even true love may not so reveal itself on earth.   Is there, then, no consolation for the

lonely and loveless heart ?   Here is Maurice Baring's
answer :

> " We drift apart, nor can we quite forget ;—
> Some link is lost and that affinity,
> That binds us not and will not set us free,
> Still tinges all our friendship with regret.
> And now I feel our hearts at last have met
> In perfect tune ; that God made you for me
> And me for you, and now that He has set
> This veil between us, this mute mystery.
> Yet when I wash away the dust of earth
> In the cool kingdoms of celestial dew,
> I think that you will meet me with a smile,
> The old smile made undying with new birth ;
> And I'll say this : ' I loved you all the while.'
> And you will say : ' I loved you and I knew.' "

In every love poem of Maurice Baring's, the love
is that by which the loved one is alike worshipped
and honoured.   Could love be more courtly than
in this portion of a sestette of a sonnet ?

> " You moved like music, and you smiled like dawn,—
> The leaves, the flowers, the dragon-flies, the dew,
> Beside you seemed the stuff of coarser clay ;
> And all the glory of the summer day
> A background for the wonder that was you."

In the following lines (*Collected Poems by Maurice
Baring*) the poet brings his love songs, and all that
he holds beautiful on earth, to lay at the loved
one's feet :

> " I have loved summer and the longest day ;
> The leaves of June, the slumberous film of heat,
> The bees, the swallow, and the waving wheat,
> The whistling of the mowers in the hay.
> I have loved words which lift the soul with wings,
> Words that are windows to eternal things.
> I have loved souls that to themselves are true,
> Who cannot stoop, and know not how to fear,
> Yet hold the talisman of pity's tear :
> I have loved these because I have loved you."

And what woman, not so superhuman as not to wish to be told that she is loved, will deny that a poet can on occasion be the most adorable of lovers ?

> " Your eyes, your eyes, divide me from my sleep ;
> The echo of your laughter makes me weep,
> You fill the measureless world, you fragile thing !
> And in the silence of my deepest dream,
> Your beauty wanders like a whispering stream,
> And brushes past me like an angel's wing."

Yet love can gently reprove the love that is not set on the things which are more excellent :

> " I think God made your soul for better things.
> .   .   .   .   .   .
> I think He meant the spirit that is you
> To soar above the world with silver wings ;
> To hear the music of celestial strings ;
> To keep the flame within you always true
> Unto your own high pole ; and pure as dew
> The fountain that within you sometimes sings."

" Fifty Sonnets "

All that has been quoted is from *Poems :* 1914-1917. Nature and Love are very near in a poet's heart, as witness the octave of this tender sonnet now included in the volume of " Collected Poems " :

> " She is a vessel of mysterious snow,
> A water-lily anchored in dark weeds,
> That in the evening's violet afterglow
> Unfolds its hidden heart of flaming seeds.
> She has the halo of the lonely moon,
> And round her floats the jessamine's faint musk,
> With summer birds and bees she is in tune,
> And silvery moths and the delirious dusk."

In Praise of Music

To love of Nature, the passionate love of noble music must be added in an attempt to interpret the personality of Maurice Baring as revealed in his poems. Of all that has been said in praise of music, can anything equal the words of Emerson ? I quote only from memory, but the thought, if not the wording, is exact : " O Music, how wonderful thou art :— so *absolutely impersonal, yet every sufferer feels his secret sorrow reached."*

A musician may have many persons in his audience. Here sits a man whose life had once hopes and aspirations which he now despairs ever to see fulfilled ; there, one who hides away, unsuspected even by his friends, the secret of a miserably unhappy marriage. Yonder girl's hopes lie in a soldier's grave in France ; beyond her is a woman whose heart has never healed of the wound inflicted by one she loved and trusted ; and near by, another, a childless wife, to whose ears the murmur of rocking cradles ever calls.

There are many hearers, but only one strain of music, yet that single strain holds the key to every wounded heart.

Some such thought as this was surely in the mind of Mr. Maurice Baring when, in the following sonnet *Beethoven,* he seeks to interpret the swiftly coming and passing moods, impressions and pictures, called up by the music of the master. Thus to convey, within the fourteen lines of a sonnet, the tragic hurling of massed legions in battle, no less than the trivial piping of a shepherd in the peaceful fields, the roar of guns, the *lin, lan, lone* of distant bells, and the dying down, and away, alike of the roar of battle and the far rumour of the bells, into the benediction of oncoming evening, is no small accomplishment of poetic art :

BEETHOVEN.

" More mighty than the hosts of mortal kings,
I hear the legions gathering to their goal ;
The tramping millions drifting from one pole,
The march, the counter-march, the flank that swings.

I hear the beating of tremendous wings,
The shock of battle and the drums that roll ;
And far away the solemn belfries toll,
And in the field the careless shepherd sings.

There is an end unto the longest day.
The echoes of the fighting die away.
The evening breathes a benediction mild.
The sunset fades. There is no need to weep,
For night has come, and with the night is sleep,
And now the fiercest foes are reconciled."

From the sternness of Beethoven to the tripping gaiety of Mozart, " and all that bears the signature of ease," is a far cry, but as an interpretation, the Mozart sonnet is equally successful :

MOZART.

" The sunshine, and the grace of falling rain,
The fluttering daffodil, the lilt of bees,
The blossom on the boughs of almond trees,
The waving of the wheat upon the plain—
And all that knows not effort, strife, or strain,
And all that bears the signature of ease,
The plunge of ships that dance before the breeze,
The flight across the twilight of the crane ;
And all that joyous is, and young and free,
That tastes of morning and the laughing surf ;
The dawn, the dew, the newly turned-up turf,
The sudden smile, the unexpressive prayer,
The artless act, the untaught dignity—
You speak them in the passage of an air."

These sonnet interpretations of musicians are followed by similar sonnet interpretations of masters of literature and thereafter by travel pictures, one of *Italy* in which we read :

" And Venice like a bubble made of dew."

Further Extracts from
Love Poems

Maurice Baring's love poems I have quoted so fully that in turning the pages of his Collected

Photo
Swaine

Maurice Baring

Poems I must do no more than quote an occasional
line or verse :

"The hours when you are with me cease to chime.

. . . . . .

You were a summer's day, all warmth and tune ;
Your soul a harbour, dark beneath the moon,
And flashing with soft lights of sympathy.

. . . . . .
Your quiet eyes
Had robbed the moon of her tranquillity.

. . . . . .

You are the million melodies that ring
At dawn, in dew-drenched woods. You are the hour
When the frail almond blossom breaks in flower,
And you are sweeter than that blossoming."

Elsewhere he says :

"I loved—and in the Eastern skies
A million morning stars arise."

Some of these stars Maurice Baring has translated
into love songs and sonnets for our benefit.

The sonnet *Harvest in Russia* is not a love poem ;
but even here, in passing, the poet bares his head,
as it were, and reverently, to womanhood—this
time to womanhood, dignified, not by beauty of
face and form, high bearing, or gracious mien, but
by the sacramental dignity of daily toil, humble
drudgery, done as service, and done cheerfully :

"And through the trees the stately shapes I see
Of women with their instruments of toil,
Calm in their sacerdotal majesty."

Here is a fragment from another Russian sonnet,
A June Night :

"Like water bubbling in a crystal jar
The nightingale begins a liquid trill,
Another answers : now the world is still :
You'd think that you could hear that falling star.

. . . .

The women's voices echo far away ;
And in the road two lovers sing a song ;
They sing the joy of love that lasts a day,
The sorrow of love that lasts a whole life long."

This, which has no title, is surely a man's, a patriot's, and a poet's answer to a Conscientious Objector :

" It were disloyalty, you say, to change
Your roving birthright for a paper rose,
And for a silver penny and brave clothes
To swear away your spirit's reckless range,
You will not sell your freedom for a plume,
Nor let your soul be brutalised in drill,
Nor break you to a meddling sergeant's will ;
You that have access to the General's room.

I crave a larger freedom.   If in line
I serve with others, all their strength is mine.
The large consent uplifts me upon wings.
And in the faces of the men that die,
Obedient to the bugle, I descry
The seal and mandate of the King of Kings."

The Shyness of
The Humorist

In Maurice Baring's prose-sketches and stories, especially in *Orpheus in Mayfair* and *Lost Diaries*, as well as in his travel books, we find ourselves in the company of a polished man of the world, under whose easy and courteous bearing a certain native modesty and shyness are not entirely to be concealed. This last may be due to the sense of humour which, in his prose, is everywhere evident.

Just as the picture taken by the photographer can record itself only upon a " sensitised " plate, so only upon the highly sensitised negative of a humorist's mind can the light and shadow play of humour register itself in true perspective.

In Maurice Baring's poems, strange to say, there is, with one exception, scarcely a glint of this quality

of humour, so evident in his prose. That being so,
I will quote part of the exception here. It is
entitled *To Juliet's Owl* :

> " Juliet has lost her little downy owl,
> The bird she loved more than all other birds.
> He was a darling bird, so white, so wise,
> Like a monk hooded in a snowy cowl,
> With sun-shy scholar's eyes,
> He hooted softly in diminished thirds ;
> And when he asked for mice,
> He took refusal with a silent pride—
> And never pleaded twice.
> He was a wondrous bird, as dignified
> As any Diplomat
> That ever sat
> By the round table of a Conference.
>
> His was the art
> Of pleasing without effort easily.
> His fluffy throat,
> His sage round eye,
> Sad with old knowledge, bright with young amaze,
> Where are they now ? Ah ! where ?
> Perchance in the pale halls of Hecate,
> Or in the poplars of Elysium,
> He wanders careless and completely free.
> But in the regions dumb,
> And in the pallid air,
> He will not find a sweet caressing hand
> Like Juliet's ; nor in all that glimmering land
> Shall he behold a silver planet rise
> As splendid as the light in Juliet's eyes.
> Therefore in weeping with you, Juliet,
> Oh ! let us not forget,
> To drop with sprigs of rosemary and rue,
> A not untimely tear,
> Upon the bier,
> Of him who lost so much in losing you."

This seems to me so perfect a specimen of courtly,
delightfully-turned *vers de société*, and with such a
pretty humour, that one sighs to think it is the only
humorous piece in the book from which it is taken,

if not indeed in the whole of the author's poems. Nor is humour all we miss. The *motif* of Maurice Baring's poems is, for the most part, either Love or Friendship. In the book of the Human Heart, it is the chapters dealing with love or friendship of which he has entire understanding. But in the book of the Human Heart there are many pages, and some of these, Maurice Baring seems, as a poet at least, hardly to have turned.

Of Motherhood, Fatherhood, Childhood, I do not recall one supreme or illuminating word. In his Fairy Stories and in the dedication to a Fairy Story, he shows that he understands and loves children. We should not have gathered as much from the study of his poems. The child figure of the little Prince Richard is brought upon the stage in the play *The Black Prince*, but whether the figure stays or goes, the reader is not likely to care. It does not appear to interest the author, and so does not interest us. But let Maurice Baring write of lovers—and instantly our world is aglow. He can make lovers live for us, as Shakespeare makes them live in *Romeo and Juliet*, as Stephen Phillips calls them into passionate, pulsing life in *Paolo and Francesca*.

Romance and Chivalry ; Love that triumphs over death and endures throughout eternity ; Friendship, fixed and faithful as the stars, these are the themes which most inspire Maurice Baring's muse.

Just as in his prose, and in his travels, we find him equally himself and at home in any company, any city, any continent, either hemisphere, so, in his poems, he seems sometimes of the West and all Modern, sometimes his inspiration is all Mediæval ; sometimes it is all of the East. Yesterday he was an Air-soldier in France, to-morrow, in his passionate love for beauty, we think of him as one walking in spirit the classic groves of Ancient Greece. Reading

his romantic plays on yet another day, we hold him
as none other than a Norman and a knight with
lance lowered and ready to meet all comers in the
Tourney of Chivalry and Love.

The Fairy
Stories

Except in respect to form, Maurice Baring's
Fairy Stories—prose though the medium be—are
essentially poetry. That not all which is metrical is
poetry, nor all that is unmetrical, necessarily prose,
even my youngest reader will scarcely need to be
reminded.   I was once asked by an old-fashioned girl
child, with thoughts beyond her years, " When
God makes any of us, which does He make first—
the body or the soul ? "

The quaint question cornered me at first, but I
answered, " I think the soul, because something
pure and beautiful seems to look at us from the
eyes of every little child. By and by the frail and
tiny body, which it would be as easy to kill and to
crush as to destroy a flower, grows bigger and stronger,
and begins selfishly to grab at things. Then, if
the child be taught and trained properly and be
sweet-natured, the soul will check and rule the body,
and the beauty and purity we see in the child's eyes
will remain, even if the child be not otherwise
beautiful. Yes, I think—I feel sure—that the soul
was made first, especially as it is the soul which
survives."

And of all true poetry, may not one say, too, that
it began in the birth of a beautiful thought, just as
the soul of a child was first of all a thought in the
mind of God ?   The expression of a poet's beautiful
thought must, like the child's life, be " ordered,"
restrained within certain wise limits, and must
conform to certain wise rules. No one wishes to
check the development of individuality and origin-

ality in either child or poem, but neither must run wild, and set law and order at naught. Hence it is that by common consent certain rules and regulations have come into being concerning poetry. Maurice Baring's *Fairy Stories* being unmetrical, are outside the range of an article on his poems, but that each Fairy Story of his writing has its origin in the birth of a beautiful thought, every reader of *The Glass Mender and other Stories, Forget-me-not and Lily of the Valley* will agree. It is fitting that the author has served in the Air Force, for just as the war has called into being fighting men whom you cannot count among " Foot, Gun, or Horse "—so Maurice Baring has created a Fairy Story which is part poetry, part prose, and all a winged creature of the Air.

His Dramatic
Poems

In writing of Mr. Baring's dramatic work, I propose merely to give a summary, with selected passages or lyrics. The public which reads drama is (I am assured) pitifully small, and that for every one reader who knows and loves Mr. Baring's plays, thousands know and love his shorter poems. Not to know Mr. Baring's dramatic work is a heavy and grievous loss for those thousands ; and is attributable, possibly, to the fact that so many of us are of opinion that (always excepting Shakespeare) plays should be acted, not read. Bald as my summaries, brief as my extracts must necessarily be, I believe that in the case of Maurice Baring, every reader of these pages will be converted to the opposite view.

No student of Shakespeare's plays, of Milton's Masques, no lover of poetry who has the dramatic sense and knows Mr. Baring's work is likely to differ when I say that it is by his dramatic work that Maurice Baring's name will live in literature. The

poet himself would agree that his most characteristic
and individual work is to be found in his dramas,
and I think, too, that he would agree in placing, as
I unhesitatingly do, the plays of his own making
before those in which the plot is founded upon
history. In the latter, the plot is more or less
arbitrarily laid down for him by historical facts,
and though, as poetry, these plays equal anything
he has written in the matter of dramatic power,
skilful stagecraft, and beauty of expression, they
are less Baringesque than are *Proserpine*, *Dusk*,
Mahasena and *Desiderio*, all four of which owe everything to himself. He is a born plot-maker as well
as a born poet, and one day may write a great novel.
The essence of a good plot is surprise, and surprise is
not possible in a play, the plot of which follows history.

No poet known to me personally is more shy of
talking of his own work than Maurice Baring ;
but I have the impression that he considers two
scenes from *The Black Prince*—that with the astro-
loger, and the closing scene—as touching a higher
note in dramatic poetry than he believes he has
elsewhere attained. Of *The Black Prince* as a
whole I would add only that in the plays, the plot
of which is founded upon history, the poet must
necessarily follow lines already laid down for him.
The bird of his imagination, if I may so word my
thought, has small space in which to soar. The bird
takes far flights and lofty, but may not for long arise
above the mists of earth. It is a falcon, strong of
wing, bold of sweep, but poised, as it were, in mid-
air, intent on every movement, every stir in the grass
of the world below, and ready on the instant to
swoop to earth upon its quarry. In *Proserpine*,
and in *Dusk*, the author's imagination is a lark rising
in utter abandonment, in sheer ecstasy of song, and
soaring, forgetful of old earth, into new and un-
dreamed-of cloud worlds of marvel and fantasy.

"Ye ha'e music ; mak the maist o' it," says Alan Breck to Rob Roy's son. To Maurice Baring, as his friend, admirer and critic, I make bold to say: "You have a great imagination : make the most of it."

Dusk

The prologue of *Dusk* takes us to a Water Under-world, beneath a lake, where the Queen of the Water-Spirits is discovered, throned. Only at dusk, only in the " emerald evening " do the water-spirits seek the surface of the lake and wander with the spirits of the air.

But one water-spirit, Jessamine, greatly daring, has ventured out of her under-water home and into the world above. To water-spirits is given power to lay a spell upon women and men, beast and bird of the earth-world, and to compel them to the water-spirit's will. But Jessamine has forgotten her Queen's commands, and has disobeyed the conditions under which water-spirits are permitted upon earth :

" JESSAMINE.   Queen, when I left my watery home to seek
The world of men, and test the power of spells,
You said my birthright would be mine, so long
I yielded not to kiss of mortal man.
Queen, when I wandered through the singing world
Amid the happy fields and flowers of spring,
And saw that all the creatures of the world
Obeyed me, I forgot the warning words,
And having proved my power on beast and bird,
I could not rest till I had tried to charm
A mortal man.   I met a wandering knight ;
I lured him with strange song and subtle speech,
And he grew mad, and, Queen, I know not how,
I know not why, I yielded to his kiss.
   QUEEN.   Ill-starred, unhappy child ; for you have lost
The spirit's birthright, and yet have not won
The thoughtless happiness of mortals, though
A mortal now.
   JESSAMINE.   Ah woe ! Ah misery !

The bitterness, the anger and the shame !
Though all the hidden spirits of the earth
Obeyed me, yet the essence of my might
Has fled ; for I, the unearthly flower of dusk,
Must needs submit unto a mortal man.
He bade me be his bride, his Queen, and I
Was forced to bow to his imperious will,
And suffer the great horror of his love.

       .   .   .   .

   QUEEN.   But though a mortal you shall still have power
Upon the spirits and the Sons of earth.
   JESSAMINE.   Oh, Queen, that is the bitterest thing of all !
I still retain my old divinity ;
All creatures of the world, all other men
Bow to me ; he unconquered keeps his sway.
O great my folly ! Sweet had been the life
Upon that world with every man my slave ;
But I no longer find delight in power ;
I am shamed and slighted, mad with bitter grief ;
Queen, from this hateful bondage set me free."

The Queen tells Jessamine that there is on earth
a knight of stainless honour and giant strength.
If she win his love, she is saved, and he and she will
be released from the mortal chain.   This knight,
Jessamine returns to the upper world to seek.   Act I
ends with the Queen's words :

   " She seeks the world of men ! Ah, wiser far
     To linger in the emerald haunts of dusk,
     To dream among the cool and silent deeps,
     And caverns of soft flowers ; only to seek
     The world when skies are dark and spirits roam
     And not to face the cruel light of day."

In Act I we read of the meeting of Jessamine and
this knight, Sir Yvain.   He is journeying to the city
" beyond the violet hills " where dwells his betrothed.
Jessamine who is as wickedly heartless as she is
beautiful, entices him to stay as the guest of her
mortal Lord and Master, Sir Peridure.   She hopes to
persuade Yvain to kill Peridure, by becoming whose
wife she lost her spirit birthright.   But Yvain is

I

true knight and says he must continue his journey
to the " violet hills." Then Jessamine summons
to her aid those powers of sorcery against which
he is helpless. He rescues her from drowning in
the lake, and by his words as he carries her unconscious body to safety we realize that the spell
Jessamine has laid upon him is doing its evil work :

> " She does not stir, her eyes are closed, her face
> Is white with deathly pallor, and she lies
> So frail upon my arms, a sleeping flower—
> Surely too frail for mortal scythe to mow—
> The ghost of some dead lily of the valley.
> It cannot be that she is dead ! Awake,
> Wake, lovely Jessamine. Thou art too fair
> To wander in the sunless halls of Death.
> Alas ! she will not wake, the frailest flower
> Of all the world has been untimely mown."

In Act II we are at the castle of Sir Peridure, where
are Robin the Minstrel, Jason, and other unhappy
knights over whom Jessamine has wantonly cast her
spell, so that, for love of her, they forget manhood
and knighthood, as Jason confesses :

> " I, as all men here, wander in a dream
> Of twilight, that is full of piteous sounds.
> I am no more a knight, no more a man,
> Naught but a helpless harp hung in the air,
> Whose trembling strings obey a wayward breeze ;
> And yet a vision lit my life of dream,
> A hope, a wonderful felicity."

The wicked and heartless Jessamine remains indifferent, even when her jealous Peridure orders
the murder of one of her love-sick worshippers,
Robin the Minstrel. The story of Robin's passing,
as he knew, to death for her sake is told with pathos
and beauty. As he leaves her presence for ever,
he looks her in the face, and repeats the last stanza
of the song he has just sung :

> " I perish for a prayer, a gleam
> Of hope that soared too high,
> But since, most dear, you were my dream,
> What does death signify ? "

Then Jessamine deliberately sets herself to simulate love for Yvain that she may incite him to the slaying of Peridure.

" JESSAMINE (*going to the window*). Come to me now, Yvain, the moon has risen
And spirits whisper in the rustling trees ;
It is my hour, the magic of the waters
Is o'er me. Come and bend unto my will.

(*Enter* YVAIN.)

JESSAMINE. The night is still
And through the lattice comes the breath of flowers.
Feel you the fragrance of the jessamine,
My flower ?
YVAIN. Oh ! clear amidst the heavy scent
Of lilies I can trace its fragrant speech.
JESSAMINE. And I am even such a helpless flower
Whose tide is lost midst richer tides of scent.
YVAIN. You are the spirit and the deity
Of flowers, the rose and lily bend to you.

.   .   .   .

Heed ! Jessamine, until this hour I saw
My life before me like a dreary sea,
A grey unending ocean cold and dark ;
But now some magic footfall skims the waves ;
The surf is glistening and no longer moans,
But whispers a soft sob of ecstasy ;
And slow and gradual over the wide sea
A breeze has stirred the petals of the foam ;
And all the ocean seems a fiery chalice,
Opening to catch a drop of holy rain.
JESSAMINE. Your dream had lit a dream within my heart ;
I see a wonder in the eastern sky,
The vault of heaven trembles into fire
Brighter than sunset, softer than the dawn,
As though the skies had melted into mist
And all the stars were shattered into dust,
I hear the motion of unearthly sails,

I see a ship that comes across the sea
And turns the sapphire wave to living flame;
And at the helm a spirit like the sun
Strikes a gold harp, and wakes the echoing sea.
Oh! take me to that ship, Yvain the Strong,
And let us seek the islands of the dead;
And now the ship has vanished into light,
The world grows dim, and like a great dark rose
It folds its petals over you and me;
And in the burning fire that is its heart,
Let us be drowned and die in blinding light.
    YVAIN.   You were the footfall on my twilight sea.
    JESSAMINE.   You dragged my sunrise from the nether world.
    YVAIN.   You were the breeze that brought the blush of dawn.
    JESSAMINE.   And you the spirit harping on the waves.
    YVAIN.   And you the chalice of mysterious fire,
The heart of that dark rose which is the world.
    JESSAMINE.   You built me a new world, Yvain the Strong,
And filled it with the lightnings of your eyes.
    YVAIN.   You smiled upon my midnight, Jessamine,
And the dark spaces blossomed into stars.
O moon, stand still! O dream, fold thy dim wings."

And so, by other exquisitely beautiful love scenes,
the poet pictures Yvain and his temptress in a very
garden of Eden of love—until, as in that older
Eden, again is heard the hissed serpent-word
of deadly sin.

" JESSAMINE.   Speak now no longer of the vanished dream
Nor of the hour which never more can be.
    YVAIN.   The word I spoke in my divine soft dream
I speak in the cold light of day.   Oh hear!
I love you while I breathe, sun of my day;
I'll love you when I die, star of my dusk;
I'll love you after death, moon of my night;
Through all the trackless ways and deeps of space,
Amidst the murmur of this clamorous world,
And in the silence of eternity.
    JESSAMINE.   Yvain, Yvain, there is no man on earth
Whose love would drive him to do all for me.
    YVAIN.   What is this little thing?   For every deed
Done for you can be but a little thing.
Speak quickly, for they come.
    JESSAMINE.   Kill Peridure."

Act III is extraordinarily powerful. Yvain has thrust away and with horror Jessamine's wicked suggestion. Away from her presence the spell she has put upon him begins to weaken. His knightliness and his manhood return, and he comes to bid her good-bye for ever. Again she tempts him to the crime by telling him of Peridure's plan to kill both Yvain and Jessamine. As the two talk, Peridure steals on them, unaware, and rushes suddenly upon Yvain to kill him. Yvain defends himself, and Peridure falls.

Again, as of old, evil seems to have prevailed, for Jessamine's wicked ends have been attained. But wait. Though the poison of her spells and her simulated love have set something like madness working in Yvain's blood, at last the scales fall from his eyes, and he knows her for the evil thing she is.

As Peridure fell dead, the treacherous Jessamine called to her men-at-arms :

> " Help ! Help ! and save me ! for they kill my lord !
> Help ! Yvain is slaying Peridure."

To the men-at-arms she says :

> " Bind him and take him to the castle dungeon !
> Let him be hanged before the break of day."

And to herself she says :

> " Free ! Free ! O lake, now I may come to you,
> And seek unshamed my buried crown of light,
> My robe of moonshine and my wings of dew."

Here is the last scene of all. It is in Jessamine's garden, and before she has returned to her Water Underworld to regain immortality.

> " (*Enter* YVAIN, *carrying* JESSAMINE'S *body in his arms.*)
>
> YVAIN. A second time I bear you in my arms ;
> Pale were you then ; now you are paler still.
> Even as then your eyes were closed, as then
> You lie within my arms like a fair flower,

Surely too frail for mortal scythe to mow ;
The ghost of some dead lily of the valley.

(*He lays the body on the ground.*)

Knight that now watch by Peridure's cold corpse,
Come hither, Modred, Sintram, Jason, come !

(*Enter* JASON, SINTRAM, *and* MEN-AT-ARMS *with torches.*)

I broke my bonds. I went to Jessamine.
Amidst the slumbering lilies and the leaves,
Asleep she lay like a soft bell of dew.
Softly I lifted her. She did not stir,
I breathed one kiss upon her sleeping lips ;
And then men called me, Sirs, Yvain the Strong—
Across my knees I broke that frailest thing.
Do you not heed ? I broke her with these hands :
There lies her body, stiff, and cold, and dead. (*Pause.*)
Tell me the road now to the violet hills."

A terrible ending this ! the swift falling of inexor-
able judgment upon the frail and beautiful being—
be she spirit or be she mortal—who can thus deliberately set out to tempt, to ruin, and to destroy.
" Dusk " may be no more than a bubble blown by
a poet's fancy, but gossamer-slight and rainbow-
ephemeral as the fancy may be, it seems to me as
perfect, after its kind, as a floating bubble or a
flower in bloom.   Nor is it without symbolism, for
as the bubble crashes into nothing, so with the
swift execution of judgment, one hears, in imagination, the far-away thunder-reverberations of eternal
law.

Mahasensa

" Mahasena " is a great play, not only in construction and characterization, but in its subtle psychological analysis. Mahasena, Ruler of Lanka, is
clearly a king among kings—just, beneficent, merciful, noble, and great.   Of him, the prophet Mahinda
speaks :

> " Thou, void of passion, with all virtue blest,
> Boldest among the bold in the field of war,
> Sedate and seeking still the holy path,
> Taught by the elders in our ancient rite ;
> Thou, who with voice of pealing thunder spakest
> Among a doubtful people, Priest and pattern
> Of Law and Duty."

Next we read of Chandra whom the King loves. She is young and exquisitely lovely, but chaste and cold of heart as the moon, after whom she is called.

> " Chandra is still a child,
> Yet envious years would weigh on her in vain ;—
> She is not wrought of perishable clay,
> But of some delicate essence thin and rare,
> Some texture whereof iris-dews are made,
> Or wings of dragon-flies, or petals of foam,
> Or the frail, iridescent, floating shell.
> In vain we liken her to star or flower ;
> Fairer is she than earthly semblances,
> She is a spirit wandered from the moon ;—
> A sigh, a melody made palpable.
> She moves as though she floated o'er the flowers,
> And the earth seems to fawn beneath her feet,
> And the sky seems to crown her as a Queen."

Here is a snatch of the song with which her women await her coming :

> " Come, for the darkness has risen from earth,
> And the moon has breathed o'er the sleeping sea ;
> We are weary of toil, we are sated with mirth,
> We are fain to dream, and our dream is of thee.
> The moon and the stars and the lotus flower,
> The lilies and dusk are of no avail,
> For thou art the dream of the twilight hour
> And lotus and lily, O fair ! O frail ! "

Her husband had some years ago been slain in the wars, and now she has given her cold heart entirely to the King, whom she honours for his high and noble nature. She and her friend Anoula are poles apart by nature, as witness this fragment of conversation :

" CHANDRA. If I loved one for truth or bravery,
And he proved false or cowardly or base,
I from my bleeding heart would tear the love,
And trample on it like a festering weed.
ANOULA. I loving, for his whole self, love a man,
And nought could then deceive me ; if he stooped
To baseness, as strange laws may haply lurk
In brightest rubies, my unconquered love
Would, like an ocean, rise to wash the stain.
Even though the flaw be deep and past all healing,
The ruby still a blood-red ruby shines ;
The man is still the man I loved and love ;
Because I gave his glory all my praise,
Must I refuse my pity to his shame ?
Then, more than ever, would he need my love,
And then most rich would its abundance be.
CHANDRA. If I loved one who seemed to me all bright,
And found the gem was false, the gold mere clay,
Not him, nor yet myself, could I forgive.
ANOULA. I would not love false gold nor lying gems ;
Yet if I found commingled with the metal
Thin streaks of baser clay, it would not prove
Gold to be tinsel, nor destroy my love.
CHANDRA. The man you speak of is a living lie.
ANOULA. You have no knowledge of the deeps of love.
CHANDRA. My love must rise like worship to a god.
ANOULA. Ah ! prayer is cold, your heart a tranquil temple."

Anoula's lover, Virata, is drawn into a quarrel
with his rival, and kills him. According to the laws
of Lanka, he who takes life must forfeit his own
life, but Anoula pleads with the King to spare
Virata's life, and the King consents. Chandra,
who is now the King's wife, and the Chief Ministers
protest that he cannot thus set aside the laws of
which he is the maker and representative, and that
Virata must die.

" CHANDRA.   How can'st thou as King
O'erlook the crime ?
KING.   Such is the voice of reason ;
But can thy woman's heart not understand
That blood for blood is but a cruel law ?
I strive to frame new laws of right and truth.

CHANDRA. Thou speakest ever of necessity,
How retribution followed every crime.
KING. But in Virata's deed there is no crime ;
He slew Sugriva in fair fight, and men
Have done worse things than he for those they loved,
  And yet proved guiltless in the eyes of heaven."

Chandra insists, and then the King makes terrible
confession. Like David of old he had coveted the
wife of another, and like David he had sent that
other to his death.

" KING.   A straggler brought me word
At nightfall that some rebels still lay hid
Among the rocks. I sought thy husband's tent ;
I bade him seek the rocky hills, and see
If any remnant of the foe still lived ;
He thought there was no peril in the task.
He said that he would seek the hills alone ;
I bade him go.
CHANDRA. Thou badest him scour the hills ?
What meanest thou ? No, not that thou didst hope
That he might die ?
KING. I bade him seek the hills ;
He said that he would seek the hills alone.
I bade him go. I knew the hidden peril.
Thou sayest I hoped that he might die ? I knew
That he would die ; I sent him to his death.
I knew I could not win thee otherwise,
Thou chaste as dew and colder than the moon !
CHANDRA. O Powers of Heaven, have pity on my heart !
My Lord is mad ; Yassa, the King is mad !
Or I am mad.
KING. No, hear me to the end—
I waited until time had healed thy sorrow,
And then I wedded thee ; and therefore I
In my great guilt, refuse to slay Virata,
Who, side by side with me, is innocent.
Chandra——
CHANDRA. Is dead ; you speak with her in vain.
KING. No, you shall hear me. 'Tis not now alone
Because of this my crime, that I make haste
To save Virata. I to the great hall
Will go, where the high elders now are met.
Before them all I will reveal the truth ;
And if they wish, I die."

It is as terrible and tremendous a scene as the mind of dramatist or novelist ever conceived, for the King's long past, but terrible, even if repented sin notwithstanding,—the agony of his remorse, and his longing to make reparation with his own life convince us of the sincerity of his repentance. Evil as was his deed, we realize that here is a man who though he has fallen as David fell, into terrible sin, is by nature noble and kingly. But Chandra has no mercy. In her hatred and scorn, she insists not only that he shall not escape his agony of mind, by death, but also insists that to live and to endure is the greater punishment. She insists, too, that if only for the people's sake, the King and she must continue on the throne. Again the broken-hearted King begs at least that he be permitted the relief of confession before the people, and acceptance of his punishment at their hands, but Yassa, his Minister, supports Chandra.

" YASSA. Thou canst not overturn a people's faith
And break their idol and destroy their trust.
There would be no more faith in right and truth,
No more obedience unto any law.
    KING. Chandra, speak thou.
    CHANDRA.   I have no words to speak.
Oh ! see you not that I am dumb and blind,
Senseless and dead ?   Above me and beneath
Is nothingness. The universe has crumbled.
Stay ! Heed ! It is not true : my words are false.
Nothing is fallen, nothing is dark, the world,
The ordered universe is in its place,
And only thou art fallen !
    KING.   I go to speak.
    CHANDRA. To ease thy conscience and to make amends !
To live hereafter with an easy heart.
    YASSA. Rather than thou shouldst go and tell this tale
I'll draw my sword and kill thee where thou standest.
This cannot be.
    KING. Strike, gladly would I die !
    CHANDRA. Yes, thou wouldst die, and from thy shameful life
Flee like a renegade. O coward soul !

All are prepared to face extremest pain
Save Mahasena !
    KING. All thy taunts are vain.
It is no coward fear that prompts my speech.
    CHANDRA. If I can make the supreme sacrifice,
To live in spite of all, thy wife, with thee,
If I can do this, canst thou not achieve
One slender sacrifice ?
    KING. Then let him die ;
I wish no longer to reveal the truth,
Seeing that men are blind, and tender women
Have hearts of ice and iron. I will go
And climb the temple steps, and don my crown
And cry aloud : ' People, acclaim your King ! '

(*Enter* ANOULA, *who rushes up to* MAHASENA *and falls on her knees.*)

    ANOULA. King, I have heard, I understand thy soul !
And never nobler seemedst thou to me
Than when thou didst unfold thy bitter tale.
Ah ! find a way to spare Virata's life ! "

And so the Second Act closes, Chandra ice-cold
and scornful, the broken and sorely repentant King
pleading—not to escape the consequences of his
sin, but for a look, a word, from the wife he loves
and worships, but pleading so vainly that even the
woman whose lover he is condemning to death, is
compelled to pity. I know no more striking picture
of kingly ruin, and of contrasted woman-natures,
outside the pages of King Lear.

There—a great and closing Third Act follows—
I leave the tragedy of Mahasena for my readers
to study for themselves, and would add only that,
compared with Maurice Baring, our so-called popular
" dramatists " of to-day seem to me of small significance.

Tristram and Iseult

The story of *Tristram and Iseult* has been the
subject of many plays and poems. Interwoven

with Maurice Baring's beautiful love story (perhaps
the most romantic and beautiful of all his dramatic
works) of the most unhappy Knight and Queen
of whom Fate made sport, by causing them, unwittingly to drink of a love potion, brewed for other
purposes, is an old Cornish legend :

> " ISEULT.   Say not the sea folk that Tintagel's towers
> Are spellbound, and by magic melt away
> Twice in the year ?   That breathless hour has come ;
> Tintagel's walls have vanished and these trees,
> This orchard, is the orchard of the song.
>   TRISTRAM.   Whisper the story softly in my ear,
> Thy voice is sweeter than all song to me.
>   ISEULT.   It tells of a strange orchard walled around
> With wizard air, and starred with shining flowers ;
> There the frail blossom falls not from the tree,
> And there the warrior wanders with his love.
> Nought can molest their dream, no enemy
> Can break the wall of air."

To quote exquisite scenes and passages would
mean transcribing the half of the play, so I stay
my hand.

But here I may incidentally observe that certain
songs and snatches from songs recur in Maurice
Baring's dramas, as if the poems were written to a
musical accompaniment which, while continuing
throughout, is for the most part inaudible, and
only now and then deepens into heard music.

Sometimes, too, he interweaves a song or snatch,
taken from one play, into another. When, in
Dusk, Jessamine's song, " My eyes are dim and my
wound is sore," appears by itself as a " Ballad "
in *Collected Poems*, one wonders why he omits the
song from *Tristram and Iseult*, for which surely
it was written ?   Tristram is dying in Brittany as
the play is closing.   He has sent for Iseult who has
pledged herself to come to him when summoned.
As he lies on his couch, looking out to sea, he watches

feverishly for the sign of a sail. If she be on board, a white sail is to be hoisted, if not the sail is to be black :

> " My eyes are dim and my wound is sore,
>   White sail, will you come to me ?
> My Friend, shall I never see thee more ?
>   Be still, O moaning sea.
>
> Have you forgotten the cup of bliss ?
>   White sail, will you come to me ?
> On the flying ship, and the first long kiss ?
>   Be still, O moaning sea.
>
> Have you forgotten the forest trees ?
>   White sail, will you come to me ?
> The vows we spoke to the stars and seas ?
>   Be still, O moaning sea.
>
> I sought you once in a strange disguise ;
>   White sail, will you come to me ?
> You knew not even my sad, sad eyes ;
>   Be still, O moaning sea.
>
> ' Call when you will, I'll come,' you said ;
>   White sail, will you come to me ?
> Come swiftly, or you will find me dead ;
>   Be still, O moaning sea.
>
> The sail is black, they have hauled it high ;
>   White sail, you came not to me ;
> I'll turn my face to the wall and die ;
>   Be still, O moaning sea.
>
> O Iseult, my life, my death, my friend !
>   White sail, there's no need for thee ;
> I waited for you until the end . . .
>   Still is the moaning sea."

Gaston de Foix

Yet another play, *Gaston de Foix*, is inspired by the same knightly chivalrous spirit which animates Tennyson's *Idylls of the Kings*. Mary, whom Gaston

loves, is speaking to him of his cousin and says that
she is fair.   Gaston replies :

> " Yes, like an ivory statue set in gems.
> But I know one who brings, where'er she goes,
> The freshness of the forest, the glad air
> Of beaches, clamorous with breaking surf.
> The thought of her is tranquil as the star
> That trembles through the wet tempestuous twilight,
> Piercing the vault of the blue firmament ;
> Yet is she fashioned like an April hour
> Of storm and sudden sunshine, and her voice
> Is like the wild appeal of sighing winds ;
> Her soul is filled with warmth and restless fire,
> And charged with shadow and with mystery."

Mary returns Gaston's love ; but at her birth it
had been foretold that the man to whom she gives
her hand, Death shall soon strike down.   So to his
love pleading, she makes piteous reply :

> " O Gaston, thou art like a tall white flower !
> I will not put the sickle in Death's hand.
> No, Gaston, thou shalt never die through me.
>
> .   .   .   .
>
> You, to whom life lies open like the lists,
> Where every honoured prize the world can give
> Awaits you—you, who scarce more than a boy
> Are the first Captain of a mighty nation ;
> So that, if you should die to-day, your death
> Would live like an immortal drop of blood
> Upon the scroll of history ; your name
> Would echo down the winding stair of time,
> And moisten the hard eyes of men with the sight
> Of those who wander in the happy fields
> With Hector and Achilles, those whose names
> Speak to the world of wasted bravery,
> Of fleeting splendour and unfinished song ;
> Of those who on the altar of all time,
> Like lilies lie, a silver sacrifice,
> Most beautiful, most piteous, and most calm ;
> Smiling with Death's triumphant listlessness,
> And crowned with immortality of Fame."

Thereafter, torn betwixt love and fear for him she loves (lest she bring death with her love), she says :

" My thoughts are tossed about like perished leaves ;
They shift like water, and like fire they burn."

And so she falls upon her knees in prayer :

" O hear !
O help me in this hour of anguish, help !
O, Thou, Who in the Garden once didst pray
For strength to drink the bitter cup of death,
Hear me ; the cup I ask Thee to remove
Is one of rapture, not of bitterness ;
I ask : I call : I cry out from the depth
Of agony and anguish. Help me ! Help ! "

But Gaston is too true knight and lover to let fear of death part lovers, and so the two come together.

" GASTON.   See, Mary, see,
The Universe has melted like a dream,
Earth has dissolved, and in the starless place
There are but you and my eternal love.
           .   .   .   .   .
MARY. It is as though we'd left the restless world,
And wandered in the happy fields of Death.
GASTON. As though we had been dead for centuries,
And could no more recall the dreams of earth.
MARY. As though we had been drowned in heavy seas.
GASTON. Beyond the river of oblivion.
MARY. Or as though we had slumbered in a tomb
For æons, and awakened full of peace.
GASTON. And we have soared through vasts of blinding light,
And moved in dazzling firmaments of flame.
MARY. And then we sought once more the place of dusk.
GASTON. And in our dim eternity of dusk,
There is no light, no sound, no voice of man,
Nor song of angel ; only I and you
Still in our everlasting ecstasy.
MARY. Yes ; only you and I. Content ! Content ! "

A second warning comes, this time from a Sooth-sayer, and this time to Gaston himself :

" Thou shalt be rich in valour and in merit ;
But thy reward shall be thy deathless fame ;
Thy prize shall be no earthly crown of gold,
But the unfading laurel leaves of glory.
As long as men are born to fight and die,
Thy name shall live, and where men meet to fight,
Thy name, more than the trumpet or the drum,
Shall stir their hearts, and when they face their death,
Thy name shall make that dreadful minute calm.
Amidst the sordid refuse of the world,
Thy memory shall flourish like a flower,
The stainless lily of the fields of blood ;
And in all time the fragrance of that flower
Shall rise into the nostrils of the brave,
And sweeten bitter death to dying men—
O Knight, made of pure gold without alloy."

Gaston is called away to the wars. Mary follows
him. He returns to her, safe from the first desperate
affray, but he has heard Death's summons.

" GASTON. Just now in the loud battle, while I fought,
Between the spears I saw the face of Death ;
Then twilight seemed to brood upon the battle ;
Above, amid the dimness and the hush,
The face of Death shone like the silent snow.
Oh, Mary, very glorious was that face,
And for one moment peace was in my soul,
And I was one with all calm sleeping things ;
And then I heard a voice which filled the skies,
Which called me by my name and bade me come
Unto a kingdom of divine strange light.

.   .   .   .   .   .

And yet when I shall sink beyond the day,
I dream I shall not find the darkness there,
But twilight, lustrous without star or moon.
My soul shall fly back to its ancient home,
And when you feel the hush of dawn or eve,
Then you will say that Gaston whom you loved,
Is sleeping somewhere on untrodden hills,
Beyond the sun."

Mary seeks, wifelike, womanlike, to hold him
back from going again to battle, but vainly ; and

so, his love being eternally hers, she bows to what she believes to be the Hand of God :

" (*Kneeling*) O God ! grant Gaston what his heart desires ;
Give him the peace he found not on the earth—
The stillness that is nowhere in the world,
Receive him into Thy tranquillity."

And so the drama ends with the bearing in of the body of Gaston, and the noble Bayart's salute to the fallen Prince :

" All you take off your helmets, bare your heads.
Your Prince is dead. Salute the noblest man
Of France, and of the world, who here lies low.
Bring honour. In the loveliness of youth
Gaston has now assumed the majesty
Of Death, and entered into deathless fame.
Our Prince has fallen."

Gaston de Foix seems to me not unworthy of the hand that penned *Idylls of the King*.

Proserpine :
A Masque

To the poet who is a scholar as well as a singer, and is familiar with his classics, the legend of Proserpine has always had peculiar fascination. That legend had its origin far back in the morning of the world, when the miracle of the new birth and return of the flowers to earth each spring—to be followed by their passing and by the mystery of seeming death each autumn—was all unapprehended by a pagan world. By that pagan world, all that was marvellous on earth was explainable only as some manifestation of the birth, the life, the loves, the anger, and the semi-human passion of the gods. So it may be that, out of the mystery of the seasons arose a legend of a daughter of the gods who, as she was gathering flowers with her maidens in the fields

K

of Sicily, was carried off by Pluto (enamoured of her
glorious beauty) to the realms below.   Though Proserpine, by the plea of her mother Demeter or Ceres,
and at the demand of Jupiter or Zeus, her father,
was permitted by Pluto the Lord of the Dead to
return to earth for a season, yet because in the World
of Shades she had eaten of the mystic food of the
Dead, the pomegranate, she was compelled again,
for a season, to return to the Underworld, taking
with her—so it seemed to the poet-pagan world
—the greenness and the flower glory of Old
Earth.

Maurice Baring's rendering of the lovely legend
opens in a cypress grove among the purple mountains of Sicily, and before the Temple of Proserpine.
The goddess when she comes to earth comes disguised as a mortal, and is known as Rosemary to
her maidens, who believe her to be a mortal and
are, in the first scene, awaiting her coming.   It is
a strange song that they sing to her :

> " Where does the Queen of the Fairies dwell ?
>   East of the sun and west of the moon :
> Whisper her name by the wishing well,
>   Curtsey and dance to the tinkling tune.
>
> Why is her garland of petals red ?
>   East of the sun and west of the moon :
> They grew in the sunless fields of the dead,
>   Curtsey and dance to the tinkling tune.
>
> Why is she pale as the marble stone ?
>   East of the sun and west of the moon :
> Never a sun on the sable throne ;
>   Curtsey and dance to the tinkling tune."

．　　．　　．　　．　　．　　．　　．

Then there enters the Prince who is to win the
love of the goddess, and thereafter, for love of her,
will be willing to forego the light, warmth and life
of Earth, and to accompany her to the sunless halls

of Death. But as yet he has not seen, and so not
come under the spell of, Proserpine. He is warned
that they who behold her mortal shape must die
ere the year be out :

> "They say that flames, lit by no mortal hand,
> Are seen here in the first warm nights of spring ;
> And that the dead in legions numberless
> March to the temple through autumnal mists ;
> The tales they tell are many, many, many,
> Of visions, and of elfin voices heard.
> Lately new rumours to the village came
> Of how the ancient gods had been dethroned,
> And wandered homeless in the haunts of men.
> Of how the elves of meadow and of wood
> Begged Proserpine to come and be their Queen.
> Some say in this green cirque of cypresses
> Before the temple on Midsummer Night,
> The faëry people worship Proserpine ;
> That mortals who behold this mystery
> Must die within the year. And Rosalind,
> One of the suppliants, saw the shadowy dance ;
> The elves, like fireflies, twinkled in the grass,
> And Proserpine walked down the temple steps."

Then, from the Temple, Proserpine herself, disguised as Rosemary, enters, singing :

> "I came with the swallow and with the swallow I go,
> Nevermore shall I see you, friend ;
> Softly over whatever was here the waters flow,
> The evening has come and the end.
>
> The hemlock flute in the spring and the grasshopper's song
> For ever shall sound in your dream ;
> My dream is dark, my dream is silent, my dream is long,
> By the reeds of the sable stream."

Rosemary and the Prince are left alone, and she
inquires whether he has come as a suppliant to the
Temple. He replies that he is bound for the sea-
girt city of King Pharamond. It is to Pharamond's
daughter that the Prince is betrothed, but already
the spell of Proserpine is upon him :

" ROSEMARY.

.   .   .   .

Ah ! bright the lot of mortals born to love !
THE PRINCE.   Is not your lot to love ?
ROSEMARY.   My lot is dark ;
Alien to mortal joy my destiny.
THE PRINCE.   May you not love ?
ROSEMARY.   Unearthly is my fate.
I serve a jealous goddess.
THE PRINCE.   Mortals say
The gods have been dethroned and cast from Heaven.
ROSEMARY.   Immortal are the gods ; though cast from
    Heaven,
They still shall find on earth a dwelling place.
Albeit men forsake the broken altars,
And seek strange gods and raise new images,
Yet shall the ancient gods endure, nor pass.
So long as men shall live and men shall die
So long in majesty shall Proserpine
Await their shades beyond the Stygian stream.
THE PRINCE.   Though all mankind should follow the new
    gods,
I still shall kneel and worship Proserpine !

.   .   .   .   .   .

What other gods have gifts to give like hers ?
Their gifts are crowns of laurel, myrtle crowns.
I do not need these things ; I yearn and seek.
But Proserpine bestows the great reprieve—
The sleep that hath no ending and no dream.
ROSEMARY.   The sleep is endless, endless too the dream.
THE PRINCE.   Who knows what lies beyond the gates of
    Death ?
ROSEMARY.   The pale dominions of Queen Proserpine ;
The waters of white Lethe, where the soul
Washes away remembrance of this earth,
A life of shadows and a silent world.
THE PRINCE.   My soul is drawn towards that silent world,
And if I could escape the dream of life
I would yield gladly to the dream of death.
ROSEMARY.   There is no springtide in the dream of death

.   .   .   .   .   .

There is no sorrow in the dream of death ;
There is no mirth, no laughter, and no song.
THE PRINCE.   How do you know the secrets of the tomb ?

ROSEMARY. I am the votaress of Proserpine,
She favours me, she visits me in dreams.
But lieth life, then, heavily on you ?
THE PRINCE. I know not ; I am haunted by a voice
That comes I know not whence, a silvery voice
That steals towards me over the high hills,
And speaks of spacious cool immensities,
And forests dense and endless aisles of night,
And glassy reaches of a sunless river
Dim and more broad than any earthly sea ;
Of harbours dark where many silent ships
At anchor ride, and stir not in the night.
A land beyond the sunset and the clouds,
East of the sun and westward of the moon.
ROSEMARY. East of the sun and westward of the moon
Dwells Proserpine, the sovran of the dusk."

Rosemary bids the Prince farewell. He makes
his obeisance and departs. The moon rises and
lights up the figure of Rosemary, which becomes
spectral and majestic. A silver halo shines around
her head, and a crown of red flowers is seen in her
hair. From the temple a chorus of voices is heard
singing. The spring has come, and with the spring
comes Proserpine. This is the invocation :

" The moon has risen in the night of spring,
   The sea is marble smooth, and dark as wine,
Oh ! hoist on thy dark ship a silver wing,
   Come to the slumbering earth, Queen Proserpine.

Bring the swift fireflies, bring the nightingale,
   And on the furrowed hills of corn and vine
Scatter red poppies and wild roses frail,
   Upon the slumbering earth, Queen Proserpine.

Come ! Leave the woods and valleys of the night ;
   The world is breathless with a hope divine.
A million swallows from the south take flight,
   Come, Queen of spring and swallows, Proserpine.

Beneath thy footsteps, like the milky way,
   The little twinkling asphodels shall shine ;
With flutes of June and cymbals of glad May,
   Come, wake the slumbering earth, Queen Proserpine."

In Scene II the Prince is at the palace of King
Pharamond, to whose lovely daughter he is betrothed.
As the ceremony is about to be celebrated, the
Princess and the courtiers are dismayed by the ill
omen of a passing funeral.   On a bier lies the Maiden
Rosalind.   She, a mortal, had, on Midsummer
Night witnessed, within the Temple, the mystic
worship of Proserpine, and so her life was forfeit.
The mourners are heard singing :

> " Drop lilies of the valley on her bier,
>   For Rosalind is dead, fair Rosalind;
>   Fair as the first white windflower in the wind,
> And frail as the first windflower of the year. . . .
>
> Ah ! weep, for she was young and she was fair ;
>   She was athirst for sunshine and for mirth,
>   For the glad sights and sounds of the sweet earth,
> And now she wanders cold in the pale air.
>
> Have pity on the shade of Rosalind,
>   She stretches out her hands in vain regret,
> For in thy kingdom there is no west wind,
>   No wheat, nor any roses, and no vine ;
>   She loved these things ; grant that she may forget,
>   And drown her dreams in sleep, calm Proserpine."

As the voices die, the Prince, like a man in a
dream, steals away from his bride and disappears.
The spell of Proserpine is upon him, and he must
seek the goddess.

In Act II we hear the strange disappearance of
the Prince discussed by the populace.   They go
on to speak of the coming Tournament of Life and
Death :

> " There is a tournament where Death himself
>   Answers the challenge of a mortal knight,
>   And meets him in the lists. . . .
>   He who would win needs more than fearlessness.
>   He must renounce all longing for the day,
>   Desire the life in death ; thus only he
>   Who vanquishes and kills his love of life
>   And longs for Death and for the life in Death,
>   Shall vanquish Death."

Then follows an exquisite love scene between Heartease, one of Rosemary's maidens, and her shepherd lover. But here I must confine myself to the story of Proserpine and the Prince. Again the two meet before the Temple, and the Prince declares his love :

" THE PRINCE. I love you for your sorrowful soft eyes,
I love you for your pale unaltered face,
I love you for your wide and dusky hair,
I love you for your voice which is the world's.
ROSEMARY. I love you, friend, I who have never loved!
THE PRINCE. Long have I dreamed of you throughout the
  world.
Far have I wandered, seeking for this face ;
Ah ! I have snatched the mask from many a face,
Yearning to find the twilight-laden eyes
That haunted me and never let me rest !
Now have I found my dream ; my quest is done.

ROSEMARY. O precious vision, O fugitive frail dream !
O would that you could last ! O would that we
Might hoist your wings for sails, and say farewell
Forever to the harbours of this world.
THE PRINCE. So shall it be. The vision shall come true.
We shall sail down the estuaries of time,
And reach the ocean of eternity.

ROSEMARY. There is one mortal man whom I may love,
That man must challenge Death and fight with him ;
That man must vanquish Death, and if he fails,
He dies, he passes to oblivion ;
He wanders lost to me for evermore.

THE PRINCE. But I shall challenge Death and vanquish him."

Rosemary looks at the Prince and bows her head. Again she reminds him that her kingdom is cold and grey, the kingdom of this world joyous and warm.

" ROSEMARY. Sweet is the fragrance of the wild white rose,
The honeysuckle and the new-mown hay.
THE PRINCE. I crave the scentless slumber-laden flowers.

ROSEMARY. Soft are the hollow wood-notes of the dove,
And low the flight of swallows in the dusk.
THE PRINCE.   I crave the woods unvexed by noise of wings.
ROSEMARY.   Glad is the sight of scarlet-flaunted fields,
The waving wheat, the dancing cornflowers,
The summer lightning, and the falling stars,
The flickering of the fireflies in the wheat,
The hot green spaces of midsummer darkness.
Can you forego for ever these fair sights ?
THE PRINCE.   The sights I need are mirrored in your eyes.
ROSEMARY.   The sighing of the wind, the whispering sea,
The noise and laughter of the busy street,
The song of lovers and the shepherd's reed.
Can you forego for ever these sweet sounds ?
THE PRINCE.   The sounds I need are echoed in your speech ;
The sights and sounds of life shall pass away,
And in the sunless place, for you and me
There shall be no more life and no more death,
No days, no hours, no seasons, and no time,
But only love for all eternity."

In Act III the populace are speaking of the
Tournament of Life and Death. A mortal, an
unknown knight, has vanquished Death.

" ' Some say
It was the lost betrothed of the Princess,
Who fought to win forgiveness and new love,' "

says a merchant. His companion, an old man,
replies :

" ' That cannot be, for when black-armoured Death
Fell rattling from his steed, a skeleton,
When that loud crash of thunder filled the air,
When the knight took the coal-black plumes of Death,
And marching to the maiden in her place,
Received of her the crown of victory,
With eyes that did not look he grasped the laurel,
And left the lists. He was so heedless, he ;—
Nor set the leaves upon his conquering brow,
Nor cast one glance upon the peerless face.' "

In the last scene Proserpine appears in all her
glory as a goddess. In the spring the voices of

the living were heard within the Temple, calling her
back to earth. Now, summer is dead, the autumn
has come, and the ghosts of the dead are here to
call Proserpine back to their Kingdom of the Dead.
They bow before her and sing :

> " The swallow seeks the southern land again,
>   The trees, but not the cypress and the pine,
> Are splashed and dyed with autumn's crimson stain ;
>   Come back unto thy dead, Queen Proserpine.
>
> The fruit has fallen from the orchard trees,
>   And on the mountain-ash red berries shine ;
> The ship awaits thee and the ghostly breeze ;
>   Come back unto thy dead, Queen Proserpine.
>
> The golden wheat was garnered long ago,
>   And ended is the harvest of the vine ;
> Through ragged woods the winds of autumn blow ;
>   Come back unto thy dead, Queen Proserpine."

The Prince, dazed and dazzled, kneels before the
goddess who declares herself as Queen Proserpine.
He tells her he has conquered Death, and offers
her the helm.   She asks what recompense he
craves.

> " THE PRINCE.   To follow to your everlasting home,
> To dwell for ever in the dream of you.
> This is the only recompense I crave—
> Ah ! you know well what is my heart's desire.
>   PROSERPINE.   In my pale kingdom on a pillared throne,
> I shall be far removed from you, for you
> Shall dwell amid the myriads of the dead ;—
> They may not even see my royal face,
> And only you, of all the endless host,
> Shall unforgetful gaze on Proserpine.
> Will you receive that for your recompense ?
>   THE PRINCE.   I shall behold your changeless face and dwell
> For ever in the dream and sight of you,
> For ever in the thought and light of you,
> For ever in the shadow of your soul,
> For ever in the stillness that is you,
> Remembering all that was ; far off, but near,
> Beyond the reach of Life and Death and Time,

And linked by chains of silent song to you.
And though the rivers and the plains of Hell
Between us lie, if I behold this face,
I shall be one with your wide majesty,
And with your mute and dark dominion one,
One with your pale, your glimmering loveliness,
One with your sorrow endless and divine,
One with the vastness of your silver dream,
And one with your eternal life in death."

Proserpine replies:

So shall it be,
For you have conquered Death, and you can choose
The fruit of darkness or the fruit of life,
The apple or the slumberous pomegranate.
So take this apple, take this pomegranate,
Await on earth the footfall of the spring,
Then, when the rapturous earth awakes from sleep,
And calls the summer to make love to her,
Look round and hear the music of the spring.
Look round and heed the glory of the world,
The pastures, the fresh woods, the cloudy hills,
The murmurous cities and the smiling sea ;
If on that day you still shall crave the dark,
The silence and the sorrow of my dream,
Taste the pomegranate ; you shall sleep to wake
Within my shadow; but if smiling Life
Be sweet to you, then taste the golden fruit,
You shall forget the dream of Proserpine,
And live contented in the world of men.
And with the spring I shall return once more,
And I shall love you with a mortal's love,
And you shall love me with a mortal's love,
With all a mortal's ecstasy of love,
With all a mortal's swift forgetfulness.
And when the summer dies, and I once more
Return to the dark realm, you shall forget ;
And, fancy-free, shall seek and find new joy.
THE PRINCE.   And if I taste the other darker fruit,
Will you return with the returning spring ?
PROSERPINE.   I shall be unaware of earth and spring,
I shall forget the vision of the world,
I shall have found the dream I sought on earth ;
I nevermore shall seek the earth in spring."

The goddess ceases, and again the ghost voices of the dead are heard in chorus.

Finally they die away, and, as she disappears, the voice of Proserpine is once again, but for the last time, heard :

> " ' Farewell. I go to my dominion,
> East of the sun and westward of the moon ;
> But you await the coming of the spring.' "

For sheer magic and beauty of language and of imagination, for Oriental splendour of sound, of sight, and of perfume, which, physically as well as intellectually, casts some subtle spell over us, I know nothing in modern dramatic poetry comparable to *Proserpine*.   Its music and its pictures haunt one.

From the beautiful poem *Blossom* (*Collected Poems*) one infers that Maurice Baring is of opinion that Poetry and Art are, for the most part, only for the day which called them forth :

> " The fashioned wonders of man's brain and hand,
> The living marble, the immortal song,
> The poet's soaring dream,
> Rise like the blossom, like the blossom wane ;
> And on the moving surface of Time's stream
> Their life is neither briefer nor more long."

We all agree that each generation demands its own poet, to express in the language of the day the perhaps passing phases of life as viewed from the standpoint of that generation ; and also newly to interpret many things of the spiritual and the natural world.   But with such poets Maurice Baring has no part.   His poetry is, in no sense, merely of to-day.   It will endure.   I conclude with the last stanza of *Blossom* :

> " Sorrow descends upon the mortal sight,
> Sorrow for beauty of fair things that fade,
> Till one strong thought consoles the hopeless night,
> That from the wealth of God, where worlds are made,

(The Treasure-house that nothing can decrease)
A never-ending tide shall ebb and flow ;
  The note must sound and die,—
The eternal symphony shall never cease ;
  Divinely made, thought, shape, and melody
Shall come like blossom and like blossom go."

Alfred Noyes

Alfred Noyes

PART I

M R. ALFRED NOYES is not a poet of the
" scarlet word " school. I mean by this
that, just as one make of typing-machine
has not only a black but also a scarlet ribbon, by
which so to startle and to compel attention that
certain words leap to the eye from the page, so some
poets, generally of a small clique—" impressionists,"
" cubists," or whatever the latest *cachet* may be—
pride themselves on the use, the artifice really,
of the scarlet word.

The " golden " word, a true poet, even if unconsciously, finds for himself. We say of some lovers
that the one was born for the other. So, too, the
golden and inevitable word meets with and expresses
its thought-affinity as its one and only complement
and mate. The scarlet word is self-consciously
sought after (even hunted down as a butterfly is
hunted down by a school-boy), to be pinned, butter-
fly-wise, to the page. The scarlet word is pinned
there thus, partly to attract to itself, and so to dis-
tract, the reader's attention away from the paucity of
the thought, the general drabness of the so-called
poetry; and partly, assertively, to advertise that
here, at least, is nothing obvious or commonplace,
here is only what is " precious," original, and
superior.

In all Mr. Noyes's poems I do not recall a single

scarlet word, one strained fancy, one bizarre metaphor. Those who set store by the proverb, " Nothing dare, nothing do," must not for that reason suppose that in his work there is anything that is timid, tame, hesitating.

Timid ? Turn to the first of the two volumes of *Collected Poems*, page 83, and read the last stanza of the song which pictures England as " The World's May Queen " :

> " And round the fairy revels whirl
>   In England, in England !
> And the buds outbreak and the leaves unfurl,
> And where the crisp white cloudlets curl
> The Dawn comes up like a primrose girl
> With a crowd of flowers in a basket of pearl
>   For England ! "

Where, even in the work of Mr. Kipling, will you find a simile more daring than that in these last three lines ? The simile is so daring that it takes the critic in us—as a sentry is sometimes taken in warfare—by surprise. Just as the sentry, hearing an unexpected step, springs forward with rifle ready to bayonet or to shoot ; and then recognizing his commander-in-chief, brings his rifle to " the slope " and thence to " the present "—so, startled by the daring of the simile, the critic in us for one moment stands to arms, and the next moment, realizing that he is in the presence of a true poet, a master of new and happy imagery, springs to the salute.

Only to one simile do I take exception. In that terrible picture of war, *The Wine Press*, Mr. Noyes says :

> "The maxims cracked like cattle whips."

I have heard the Maxim gun in action, near by as well as afar, and have on occasion fired one myself, but I should not describe Maxims as cracking like cattle whips. That might apply to rifle fire, but when Maxims " speak," they do so in a voice in which is a stutter, almost a stammer : " Tt-ttt-tt-ttttttt-tt."

Since the Balkan War, of which Mr. Noyes was writing, the Maxim has been superseded by the Lewis and the Vickers guns, but what I have said applies equally to the now out-of-date Maxim.

If, in my appreciation of the poems of Mr. Noyes, I write first of *The Forest of Wild Thyme*, I do so for the following reason. Sunrays coming to us in a continuous stream from nearly 93,000,000 miles away may, by means of a glass, be concentrated into one focal point and globe (an infinitesimal reproduction of the great sun itself) of intense heat and light. Similarly, in *The Forest of Wild Thyme*, one finds, not only most, if not all the qualities which entitle Mr. Noyes to a place in the very front rank of living poets, but one also finds a reproduction, in miniature, of the poet's self and soul.

In the very beginning of *The Forest of Wild Thyme* we read :

> " When with a wild flower in your hand
> You echoed that dead poet's cry—
> ' *Little flower, but if I could understand!* '
> And you saw it had roots in the depths of the sky,
> And there in that smallest bud lay furled
> The secret and meaning of all the world."

That is the keynote to the whole poem. It is not a new note, as witness the gracefully interpolated quotation from Tennyson's lines, " Little flower in the crannied wall," but Mr. Noyes so sounds the note that it has here new depths and new meanings, which are as much of his own personality as the fragrance of a violet is of that violet's self.

And mark the courtliness of the younger poet to the older. In thus quoting his illustrious predecessor in poetry, Mr. Noyes, like a young knight setting out for the Crusades, lowers his lance-point in homage

L

when passing the grave of a great and fallen warrior.

Let no one suppose, however, that *The Forest of Wild Thyme* is in any sense an elaboration of a thought from Tennyson. The poem would have been written, and on exactly the same lines, had there been no Tennyson. Nor, though Mr. Noyes is evidently widely read in science, does he owe to science his inspiration. Poetry, by virtue of the great gift of vision, sometimes sees what science discovers only by collection and collation of data, research, and deduction.

Now I ask my readers to journey with Mr. Noyes to *The Forest of Wild Thyme.* It is again " a little child " who " shall lead them."

The children are sorely grieving at missing little brother Peterkin from their play. Whither he has gone—

> " Whether he set out to run
> By candle-light to Babylon,"—

or on what other high adventure, they do not know.

> " We just missed something father said
> About a young prince that was dead,
> A little warrior that had fought
> And failed : how hopes were brought to nought,
> He said, and mortals made to bow
>   Before the Juggernaut of Death,
> And all the world was darker now,
>   For Time's grey lips and icy breath
> Had blown out all the enchanted lights
> That burned in Love's Arabian nights ;
> And now he could not understand
> Mother's mystic fairy land,
> ' Land of the dead, poor fairy tale,'
> He murmured, and her face grew pale."

Then, in the wife's reply to the doubting husband, comes in my first quotation, given above, in which occurs Tennyson's line :

> " Little flower, but if I could understand."

Again I must say a word of the felicity with which the quotation is interpolated. It is as if Mr. Noyes had slipped upon the finger of the Muse a ring, in which gems of his own finding and fashioning form a setting for a rare gem of another and older poet's bringing.

> " He shook his head and then he tried
> To kiss her, but she only cried
> And turned her face away and said,
> ' You come between me and my dead !
> His soul is near me night and day,
> But you would drive it far away ;
> And you shall never kiss me now
> Until you lift that brave old brow
> Of faith I know so well ; or else
> Refute the tale the skylark tells,
> Tarnish the glory of that May,
> Explain the Smallest Flower away.'
> And still he said, ' Poor fairy tales,
> How terribly their starlight pales
> Before the solemn sun of truth
> That rises o'er the grave of youth ! ' "

The children overhear this, and, taking the talk of the " grown-ups " seriously, Dick, the eldest, declares that they must :

> " Seek the lost
> Smallest Flower at any cost.
> For since within its leaves lay furled
> The secret of the whole wide world,
> He thought that we might learn therein
> The whereabouts of Peterkin ;
> And if we found the Flower, we knew
> Father would be forgiven, too ;
> And mother's kiss atone for all
> The quarrel by the rose-hung wall."

And so they set off on the quest. Being wise children, not foolish grown-ups, they go, of course, by way of fairyland.

" Oh, grown-ups cannot understand
And grown-ups never will,
How short's the way to fairyland
Across the purple hill :
They smile : their smile is very bland,
Their eyes are wise and chill,
And yet—at just a child's command—
The world's an Eden still."

When children set out to seek either the Smallest
Flower or the gold that lies hidden where the greatest
and the most glorious (if the briefest in bloom) of all
God's flowers—the Rainbow-Iris—has roots in the
warm earth, we grown-ups must not follow after too
closely. By doing so we might frighten away the
fairies, or might, by our heavier breathing, shatter
the delicate rainbow-petals, frail as a floating bubble.
Hence, while the children run on ahead, I say a
few words about Mr. Noyes's poems generally, and
The Forest of Wild Thyme in particular.

The Music of
Alfred Noyes

Were some one to assure me that Mr. Noyes's poems
come to him first as music ; are set down, in terms of
music, on paper, ruled with the familiar five closely-
placed lines, which is used by musicians when
inscribing the score of a composition—were I so
assured, I should scarcely feel surprised.

One might even fancy (I do not imply, or even for
a moment suggest, that it is so) that Mr. Noyes, if he
did not actually write certain passages " to music,"
had, at least, a passage of music " running in his
head," as the homely phrase words it, when penning
this or that refrain.

If the reader happen to have Grieg's *Peer Gynt*,
Suite I (Opus 46) for violin and piano, and will run
over No. IV, " In der Halle des Bergkönigs " (In
the Hall of the King of the Mountain), popularly

known as " The Gnome's Song," the reader will, I
think, agree, either that one passage of the music
might have been written as an accompaniment to
the following refrain from Mr. Noyes's poem *The
Barrel Organ*, or that the poet might have penned his
refrain to an accompaniment of the passage from
Grieg :

> " Come down to Kew in lilac-time, in lilac-time, in lilac-time,
>   Come down to Kew in lilac-time (it isn't far from London !),
> And you shall wander hand in hand with love in summer's
>   wonderland ;
>   Come down to Kew in lilac-time (it isn't far from London !)."

Grieg's music is often weird, ghostly, grotesque, even
uncanny, but this particular passage, if played so
as to trip to a lighter measure, keeps time and keeps
tune with surprising exactness to the wonderful
" lilt " of which Mr. Noyes is so consummate a
master. One other point in connexion with *The
Forest of Wild Thyme*, I wish to make. It is that
in writing a poem the author does well to avoid anything which recalls a well-known poem by an earlier
poet. The new poem may be the finer of the two, but
if inferior work—even without direct association of
the one poem with the other by the reader ; even if
only by unconscious suggestion—be brought to mind
the new and finer poem suffers. Though possibly
unaware why he does so, the reader may associate
the new poem dimly and vaguely in his mind with
inferior work—to the new poem's detriment. It is
as if the shadow of something less worthy had been
cast from the past upon the present. On the other
hand, if the new poem be the inferior of the two, the
new poem suffers by comparison.

There are moments when the metre of *The Forest
of Wild Thyme* recalls the metre of Southey's well-
known *Battle of Blenheim*, from which I copy a
stanza :

> " With fire and sword the country round
> Was wasted far and wide,
> And many a chiding mother then,
> And new-born infant died.
> But things like this, you know must be
> At every famous victory."

And here is one of the two resembling stanzas (there are only two, so far as I remember) from *The Forest of Wild Thyme* :

> " Why, mother once had sung it us
> When, ere we went to bed,
> She told the tale of Pyramus,
> How Thisbe found him dead
> And mourned his eyes as green as leeks,
> His cherry nose, his cowslip cheeks."

Nor is this all. The refrain, " 'twas a famous victory " from Southey is, consciously or unconsciously, recalled by the haunting and melodious refrain in which Mr. Noyes mourns the lost boy ; and as Southey speaks of " brother Peterkin " and " little Peterkin," and Mr. Noyes of " little brother Peterkin," the quaint and uncommon recurrent name common to both poems recalls the earlier poem to readers of the later. Of the two poems, that by Mr. Noyes is incomparably the finer, and I make the point not in disparagement of the younger poet, but as a hint to readers who contemplate challenging the verdicts of critics with a volume of poetry.

If the reader's aim be to write musically, she or he will do well lovingly to study all that Alfred Noyes has written. His poems not only make music, but *are* music, and scarcely less so than they are poetry.

In writing of Maurice Baring's work, I said that certain songs and snatches from songs recur in the dramas, as if the songs were written to a musical accompaniment which, while continuing throughout, is, for the most part, inaudible, and only now and then deepens into heard music. In Alfred Noyes's work one is conscious of the music all the time, not, as in Maurice Baring's, intermittently, and as an occasional accompaniment, but as a dancing, lilting —always lilting, lilting, lilting—even if distant refrain.

Poems that
" Lilt "

Some of us, on a first visit to Switzerland, bring back a tiny model of one of the pine-wood chalets so common in that country. It is a musical-box, the opening of which sets the melody going. So with a book by Alfred Noyes. Open a book of his, and you are instantly aware of fairy music. Is it because the fairies, forsaking or driven from their ancient haunts, have taken to housing themselves between the pages or under the covers of Mr. Noyes's works ; and, when a book is opened, they step out to tread a measure in honour of one who still honours and believes in fairies ? Or is it that his poems come to him only when he is a-stretch beside some brooklet or stream, and so he unconsciously makes his music to keep time and tune with the ripple, tinkle and purl of running water ? Or, again, is it that, by some magic, Marconi, message-receiving system of his own invention, he can capture at will the wind-borne and distant chime of volleying bells, and compel their dancing silvern clamour to echo in his verse ?

My words may seem fanciful to a matter-of-fact reader, but are they more fanciful than—if I may be forgiven for using so great a name in such trivial connexion—Shakespeare's words of another maker of music :

> " Orpheus, with his lute, made trees
> And the mountain tops that freeze
> Bow themselves when he did sing " ?

It is at least plain fact, and no fancy, that certain of Alfred Noyes's poems float to us as lightly and as liltingly as the far chiming of vesper bells ; as if the fairies danced for him when he wrote ; as if the poem came to him, wind-carried, butterfly-borne, or as softly a-sail as a rose petal upon a stream's surface.

This is specially true of *The Forest of Wild Thyme.* Wherever that forest may be, here on old earth or in fairyland, it is within sound of a chime of bells, and a chime which rings strange, and many, changes. First, it may be, we hear some home-reminding, home-remembering strain familiar to our childhood ; after that, the call to prayer of the *Angelus,* followed by the slow tolling which tells that a soul is passing or has passed to God.   Then—is it from the belfry in the church tower, or from the organ-loft within that the music comes ?—for that surely is the roll of a great hymn, gathering in volume of sound, as if swelled by the voices of a congregation.   Next we hear the volleying of wedding bells, followed by such rippling merriment of bell-music, that every bell a-swing in the tower seems to be shaking its sounding sides, and rocking like a pendulum in one great chorus of glad bell-laughter.

But whether the music be sad and solemn, glad and gay ; whether the thought in the poet's mind be a quaintly-humorous thought, a beautiful thought, or, as it often is, a thought which opens up new worlds of thought with the suddenness and vividness of the lightning flash—thought and music alike go as it were together, hand in hand, like twin children of one father whom each in some way strangely resembles.

On to Fairyland

Now let us follow on again to *The Forest of Wild Thyme,* and Nursery Rhymeland, by way of which and of Fairyland, we go.   We also go by way of a

Photo
Chickering

Alfred Noyes

country, the frontiers of which some poets—the less poets they—never cross. They do not speak the language, and so are refused a passport—I mean the Rainbowland of Humour. It is a land of sunshine and shower, of gladness and sadness, for he or she to whom has been given the divining-rod of humour, discovers not only hidden waters of laughter, but also hidden fountains of tears. If poets are born, not made, so are humorists. One must be born in Rainbowland to be a humorist. The biographical books tell us that Mr. Noyes was born in Staffordshire, but forget to tell us in what town. It does not matter. The great house in Park Lane, London, known as the American Embassy, is a tiny bit of America. The ground it stands on is, by international law, American territory. So with the French, Italian, Spanish, and other embassies. They are part of the country which those who live in the embassy house represent.

His Humour

Alfred Noyes may have been born in Staffordshire, but Humour and Poetry have their embassies and their territory in every country. Wherever Mr. Noyes was born, it was on territory under the double sovereignty of Poetry and Humour. Every one born in the Rainbowland of Humour has a fairy for a godmother, and this lets us into the secret of Mr. Noyes's knowledge of fairies.

His sense of humour is so delightful that to read *The Forest of Wild Thyme* is sheer joy. No one without a delicate sense of humour—which means nearly always a sense of true reverence, as well as of perspective—could have harmoniously interwoven the nursery rhymes of our childhood with an intensely symbolical, spiritual—one might even say " religious—poem, and with never a shadow of offence.

The Ladybird
in Poetry

The children are now in Fairyland. How they travelled thither, and by what magic they became ever so much smaller than ladybirds, the reader must learn from the book.

> " Far off we heard a bell ;
> And suddenly a great red light
> Smouldered before our startled sight.
> Then came a cry, a fiercer flash,
>   And down between the trees
> We saw great crimson figures crash,
>   Wild-eyed monstrosities ;
> Great dragon shapes that breathed a flame
> From roaring nostrils as they came :
>   We sank upon our knees ;
> And looming o'er us ten yards high,
> Like battleships they thundered by.
> And then, as down that mighty dell
>   We followed faint with fear,
> We understood the tolling bell
>   That called the monsters there ;
> For right in front we saw a house
> Woven of wild mysterious boughs
>   Bursting out everywhere
> In crimson flames, and with a shout
> The monsters rushed to put it out."

Then the children heard a voice calling :

> " *Oh, Ladybird, Ladybird, fly away home ;*
>   *Your house is on fire and your children are gone,*"

and knew that

> " The dragons were but ladybirds."

This, the first adventure, ends, as all ends, in a crooning, lilting, longing cry after the little lost brother :

> " Peterkin, Peterkin, if you could only hear
>   And answer us ; one little word from little lonely Peterkin
> To take and comfort father, he is sitting in his chair

In the library, he's listening for your foots'ep on the stair
And your pattei down the passage, he can only think of Peterkin:
Come back, come back to father, for to-day he'd let us tear
His newest book to make a paper-boat for little Peterkin."

The Hideous Hermit

The second adventure is entitled " The Hideous Hermit."

> " Ah, what wonders round us rose
>   When we dared to pause and look,
> Curious things that seemed all toes,
>   Goblins from a picture book;
> Ants like witches, four feet high,
>   Waving all their skinny arms,
> Glared at us and wandered by
>   Muttering their ancestral charms.
>
> .   .   .   .   .   .
>
> Once a sort of devil came
>   Scattering broken trees about,
> Winged with leather, eyed with flame—
>   He was but a moth, no doubt."

First we encounter the murderer of Cock Robin :

> " ' *I !* And who are *You*, sir, pray ? '
>   Growled a voice that froze our marrow.
> ' Who ? ' we heard the murderer say,
>   ' Lord sir, I'm the famous Sparrow,
>   And this 'ere's my bow and arrow !
>   *I*
>   *killed*
>   *Cock*
>   *Robin !* ' "

But

> " The Robin and the Wren
>   Are such friends to mortal men,
> Such dear friends to mortal men "—

that the children

> " Couldn't bear to wait
>   Even to hear the murderer's fate,"

and pass on to meet creatures even more eerie than
the little bird murderer :

> " Mammoths father calls ' extinct,'
>   Creatures that the cave-men feared,
> Through that jungle walked and blinked,
>   Through that jungle crawled and leered,
> Beasts no Nimrod ever knew,
>   Woolly bears of black and red ;
> Crocodiles we wondered who
>   Ever dared to see *them* fed."

Then—

> " Faint and far
> Came the shadow of a cry,
>   Like the calling of a star
> To its brother in the sky."

Little Boy Blue

It is the horn of Little Boy Blue, and here Mr.
Noyes retells the old story exquisitely. *This* Little
Boy Blue is bidden to summon an older generation,
the tired, grown-up children of to-day—you who
read, and I who write, and others like us—to courage
and hope, and to keep the child-heart in us alive
to life's end. But alas ! much that is loveliest in
life—a flower, a sunset, a moonrise, no less than the
moment of rapt ecstasy, when we see as in a vision
the sorrowful face of One, thorn-crowned—is the
swiftest to pass. Scarcely has the brave message
reached our ears, scarcely has Mr. Noyes's angel-
messenger—

> " Straight and clad in aery blue "—

lifted the golden horn to his lips—before he is gone,
and—

> " Round him flowed the purple night."

Now the music changes, and is indeed Grieg-like
and grotesque. Yet though grey in tone (if one may

so speak of music) it is none the less reverberant
with grim humour. Enter " The Hideous Hermit."
In all the poem there is no more delightfully humorous fancy than Mr. Noyes's conception of The Sentimental Spider. I have a personal reason for so
thinking, inasmuch as, at the request of a friendly
publisher, I long ago collected verses of mine from
Punch, the *Windsor*, and other publications, into a
book about Dogs. That the contents might not
be all reprinted matter, I attempted a jingle with
the title of *The Pessimistic Poodle*, but got no farther
than the title, and the last line which ran—

"The Pessimistic Poodle had committed poodlecide."

There I stuck. The poodle had established the
remarkable record—he ought to have been an Irish
terrier by my way of wording the incident—of ending
his life before he began it. The Sentimental Spider
of Mr. Noyes's poem makes skilful use of sentiment
to end the lives of other creatures.

" Will you Walk into
my Parlour ? "

" Then from out a weird old wicket, overgrown with shaggy hair
Like a weird and wicked eyebrow round a weird and wicked eye,
 Two great eyeballs and a beard
 For one ghastly moment peered
At our faces with a sudden stealthy stare ;
 Then the door was opened wide,
 And a hideous hermit cried,
With a shy and soothing smile from out his lair,
' Won't you walk into my parlour ? I can make you cosy there ! '
 . . . .
Then we looked a little closer at the ogre as he stood
With his great red eyeballs glowing like two torches in a wood,
And his mighty speckled belly and his dreadful clutching claws,
And his nose—a horny parrot's beak—his whiskers and his
 jaws ;
Yet he seemed so sympathetic, and we saw two tears descend,
As he murmured, ' I'm so ugly, but I've lost my dearest friend !

I tell you most lymphatic'ly I've yearnings in my soul '—
And right along his parrot's beak we saw the teardrops roll.
He's an arrant sentimentalist, we heard a distant sigh,
Won't you weep upon my bosom? said the spider to the fly.

' If you'd dreamed my dreams of beauty, if you'd seen my works
      of art,
If you'd felt the cruel hunger that is gnawing at my heart,
And the grief that never leaves me, and the love I can't forget
(For I loved with all the letters in the Chinese alphabet),
Oh, you'd all come in to comfort me : you ought to help the
      weak ;
And I'm full of melting moments ; and—I—know—the—thing
      —you—seek ! '
And the haunting echo answered, *Well, I'm sure you ought
      to try ;*
There's a duty to one's neighbour, said the spider to the fly.

     .   .   .   .   .

And again the foolish echo made a far-away reply—
      Oh, don't come to me for comfort,
      Pray don't look to me for comfort,
Heavens, you mustn't be so foolish, said the spider to the fly.

     .   .   .   .   .

Then he moaned, ' My heart is hungry ; but I fear I cannot eat
(Of course, I speak entirely now of spiritual meat),
For I only fed an hour ago ; but if we calmly sat
While I told you all my troubles in a confidential chat,
It would give me *such* an appetite to hear you sympathise,
And I should sleep the better—see, the tears are in my eyes !
Dead yearnings are such dreadful things, let's keep 'em all
      alive—
Let's sit and talk awhile, my dears ; we'll dine I think at
      five.' "

Then, to enliven the time till the dinner-hour—
his dinner-hour—and to encourage the children to
persevere in the hope that some dinner is, as the
Canadians say, " coming to them," the Sympathetic
Spider tells the story of Robert the Bruce and the
spider (a near relative, it seems, of his own) as well
as of little Miss Muffet.

But again the children hear a call—the wailing,
lilting cry to little Brother Peterkin, which is as

compelling to them as the playing of the Pied Piper of Hamelin to the children of that town. Our children are now, however, in deadly danger, for the spider means mischief—in other words, a meal—but deliverance out of his clutches is at hand. A fairy battalion, led by Pease Blossom and Mustard Seed, come to succour the wanderers, and to guide them on the way to the Smallest Flower.

Pease Blossom and Mustard Seed

One longs to write fully of these fairy happenings, and of the doings and sayings of Pease Blossom and Mustard Seed, but here I must quote only a few lines from each. Pease Blossom shall speak first :

> " ' Men toil,' he said, ' from morn till night,
> With bleeding hands and blinded sight
> For gold, more gold ! They have betrayed
> The trust that in their souls was laid ;
> Their fairy birthright they have sold
> For little disks of mortal gold ;
> And now they cannot even see
> The gold upon the greenwood tree,
> The wealth of coloured lights that pass
> In soft gradations through the grass,
> The riches of the love untold
> That wakes the day from grey to gold ;
> And howsoe'er the moonlight weaves
> Magic webs among the leaves,
> Englishmen care little now
> For elves beneath the hawthorn bough :
> Nor if Robin should return
> Dare they of an outlaw learn ;
> For them the Smallest Flower is furled,
> Mute is the music of the world ;
> And unbelief has driven away
> Beauty from the blossomed spray.' "

Then Mustard Seed, who is a

> " Devil-may-care,
> Epigrammatic and pungent fellow,
> Clad in a splendid suit of yellow,"

adds his own words of wisdom :

> " ' For since the Thyme you used to know
> Seems a forest here below,
> What if you should sink again
> And find there stretched a mighty plain
> Between each grass-blade and the next ?
> You'd think till you were quite perplexed ;
> Especially if all the flowers
> That lit the sweet Thyme-forest bowers
> Were in that wild transcendent change,
> Turned to Temples, great and strange,
> With many a pillared portal high
> And domes that swelled against the sky.
> How foolish, then, you will agree,
> Are those who think that all must see
> The world alike, or those who scorn
> Another who perchance was born
> Where—in a different dream from theirs—
> What they call sins to him are prayers.' "

And so, fairy-led, and cheered by the way, the children come at last within sight of the Ivory Gates which guard the City of Sleep. Others—a mighty throng of which the children are now a part—are journeying thither.

The Ivory Gate
of Sleep

> " And lo, as we neared that mighty crowd
> An old blind man came, crying aloud
> To greet us, as once the blind man cried
> In the Bible picture—you know we tried
> To paint that print, with its Eastern sun ;
> But the reds and the yellows *would* mix and run.
>
> .   .   .   .   .   .
>
> And the blind man cried, ' Our help is at hand,
> Oh, brothers, remember the old command,
> Remember the frankincense and myrrh,
> Make way, make way, for those little ones there ;
> Make way, make way, I have seen them afar
> Under a great white Eastern star ;

For I am the mad blind man who sees ! '
Then he whispered softly—' *Of such as these.*'

· · · · · · ·

And then, in one splendid marching stream
The whole of that host came following through.
We were only children, just like you ;
Children, ah, but we felt so grand
As we led them—although we could understand
Nothing at all of the wonderful song
That rose all round as we marched along.

Song.

" ' You that have seen how the world and its glory
  Change and grow old like the love of a friend ;
You that have come to the end of the story ;
  You that were tired ere you came to the end ;
You that are weary of laughter and sorrow,
  Pain and pleasure, labour and sin,
Sick of the midnight and dreading the morrow,
  Ah, come in ; come in.

' You that are bearing the load of the ages ;
  You that have loved overmuch and too late ;
You that confute all the saws of the sages ;
  You that have served only because you must wait,
Knowing your work was a wasted endeavour ;
  You that have lost and yet triumphed ´therein.
Add loss to your losses and triumph for ever,
  Ah, come in, come in.' "

After this poignant song, and when the poem as
a whole is nearing a close, the reintroduction of
nursery rhymes, See-Saw, Margery Daw, Little Boy
Blue, Dickery Dock, and the like, would—were not
Mr. Noyes a poet whose every thought is as reverent
as his art is exquisite—seem to jar.   Far from being
conscious of discord, however, one is aware only of
harmony, for—

" We saw that the tunes of the world were one ;
  And the metre that guided the rhythmic sun
  Was at one, like the ebb and the flow of the sea,
  With the tunes that we learned at our mother's knee."

M

Motherhood

It is, indeed, back to the knee of Motherhood that Mr. Noyes leads us.   Now and then we seem to come a-near the haunts of mankind again, and to pass the outskirts of a dark and sleeping city.   But our leader has gone before to set, here and there, in a window, a light kindled by the fire of his own imagination ; and by parable and symbol to illumine the way.   For the most part, our path lies through the forests and misted valleys ; but in the eastern sky, the poet points us to a star, by following which we come at last to kneel in one of the world's holiest places.

" A Child was born in Bethlehem, in Bethlehem, in Bethlehem,
    The wise men came to welcome Him, a star stood o'er the
        gable ;
    And there they saw the King of Kings,
    No longer throned with angel wings,
But croodling like a little babe, and cradled in a stable.

    The wise men came to greet Him with their gifts of myrrh and
        frankincense—
    Gold and myrrh and frankincense they brought to make Him
        mirth ;
    And would you know the way to win to little brother Peterkin,
    My childhood's heart shall guide you through the glories of
        the earth."

If, with the children, we have travelled back to a time two thousand years ago, we have travelled far forward with them in wisdom by learning that only by the child-heart within us, may the riddle of Life be answered, the things that are of God be discerned.

They are now nearing the end of their quest, and are about to enter the Temple of the Smallest Flower.

The Temple of the Smallest Flower

" There above the woods in state
 Many a temple dome that glows
Delicately like a great
 Rainbow-coloured bubble rose :
Though they were but flowers on earth,
 Oh, we dared not enter in :
For in that Divine re-birth,
 Less than awe were more than sin.

 .   .   .   .   .   .

And then we strangely seemed to hear
 The shadow of a mighty psalm,
A sound as if a golden sea
 Of music swung in utter calm
Against the shores of Eternity ;
 And then we saw the mighty dome
Of some mysterious Temple tower
 On high ; and knew that we had come
 At last to that sweet House of Grace
 Which wise men find in every place—
 The Temple of the Smallest Flower.

 .   .   .   .   .   .

Only a flower ? Those carven walls,
Those cornices and coronals,
The splendid crimson porch, the thin
Strange sounds of singing from within.

Through the scented arch we stept,
 Pushed back the soft petallic door,
And down the velvet aisles we crept ;
 Was it a Flower—no more ?

For one of the voices that we heard,
A child's voice clear as the voice of a bird,
Was it not ? Nay it could not be ;
And a woman's voice that tenderly
Answered him in fond refrain,
And pierced our hearts with sweet sweet pain—

' What is there hid in the heart of a rose, Mother mine ? '
' Ah, who knows, who knows, who knows ?
A Man that died on a lonely hill
May tell you, perhaps, but none other will, Little child.'

'What does it take to make a rose, Mother mine?'
'The God that died to make it knows.
It takes the world's eternal wars,
It takes the moon and all the stars,
It takes the might of Heaven and Hell,
And the everlasting Love as well, Little child.'"

The Answer to all
Our Questioning

Here, in the divine philosophy of Motherhood—
surely the holiest and most beautiful earthly type
of vicarious sacrifice, the suffering which gives life
to another in this world, even as the Christ suffered
upon the Cross that all God's children might be born
into eternal life—we have the answer to all our
questionings. Elsewhere—in a poem which is a
marvel of insight, by symbolism—the same thought
is more fully expressed.

Mystical the poem in question—it is entitled
Creation—may be, but those who lightly dismiss such
visions of the Unseen as mere " mysticism " would
do well to ponder the words of a great spiritual
teacher, George MacDonald.

In *Unspoken Sermons* he says : " A mystical
mind is one which, having perceived that the highest
expression of which the truth admits lies in the
symbolism of Nature, and the human customs
which result from human necessities, prosecutes
thought about truth, so embodied, by dealing with
the symbols themselves, after logical forms.   This is
the highest mode of conveying the deepest truth,
and the Lord Himself often employed it, as, for
instance, in the whole passage ending with the words :
' If, therefore, the light that is in thee be darkness,
how great is the darkness.' "

Mysticism

The mystical poem *Creation*, of which I have
spoken (it should be read with George MacDonald's

555

words in mind), will be found in *Collected Poems*, Volume II, page 348. I do not think I am betraying a confidence in adding that Mr. Noyes tells me that it is one of three poems of his writing for which he cares most.

"In the beginning, there was nought
    But heaven, one Majesty of Light,
Beyond all speech, beyond all thought,
    Beyond all depth, beyond all height,
Consummate heaven, the first and last,
    Enfolding in its perfect prime
No future rushing to the past,
    But one rapt Now, that knew not Space or Time.

Formless it was, being gold on gold,
    And void—but with that complete Life
Where music could no wings unfold
    Till lo, God smote the strings of strife.
'Myself unto Myself am Throne,
    Myself unto Myself am Thrall,
I am that All am all alone,'
    He said : ' Yea, I have nothing, having all.'

And, gathering round His mount of bliss
    The angel-squadrons of His will,
He said, ' One battle yet there is
    To win, one vision to fulfil ;
Since Heaven, where'er I gaze, expands,
    And power that knows no strife or cry,
Weakness shall bind and pierce My hands
    And make a world for Me wherein to die.

' All might, all vastness and all glory
    Being Mine, I must descend and make
Out of My heart a song, a story,
    Of little hearts that burn and break ;
Out of My passion without end
    I will make little azure seas,
And into small sad fields descend
    And make green grass, white daisies, rustling trees.

Then shrank His angels, knowing He thrust
    His arms out East and West and gave
For every little dream of dust
    Part of His Life as to a grave !

' *Enough, O Father, for Thy words*
    Have pierced Thy hands! '   But low and sweet
He said, ' Sunsets and streams and birds,
    And drifting clouds ! '—The purple stained His feet.

' Enough ? '   His angels moaned in fear,
    ' *Father, Thy words have pierced Thy side!* '
He whispered, ' Roses shall grow there,
    And there must be a hawthorn-tide,
And ferns, dewy at dawn,' and still
    They moaned—' *Enough, the red drops bleed!* '
' And,' sweet and low, ' on every hill,'
    He said, ' I will have flocks and lambs to lead.'

His angels bowed their heads beneath
    Their wings till that great pang was gone :
' *Pour not Thy soul out unto Death!* '
    They moaned, and still His Love flowed on,
' There shall be small white wings to stray
    From bliss to bliss, from bloom to bloom,
And blue flowers in the wheat ; and—' Stay !
    ' *Speak not*,' they cried, ' *the word that seals Thy tomb!* '

He spake : ' I have thought of a little child
    That I will have there to embark
On small adventures in the wild,
    And front slight perils in the dark ;
And I will hide from him and lure
    His laughing eyes with suns and moons,
And rainbows that shall not endure ;
    And—when he is weary sing him drowsy tunes.'

His angels fell before Him weeping,
    ' *Enough! Tempt not the Gates of Hell!* '
He said, ' His soul is in his keeping
    That we may love each other well,
And, lest the dark too much affright him,
    I will strow countless little stars
Across his childish skies to light him
    That he may wage in peace his mimic wars ;

' And oft forget Me as he plays
    With sword and childish merchandise,
Or with his elfin balance weighs,
    Or with his foot-rule metes the skies ;

Or builds his castle by the deep,
  Or tunnels through the rocks, and then—
Turn to Me as he falls asleep,
  And in his dreams, feel for My hand again.

'And when he is older he shall be
  My friend and walk here at My side ;
Or—when he wills—grow young with Me,
  And, to that happy world where once we died,
Descending through the calm blue weather,
  Buy life once more with our immortal breath,
And wander through the little fields together,
  And taste of Love and Death.' "

I quote this poem—one of the profoundest mystical utterances of our time—here, because the low and tender strain which, softly played as it is, forms the theme, as it were, of *The Forest of Wild Thyme,* deepens, in the poem *Creation,* into rolling and majestic organ music.

The Journey's End

The children's journey is nearly ended, for as they listen to the song *Mother mine,* they see :

" Four angels, great and sweet,
  With outspread wings and folded feet,
  Come gliding down from a heaven within
  The golden heart of Paradise ;
  And in their hands, with laughing eyes,
  Lay little brother Peterkin."

Then comes the awakening, and the end of the beautiful dream. The children had wandered no farther than the grave of their little lost brother, where, tired out, they had fallen asleep.

" And then a voice, ' Why here they are ! '
  And—as it seemed—we woke :
  The sweet old skies, great star by star
  Upon our vision broke ;

Field over field of heavenly blue
Rose over us ; then a voice we knew
  Softly and gently spoke—
  ' See, they are sleeping by the side
Of that dear little one—who died.' "

The last section of the poem is entitled *The
Happy Evening* :

" We told dear father all our tale
  That night before we went to bed,
And at the end his face grew pale,
  And he bent over us and said
(Was it not strange ?) he, too, was there,
  A weary, weary watch to keep
  Before the Gates of the City of Sleep ;
But, ere we came, he did not dare
Even to dream of entering in,
Or even to hope for Peterkin.
He was the poor blind man, he said,
And we—how low he bent his head !
Then he called mother near, and low
He whispered to us—' Prompt me now ;
For I forget the song we heard,
But you remember every word.'
Then memory came like a breaking morn,
And we breathed it to him—' *A Child was born !* '
And there he drew us to his breast
And softly murmured all the rest—

' *The wise men came to greet Him with their gifts of myrrh and
    frankincense—*
Gold and myrrh and frankincense they brought to make Him mirth.
And would you know the way to win to little brother Peterkin,
*My childhood's heart shall guide you through the glories of the
    earth.*'

Then he looked up and mother knelt
  Beside us, oh, her eyes were bright ;
Her arms were like a lovely belt
  All round us as we said Good-night
To father : *he* was crying now,
But they were happy tears somehow ;
For there we saw dear mother lay
Her cheek against his cheek and say—
' Hush, let me kiss those tears away.' "

So closes the little dream-drama—little only in the sense that it is comparatively brief, for has not Emerson told us that—

> " There is no great and no small
> To the Soul that maketh all,
> And where it cometh all things are,
> And it cometh everywhere " ?

If, as Alfred Noyes holds, and truly, that a rose is no less a creation than a world, so, in calling into being, in creating this lovely Flower of Song, the poet (we may well believe) penned his lines in travail of soul, even penned certain passages as if with his heart's red blood :

> " *What does it take to make a rose, Mother mine ?*
> ' *The God that died to make it knows*
> *It takes the world's eternal wars,*
> *It takes the moon and all the stars,*
> *It takes the might of Heaven and Hell,*
> *And the everlasting Love as well, Little child.'* "

PART II

An Epic of the Great Waters

" It is a noble work. How could it be otherwise ?—for a gifted painter, skilled in his craft, has, with signal success, made of the sky a studio ; and for a canvas, upon which to paint his picture, he has taken the sea."

So no less a poet and critic than Swinburne once said of Mr. Alfred Noyes's Epic of England, *Drake*.

Watts-Dunton, with whom Swinburne for many years made his home, was quick to recognize and to speak generously of the younger writers. Swinburne, on the contrary—I have many times heard him discuss his contemporaries—rarely thus delivered himself, and then only of his peers.

Remembering that the English are an island race, and that English poets of the past—Shakespeare in *The Tempest*, Coleridge in *The Ancient Mariner*, and many others—have written greatly of the sea, it is curious that so few living poets have attempted an Epic of Great Waters.

Some of our novelists have drawn for us sea-pictures of grandeur, but contemporary poets have, for the most part, been content to write only brief narrative sea-poems and sea-songs.

Alfred Noyes has " made of the sky a studio ; and for a canvas, upon which to paint his picture, he has taken the sea," said Swinburne of *Drake*.

The Navy on Alfred Noyes

I open *The Battle of the Falkland Islands* by Commodore H. Spencer-Cooper, and read in the preface :

" The words of Alfred Noyes have been referred to frequently, because they are in so many respects prophetic, and because of their influence in showing the spirit of Drake still inspires the British Navy."

Commander Spencer-Cooper then adds some sixteen quotations, all from *Drake*.

After a great poet and fine critic's sweeping hyperbole, after such tributes from a distinguished naval officer fresh from fighting his country's battles at sea, for me, a landsman and a proseman, to attempt a literary appreciation might try the patience of the reader.

I shall, therefore, add no word in praise of *Drake*. Nor, as the story of the Admiral's defeat of the Great Armada is known to every schoolgirl and schoolboy, need I outline the poem. Instead, let me here and there note a memorable passage or imagery.

**"Oh, you Beautiful
Land!"**

First, there is the almost Miltonic power and beauty
of the great Dawn poem, if I may so describe it,
with which Book IX opens.   Next, I instance the
seven stanzas of the " Song " of England, the refrain
of which is " Oh, you beautiful land! "   Here are
the last two stanzas :

> " How should we sing of thy beauty,
> England, mother of men,
> We that can look in thine eyes
> And see there the splendour of duty,
> Deep as the depth of their ken,
> Wide as the ring of thy skies ?
>
> O, you beautiful land !
> Deep-bosomed with beeches and bright
> With the flowery largesse of May,
> Sweet from the palm of her hand
> Outflung, till the hedges grew white
> As the green-arched billows with spray.
> O, you beautiful land ! "

Another " Song " of England is equally noble, as
witness the last stanza :

> " For the same Sun is o'er us,
> The same Love shall find us,
> The same and none other,
> Wherever we be ;
> With the same hope before us,
> The same home behind us,
> England, our mother,
> Ringed round with the sea."

Of *Drake*, as a poem, I say no more here ; but as
I have spoken of it as an Epic of England, let me,
before passing on, quote a few lines from three
essentially English songs included in another book
by Mr. Noyes, *A Salute from the Fleet.*

**The Coasts of
England**

" All along the white chalk coast
        The mist lifts clear ;
Wight is glimmering like a ghost ;
        The ship draws near.
Little inch-wide meadows,
        Lost so many a day,
The first time I knew you
        Was when I turned away.

.   .   .   .   .   .

Over yon green water
        Sussex lies ;
But the slow mists gather
        In our eyes.
England, little island—
        God, how dear !—
Fold me in your mighty arms ;
        Draw me near.

Little tawny roofs of home,
        Nestling in the grey,
Where the smell of Sussex loam
        Blows across the bay.
Fold me, teach me, draw me close,
        Lest in death I say,
' The first time I loved you
        Was when I turned away.' "

And here are verses which are like to jut out,
cliff-wise, in the memory of him or her who loves the
sea-coast of Devon, Cornwall, Sussex, or Kent :

" Wodin made the red cliffs, the red walls of England ;
        Round the South of Devonshire they burn against the blue.
Green is the water there, and clear as liquid sunlight ;
        Blue-green as mackerel, the bays that Raleigh knew.

Thor made the black cliffs, the battlements of England,
        Climbing to Tintagel, where the white gulls wheel.
Cold are the caverns there, and sullen as a cannon mouth,
        Booming back the grey swell that gleams like steel.

Balder made the white cliffs, the white shield of England
 (Crowned with thyme and violet where Sussex wheatears fly).
White as the White Ensign are the bouldered heights of Dover,
 Beautiful the scutcheon that they bare against the sky."

A Miniature

Most of my readers know William Allingham's
tiny lyric, a moment's tear, as it were, in the eye
of a smiling Muse :

> "Four ducks on a pond,
>   A grass bank beyond,
>   A blue sky of spring,
>   White clouds on the wing ;
>   What a little thing
>   To remember for years—
>   To remember with tears ! "

Let me present them, then, with a tiny memory-
miniature of English meadowland by Mr. Noyes.
It should find place, side by side, with Allingham's
lines in the anthologies :

> "Crimson and black on the sky, a wagon of clover,
>   Slowly goes rumbling over the white chalk road ;
> And I lie in the golden grass there, wondering why
>   So little a thing
>   As the jingle and ring of the harness,
>   The hot creak of leather,
>   The peace of the plodding,
> Should suddenly, stabbingly, make it dreadful to die."

In another poem we find the same human recoil
from the thought of death. It is common to us all,
I suppose, in moods when home-pictures and home-
thoughts make the warm life on earth so dear.
The poem is called *Ghosts* :

" Ghosts "

> " O, to creep in by candle-light,
>   When all the world is fast asleep,
> Out of the cold winds, out of the night,
>   Where the nettles wave and the rains weep !

O, to creep in, lifting the latch
So quietly that no soul could hear,
And, at those embers in the gloom,
Quietly light one careful match—
You should not hear it, have no fear—
And light the candle and look round
The old familiar room ;
To see the old books upon the wall
And lovingly take one down again,
And hear—O, strange to those that lay
So patiently underground—
The ticking of the clock, the sound
Of clicking embers . . .
                    watch the play
Of shadows . . .
                 till the implacable call
Of morning turn our faces grey ;
And, or ever we go, we lift and kiss
Some idle thing that your hands may touch,
Some paper or book that your hands let fall,
And we never—when living—had cared so much
As to glance upon twice . . .
                But now, oh, bliss
To kiss and to cherish it, moaning our pain,
Ere we creep to the silence again."

New Metres and
Lovely Refrains

Mr. Noyes has a genius for the making of new
metres. In one case he attempts (it is a novelty
to me, in the sense that I know no other instance)
a poem, *Astrid*, with rhymes at the beginning of a
line, instead of at the end (the italics are mine) :

    " *Making* her wild garland as Merlin had bidden her,
    Breaking off the milk-white horns of the honeysuckle,
    Sweetly dripped the dew upon her small white
    Feet."

He has been called " traditional " in his methods.
I dissent entirely, except in the sense that one
born of a line of kings—or poets—will not, and

may not, altogether disregard the great and classic traditions and conditions which he inherits. In that sense of the word, all true poets are traditional. There is, of course, a sense in which one might say that the miracle by which a child is born into the world, the marvel of sunset and dawn, are " traditional." They follow appointed laws, yet none the less, no little child that ever was, no sunset or dawn that was seen in the skies, was like any other child, any other sunset or dawn which came before.

So far from accounting Mr. Noyes traditional—other than in observing the great traditions of English poetry—I question whether, in the works of a living poet, there can be found so many new metres, so many new and interwoven lovely refrains, so many new and exquisite harmonies. The so-called " new " poets of the " scarlet word "—of whom I spoke when dealing with *The Forest of Wild Thyme*—adopt, for the most part, only conventional metres, or else claim the privilege to write *vers libre*, chiefly because they cannot *sing*. They produce iambic hexameters and stiffly-weird sonnets galore ; but I take leave to say that poetry is *song*, and that in singing power Mr. Noyes is not excelled by any of his contemporaries.

He uses either an entirely new metre, as in the prelude to *The Forest of Wild Thyme* (which has a recurrence of *motif* throughout), or else enriches an old metre with new harmonies in the refrain, or in variations of the refrain, in which he attains the required cumulative effect. Of skilful use of the refrain he is indeed a master.

Study for yourself, if you wish to realize how entirely new are Mr. Noyes's methods and metres, the refrain and the variations of the refrain in *The Loom of Years* (has the same metre ever been used before ?) ; *The Heart of the Woods* (note how, like a streamlet, percolating and running through one wooded copse to another, the insistent music of the refrain haunts the ear throughout) ; *The Highwayman ; The Lord of Misrule ; A Triple Ballad of Old Japan* (ten stanzas with the same rhyme) ; *Haunted in Old Japan ; A Song of England* (where there is so often an " internal " rhyme with another word in the same stanza); *The Phantom Fleet* (a combination of quatrains with Spenserian stanzas, which I have not seen elsewhere attempted) ; *The Barrel Organ* (with its incomparably beautiful and entirely original interweaving and varying of refrain) ; *Nelson's Year ; The Haunted Palace ;* and *Orpheus and Eurydice* (the first part an entirely new and recurrent metre).

Alfred Noyes and Rudyard Kipling

Once, at least, he uses a form made familiar to us by Mr. Kipling. Here is the first stanza of *The Empire Builders* :

> " Who are the Empire-builders ? They
>   Whose desperate arrogance demands
> A self-reflecting power to sway
>   A hundred little selfless lands ?
> Lord God of Battles, ere we bow
>   To these and to their soulless lust,
> Let fall Thy thunders on us now
>   And strike us equal to the dust."

Except for the fact of their common and passionate patriotism, and for their eagerness to be of " service " to their country and their fellows, no two contemporary poets are more unlike than Kipling and Noyes. I said " of service to their fellows," but it would perhaps be more exact to say of Mr. Kipling " to his fellow-Britons," and of Mr. Noyes, " to his fellow-mortals." Each is widely travelled, each is something of a cosmopolitan ; but Mr. Kipling remains sturdily British, while Mr. Noyes, for all his patriotism, is more markedly what is called humanitarian in his views. In politics and world-politics, I imagine the two poets to be as opposed, as they are opposed on the subjects of War and Imperialism. For that reason, and because I have heard Mr. Noyes's work recommended as an antidote to Mr. Kipling's Imperialism, I have sometimes wondered whether it were not of set purpose—for strategic reasons—that *The Empire Builders* is in the same metre as *Recessional*.

One other similarity there is between the two poets. My friend, Mr. Henry Chappell, the Railway porter-poet of Bath, author of *The Day*, tells me that, with Kiplingesque directness, almost the first words which the author of *Recessional* said to him were : " Chappell, why don't you make the platform speak ? " Mr. Chappell has followed that excellent advice and has made the platform speak. In a book which will soon be published, the platform, as represented by the luggage porter, the ticket collector, the carriage cleaner, and the guard, will speak for itself, and to good purpose. We all know that Mr. Kipling can make *his* platform—whether the Drill Yard, the Barrack Room, or the Battle-field—speak and in its own lingo. Nor is Mr. Noyes without gift that way. His platform is sometimes the Lower Deck, sometimes the Mercantile Marine, and his seamen speak their part to the life. Now and then Mr. Noyes introduces us to a sort of nautical Wonderland or Nonsenseland, as when his *Forty Singing Seamen* pay a visit to Prester John, in whose fabled country, red, green, black, and white lions and bears are said to abound :

" So we thought we'd up and seek it, but that forest fair defied us,—
First a crimson leopard laughed at us most horrible to see,

N

Then a seagreen lion came and sniffed and licked his chops
    and eyed us,
While a red and yellow unicorn was dancing round a tree!
We was trying to look thinner,
    Which was hard, because our dinner
Must ha' made us very tempting to a cat o' high degree!
(*Chorus*) Must ha' made us very tempting to the whole menar-
    jeree!"

This brings me once again to the subject of Mr. Noyes's humour. A humorist is humorous by nature, but never by ill-nature. This is however not always true of poets. Their humour is often most evident when they are angry. Sir William Watson, when roused, is a master of saturnine invective, as witness certain lines of his, not unconcerned with British politicians, and the Purple Thunder which he called down upon the head of Abdul-the-Doomed.

When Lord Lytton, under the pseudonym of " Timon," reviewed work of Tennyson's unfavourably, the Laureate replied (*Punch*, February 18, 1846) in a poem entitled *The New Timon*, lashing his critic's personal foppishness unmercifully, and in lines that quiver with angry scorn. I quote only two verses :

" What profits, now, to understand
    The merits of a spotless shirt,
A dapper boot—a little hand—
    If half the little soul is dirt?

A Timon, you! Nay, nay, for shame,
    It looks too arrogant a jest,
The fierce old man, to take *his* name,
    You bandbox! Off and let him rest."

Edward FitzGerald, the translator of Omar Khayyám, indulged a somewhat bitter humour—it is fair to remember that he wrote jestingly and never supposing that the matter would come to Browning's knowledge—at the expense of Mrs. Browning and her poem, *Aurora Leigh.* When Fitzgerald was dead, Browning contributed to the *Athenæum*—so much the less Browning he—a sonnet so savage that—— But why continue ? An instance or two of a poet in a tantrum was necessary in support of my contention, but the subject is not pleasant, and we will not pursue it.

The humour of Mr. Noyes is always that of a poet, but never that of a poet in a tantrum. It is irradiating, imaginative, fanciful, quaint, sometimes even nonsensical, in the sense only in which Lewis Carroll and Edward Lear wrote what is nonsensical ; but it is always sunny and never unkind.

A Master of Horror

He can, however, convey horror, terror, tragedy, with extraordinary power. It is a gift which often goes with humour. Thomas Hood's *Bridge of Sighs* is an instance. A prose example in our own day will be found in Mr. W. W. Jacobs's story, *The Monkey's Paw.* Mr. Noyes has similar power, but he is no maker of horror for horror's sake. He is a poet, a man of burning and passionate humanity, who dedicates—better still, consecrates—his God-given powers to his fellows. If in *Lucifer's Feast* and *The Wine Press : a Tale of War,* he compels horror, and creates an atmosphere sickly with the odour of blood, he does so only to make more hideous and more hateful the horrors of war. I will not harry the feelings of my readers by quoting either poem here ; but if it be possible, by means of the written word, whether in prose or in poetry, so to picture war as to cause the world to recoil in loathing, and to rise up, once and for ever, to make an end of war—Alfred Noyes has written that word. He should be the next recipient of the Nobel Peace Award.

War to End War

From Mr. Noyes's war and pre-war poems I cull
here and there a passage in which he warns us that
if a so-called civilization does not bring about an
understanding between the nations for the ending of
war, war will inevitably make an end alike of civilization and the nations. *The Wine Press*, of which I
have already spoken, is, from the opening dedication
to the last line, an indictment of the filth, the futility,
and the fiendishness of war. Remembering that it
was published in 1913, its exactness as a description
of the Great War—allowing for change of scene—is
so wonderful as to seem like prophecy. Only by
quoting one-half of the book would it be possible to
do justice to *The Wine Press* as a picture of war.
Apart from that difficulty, the picture is so terrible
that, as I have already said, I shrink from making
quotations here, so I pass on.

Swinburne once wrote of a time when—

> " As a god, self-slain, on his own strange altar,
> Death lies dead."

Mr. Noyes, too, with a poet's vision, looks for a
time when the world shall see war, " as a god, self-
slain on his own strange altar," ended for all time,
if only by the horrors of war. But he is a thinker,
which Swinburne for the most part was not, as well
as a seer. Mr. Noyes not only says, " This should be,"
or " This should not be," but proves, by calmly-
reasoned argument, why the thing should not be.
He puts a terrible question to those who acclaim
" a victory " :

> " The laugh is Death's ; he laughs as erst o'er hours that England
>   cherished,
>   ' Count up, count up the stricken homes that wail the first-born
>   son ;

Count by your starved and fatherless the tale of what hath
    perished ;
Then gather with your foes and ask if you—or I—have won.' "

For my own part, I am by no means sure that the
war through which we have just passed will end
war on this world.   I wish I could so think, but
apart from that question, every one of us must long
for, and in our own sphere work for, the attainment
of the ideal which Mr. Noyes so nobly sets before us :

" And here to us the eternal charge is given
    To rise and make our low world touch God's high :
To hasten God's own kingdom, Man's own heaven,
    And teach Love's grander army how to die."

Is there one of us who will not breathe a heartfelt
amen to that prayer ?

Part III

Tales of the
Mermaid Tavern

Keats seems to me the poet to whom Mr. Noyes
owes most, at least in craftsmanship.   His influence
is not indiscernible in that noble poem, *Mount Ida*.
But for the fact that the heart-cry is less passionate,
less personal and so less poignant, than in other
elegies, with which in art, at least, it is comparable,
Mount Ida might count among great Classic Com-
memorative Odes.   And since Keats penned the
jovial ode to poetic conviviality, which begins and
ends with the four lines :

" Souls of poets dead and gone,
    What Elysium have ye known,
    Happy field or mossy cavern,
    Choicer than the Mermaid Tavern ? "

so many poets have felt called upon to sing that
famous trysting-place, that one tires of Shakespeare

as "bright-eyed Will," of Jonson as "rare Ben," and of Marlowe as "our Kit." Only to read of the stouts of malmsey and sack consumed might rouse a toper's thirst, or a teetotaller's ire.

Hence I opened *Tales of the Mermaid Tavern* with misgivings. If only for the newer and, I believe, truer light in which Mr. Noyes reveals the soul of Marlowe, the poet whom Shakespeare loved, the poet whom, there is reason for believing, collaborated with Shakespeare in the writing of *Henry VI* and *Titus Andronicus*, the poet whose star was second only to Shakespeare's in the brilliant firmament of Elizabethan skies—if only for this reason, *Tales of the Mermaid Tavern* should be read by every student of poetry.

Mr. Noyes does not seek to excuse Marlowe's sinnings. Marlowe (I am not quoting Mr. Noyes now) is believed to have served as a soldier in Flanders ; and as no less an authority on Military history than Lord Roberts once remarked to me, British Armies in Flanders have, until recent times, borne no very good name. One of Lord Roberts's explanations was that the climatic conditions, damp and often depressing, induced the drink habit. Another was that he understood from statistics that offences of gross nature seem more prevalent in low-lying districts than in higher and more bracing climes. He added also that in those days the army was often the last resort of the least reputable members of the community. All that is now changed. No army in the world has a cleaner and more chivalrous record than the British. Naturally, however, I was much impressed by what the great Field-Marshal had to say upon a subject so interesting alike to the soldier and to the student of human nature, and I believe that Lord Roberts was right in attributing the grossness of former British Armies in Flanders to climatic and other conditions, under which weaker natures succumbed easily, especially in regard to drink. Marlowe must have gone as a soldier to Flanders as a very young man, and there possibly formed habits for which he paid later with his glad young life.

Mr. Noyes, in his noble picture of the poet, does not so much plead for a charitable judgment, as passionately and scornfully refute the current legend that Marlowe was a worthless sot, who was, not undeservedly, killed in a drunken brawl. Before writing *Tales of the Mermaid Tavern*, Mr. Noyes must have acquainted himself with every known fact of Marlowe's life, and he seems to me sufficiently to establish that, in the quarrel in which Marlowe was killed, the poet was more sinned against than sinning. The canting hypocrite, Richard Bame, who had brought the charges against Marlowe, was eventually hanged, as Mr. Noyes reminds us,

> " For thieving from an old bed-ridden dame
> With whom he prayed at supper-time on Sundays."

That Marlowe ran wild, lived loosely, and drank heavily, as was the habit of his time, Mr. Noyes plainly states. But what Ben Jonson says in the poem, of the hapless Robin Greene, is equally true of Marlowe :

> " He had the poet's heart, and God help all
> Who have that heart and somehow lose their way
> For lack of helm, souls that are blown abroad
> By the great wings of passion, without power
> To sway them, chartless captains. Multitudes ply
> Trimly enough from bank to bank of Thames
> Like shallow wherries, while tall galleons,
> Out of their very beauty driven to dare
> The uncompassed sea, founder in starless nights."

Marlowe was a cobbler's son, and was under thirty when he was killed. Speaking of him as the boy he was, when he left Cambridge, where he took his

degree, John Nash, the poet, says to his brother-
poet, Chapman, in Mr. Noyes's book :

> " He was a brave lad,
> Untamed, adventurous, but still innocent,
> O, innocent as the cobbler's little self !
> He brought to London just a bundle and stick,
> A slender purse, an Ovid, a few scraps
> Of song, and all unshielded, all unarmed
> A child's heart packed with splendid hopes and dreams.
> I say a child's heart, Chapman, and that phrase
> Crowns, not discrowns, his manhood."

Later in the poem, Chapman, as if in answer to Nash,
quotes of Marlowe, the man who had sinned away
his boy innocence, yet found not happiness, but
horror in sin, Marlowe's own lines :

> " Think'st thou that I who saw the face of God,
> And tasted the eternal joys of heaven,
> Am not tormented with ten thousand hells ? "

The poem ends with a tribute to Marlowe by
Nash. It is partly requiem, partly eulogy, as when
Nash says of the dead poet :

> " The Apollonian throat and brow,
> The lyric lips, so silent now,
> The flaming wings that heaven bestowed
>   For loftier airs than this !
> The sun-like eyes whose light and life
>   Had gazed an angel's down."

But the power of the tribute lies neither in the
requiem nor in the eulogy, but in these two stanzas :

> " And many a fool that finds it sweet
>   Through all the years to be,
> Crowning a lie with Marlowe's fame,
> Will ape the sin, will ape the shame,
> Will ape our captain in defeat ;
>   But not in victory ;
>
> Till Art becomes a leaping-house,
>   And Death be crowned as Life,

> And one wild jest outshine the soul
> Of Truth . . . O fool, is this your goal?
> You are not our Kit Marlowe,
>   But the drunkard with the knife."

Could there be more awful warning to the fool who, without Marlowe's genius, would make, and in the name of Art, the dead poet's lapses an excuse for his own drunkenness, than this picture of that fool, knife in hand, as the drunkard who murdered Marlowe? I think not; and I do not hesitate to say that, so terribly and so truly to paint the terrible picture, is an achievement not unworthy of Shakespeare. It is not because he died by a murderer's hand that the story of Christopher Marlowe is so tragic. Tragedy is of the soul, it is not a matter of sensational happenings. As Meredith says:

> " In tragic life, God wot,
> No villain need be; passions spin the plot,
> We are betrayed by what is false within."

That Mr. Noyes can interpret what Meredith called the Comic Spirit no less than the Spirit of Tragedy, is shown in the poem (no two pieces of writing could present a more complete contrast) which follows immediately after the tragedy of Marlowe. It is one mad, merry orgy of joy and of dancing delight. The title is *The Companion of a Mile*. Will Kemp, a player, made of himself a nine days' wonder by dancing from London to Norwich in as many days, as he dances for us to-day between Mr. Noyes's lilting lines. One dancing companion fell out, vowing he could dance no more, and a bouncing frolicsome milkmaid took his place.

> "' You lout!' she laughed, ' I'll leave my pail, and dance with
>   him for cakes and ale!
> I'll dance a mile for love,' she laughed, ' and win my wager,
>   too.

Your feet are shod and mine are bare, but when could leather
  dance on air ?
A milkmaid's feet can fall as fair and light as falling dew.'

.   .   .   .

And straying we went, and swaying we went, with lambkins
  round us playing we went ;
Her face uplift to drink the sun, and not for me her smile,
We danced, a king and queen of May, upon a fleeting holiday,
But O, she'd won her wager, my companion of a mile ! "

The Burial of a Queen is the story of Mary of Scot-
land which, being known to all, I leave untold.
Musical Comedy is common enough, but here is something rare—Tragedy, set to slow music—for there is
other music than that which is vocal (in the sense
of being sung) or instrumental. Poets, if not all
musicians, will acquiesce when I say that the music
which is produced by the instrumentality of words—
if different in kind, is in no less a degree, true music,
than the music which is sung or played. What
could be more essentially music than certain passages
by Shelley or Keats ? The dirge from *The Burial of
a Queen* is entirely new in its metrical and musical
aim. It seeks to convey in poetry, by means of
longer lines, the effect of an unended melody—a
melody which does not so much actually " cease
upon the midnight with no pain," as cease to be
heard by us, because it is wind-borne beyond our
hearing. It is, in a word, the Wagnerian effect in
poetry.
   Here once again, as in many other poems of his,
Mr. Noyes introduces—sometimes a line by another
poet, but in this case the very words (in French) of
Mary Queen of Scots, when as a girl, she left France
for Holyrood. He does this always with grace and
skill, as I have already said, when speaking of the
interpolation of Tennyson's " Little flower in the
crannied wall " into *The Forest of Wild Thyme*.
Once again it is as if the poet had slipped, upon

the finger of the Muse, a ring, in which gems, of his own finding and fashioning, form a setting for a rare gem, the property of another.

" Carry the queenly lass along !
—*Cold she lies, cold and dead,*—
She whose laughter was a song,
—*Lapped around with sheets of lead !*
She whose blood was wine of the South,
—*Light her down to a couch of clay !*—
And her body made of may !
—Lift your torches, weeping, weeping,
Light her down to a couch of clay.

They should have left her in her vineyards, left her heart to her
land's own keeping,
Left her white breast room to breathe, and left her light foot free
to dance !
Hush ! Between the solemn pinewoods, carry the lovely lady
sleeping,
Out of the cold grey Northern mists, with banner and scutcheon,
plume and lance,
Carry her southward, palled in purple, weeping, weeping, weeping,
weeping,—

O, ma patrie,
La plus chérie
Adieu, plaisant pays de France ! ":

PART IV

My quotations have already been so many that I must do no more than draw attention to a few poems which no reader should miss. One is *Rank and File*, with its picture of the marching armies of the battlefield and the slum :

" Drum-taps, drum-taps, where are they marching ?
Terrible, beautiful, human faces,
Common as dirt, but softer than snow,
Coarser than clay, but calm as the stars.":

By way of contrast, and as another instance of
Mr. Noyes's range of subject and versatility, let us
next read—the two poems are only a few pages
apart—*The Tramp Transfigured*. *Rank and File* has
the hopelessness and the helplessness of life's con-
scripts, of whom Mr. Noyes elsewhere says :

> " It seemed that some gigantic hand
>   Behind the veils of sky
> Was driving, herding all these men
> Like cattle into a cattle pen,
> So few of them could understand,
>   So many of them must die."

The Tramp Transfigured, though equally demo-
cratic, is the drollest Cockney comedy. The tramp-
hero makes his living by gathering cornflowers and

> " Selling little nosegays on the bare-foot Brighton beach,
>   Nosegays *and* a speech,
> All about the bright blue eyes they matched on Brighton
>   beach."

But, as a girl-child crooning a nursery rhyme at
bed-time suddenly ceases to sing, and kneels with
folded hands to pray, so Mr. Noyes in this and other
poems, sobers us, even as we smile, by some lovely
thought of human or even heavenly life. In *The
Forest of Wild Thyme* a Nursery Rhyme and a Hymn
of the Nativity follow, the one after the other, as
naturally, and with as little sense of irreverence as the
baby girl's " Our Father " follows the nursery doll-
talk. And, as in *The Forest of Wild Thyme*, Mr.
Noyes passes so naturally from one metre into another
that the reader is scarcely aware of the change,
unless it be vaguely to realize that the swing of the
poet's aim is freer in the longer lines than in those
which are shorter. In *The Tramp Transfigured* he
alternates his metres with singular felicity and
success. Here is a single specimen of a tramp's
happy philosophy :

A Tramp's Philosophy

" So the world's my sweetheart and I sort of want to squeeze 'er.
  Toffs 'ull get no chance of heaven, take 'em in the lump !
Never laid in hayfields when the dawn came over-sea, sir ?
  Guess it's true that story 'bout the needle and the hump !
Never crept into a stack because the wind was blowing,
  Hollered out a nest and closed the doorway with a clump,
Laid and heard the whisper of the silence, growing, growing,
Watched a thousand wheeling stars, and wondered if they'd
  bump ?
    What I say would stump
Joshua ! But I've done it, sir. Don't think I'm off my chump."

The Rock-Pool, Butterflies, Gorse, and *The Swimmer's Race,* each that rare achievement in poetry, a perfect lyric, must be read as they stand. In a sonnet, *The Scholars,* Mr. Noyes charges " old Master Science " to—

" Bid us run free with life in every limb
  To breathe the poems, and hear the last red rose
  Gossiping over God's grey garden wall."

Who that reads *The Hill Flower* will not (recalling the poem) stay a thoughtless hand outstretched lightly to pluck, and perhaps as lightly to throw away, one of the wild flowers which make lovely our world ? Or who that, having thoughtlessly plucked, will not pass on, heavy and reproachful of heart, as if he had unwittingly tossed a stone and killed a bird in song ?

" I stooped to pluck it ; but my hand
Paused, midway, o'er its fairyland.
Not of my own was that strange voice,
  ' Pluck—tear a star from heaven ! '
Mine only was the awful choice
  To scoff and be forgiven
Or hear the very grass I trod
Whispering the gentle thoughts of God."

In this poem Mr. Noyes shows his kinship with Wordsworth and Cowper.

'*Tween the Lights* is a fitting opening to a volume of *New Poems* by one who has rediscovered our long-lost fairyland :

> " Fairies come back ! Once more the gleams
> Of your lost Eden haunt our dreams,
> Where Evil, at the touch of Good,
> Withers in the Enchanted Wood :
> Fairies come back ! Drive gaunt Despair
> And Famine to their ghoulish lair !
> Tap at each heart's bright window-pane
> Thro' merry England once again."

The Loom of Years, Michael Oaktree, and *In the Heart of the Woods* are three exquisite poems, the last named having for its refrain :

> " For the Heart of the woods is the Heart of the world and the Heart of Eternity,
> Ay, and the burning passionate Heart of the heart in you and me."

The Epilogue to " The Flower of Old Japan "

The Flower of Old Japan is on similar lines to (possibly may have inspired the later and more lovely poem) *The Forest of Wild Thyme.* Here I must do no more than quote The Epilogue *To Carol* :

> " Carol, every violet has
> Heaven for a looking-glass !
> Every little valley lies
> Under many-clouded skies ;
> Every little cottage stands
> Girt about with boundless lands;
> Every little glimmering pond
> Claims the mighty shores beyond—
> Shores no seaman ever hailed,
> Seas no ship has ever sailed.
>
> All the shores when day is done
> Fade into the setting sun,

So the story tries to teach
More than can be told in speech.

Beauty is a fading flower,
Truth is but a wizard's tower,
Where a solemn death-bell tolls
And a forest round it rolls.

We have come by curious ways
To the Light that holds the days;
We have sought in haunts of fear
For that all-enfolding sphere,
And lo! it was not far, but near.
We have found, O foolish-fond,
The shore that has no shore beyond.

Deep in every heart it lies
With its untranscended skies;
For what heaven should bend above
Hearts that own the heaven of love?

Carol, Carol, we have come
Back to heaven, back to home."

Sherwood is a brave ballad of Robin Hood, and brings that stout bowman back to life as vividly as, in other poems, Mr. Noyes has called back the fairies.

The impulse here to omit no single stanza, no single line, of a poem so lovely, alike in music and in glorious pride of country, as *A Song of England*, is hard to resist. But there are eight stanzas and I must sorrowfully content myself with one:

A Song of England

" There is a song of England that haunts her hours of rest:
    The calm of it and balm of it
Are breathed from every hedgerow that blushes to the West:
    From the cottage doors that nightly
    Cast their welcome out so brightly
On the lanes where laughing children are lifted and caressed

By the tenderest hands in England, hard and blistered hands
    of England :
  And from the restful sighing
  Of the sleepers that are lying
With the arms of God around them on the night's contented
    breast."

From *The Barrel Organ* I have already filched, bee-wise, the honeyed and beautiful refrain, " Come down to Kew in lilac-time." I must not play the honey-loving bear, instead of bee, and plunder the entire hive of its sweetness.

Love-Poems

Of Afred Noyes's love-poems, as love-poems, I have said no word, not because they are less perfect—they are fewer in number—but because many poets, infinitely his inferior, have excelled in love-songs, whereas Mr. Noyes excels in writing on subjects which few poets understand or attempt. Beautiful love-songs are not uncommon, but beautiful poems in which there is breadth of vision on great matters, as well as profound insight and originality, are rare. In his love-poems Mr. Noyes sings more often of love in the ideal than of love in its more personal and passionate relations. Passion, ardent and urgent, pulses in his love-poems, and as irresistibly as an incoming tide ; but as the moon sways the tides, so the white star of a pure and transcendent ideal controls passion in the poet's conception of love.

The Progress of Love is a wonderful poem, telling as it does of one who—

" Dreams he loves but only loves his dream,"

and with the haunting symbolism of the recurring but varying refrain :

" And God sighed in the sunset, and the sea
  Grew quieter than the hills : the mystery
  Of ocean, earth, and sky was like a word
  Uttered, but all unheard."

ALFRED NOYES

Slumber Songs

Turning from love to a mother's love, I counsel the
reader to miss no stanza of the *Slumber Songs* of
the Virgin Mother to her Child. There are seven
songs in all, from which I make a quotation here
and there :

" Sleep, little baby, I love thee ;
  Sleep, little king, I am bending above thee.
    How should I know what to sing
  Here in my arms as I swing thee to sleep ?
    Hushaby low,
    Rockaby so,
  Kings may have wonderful jewels to bring,
  Mother has only a kiss for her king !
  Why should my singing so make me to weep ?
  Only I know that I love thee, I love thee,
    Love thee, my little one, sleep.

    .   .   .   .   .

See, what a wonderful smile ! Does it mean
    That my little one knows of my love ?
Was it meant for an angel that passed unseen,
    And smiled at us both from above ?
Does it mean that he knows of the birds and the flowers
That are waiting to sweeten his childhood's hours,
And the tales I shall tell and the games he will play,
And the songs we shall sing and the prayers we shall pray
    In his boyhood's May
    He and I, one day ?

For in the warm blue summer weather
We shall laugh and love together :
I shall watch my baby growing,
    I shall guide his feet,
When the orange trees are blowing
    And the winds are heavy and sweet.

    .   .   .   .   .

He shall laugh while mother sings
Tales of fishermen and kings.
He shall see them come and go
    O'er the wistful sea,
Where rosy oleanders blow
    Round blue Lake Galilee,
Kings with fishers' ragged coats
And silver nets across their boats,

Dipping through the starry glow,
  With crowns for him and me !
    Ah, no ;
  Crowns for him, not me !
Rockaby so !   Indeed it seems
A dream : yet not like other dreams !

          .   .   .   .   .   .

But when you are crowned with a golden crown
  And throned on a golden throne,
You'll forget the manger of Bethlehem town
  And your mother that sits alone
Wondering whether the mighty king
Remembers a song she used to sing,
      Long ago,
      Rockaby so,
Kings may have wonderful jewels to bring,
Mother has only a kiss for her king ! "

The Spirituality of Mr. Noyes

Need I say to those who have followed me thus far
that a marked feature of Alfred Noyes's poems is
intense spirituality ? No poet of to-day seems to
me more entirely to realize that, behind the simply
told story of the Babe of Bethlehem, Who thereafter
became the world's Redeemer—a story, the divine
and human elements in which are not beyond the
comprehension of a child—lies a meaning, so ele-
mental yet so eternal, that many of this world's
wisest and greatest have confessed that the more
closely they study, the profounder, the more marvellous and sublime, do they find the meaning which
underlies the philosophy of the Cross. To Alfred
Noyes, the Cross towers the heavens from nadir to
zenith, and spans with outstretched arms God's
visible and invisible world.

The Paradox is like no other poem known to me.
Only by printing it in full could one convey the
grandeur and the greatness of the thought. To do
otherwise would be like detaching a clause from the

context of a creed, thereby hoping to indicate the
intention and scope of that article of faith. Mr.
Noyes attempts to convey what I must call the Idea
of God. He does no more than attempt, for he
sets himself a task in which no finite human mind
can succeed. But he does succeed in carrying the
reader in thought far above the mists of our little
world, and the vision which opens up before us is
so vast that we lose ourselves in the immensity.

The Origin of
Life

The poem *Before the World* was, he tells us, written
in answer to certain statements on " the origin of
life." There is a school of thought which asserts
that Christ was no more than man, and that man
himself came into being, not by the breath of God,
but as the product of some chance combination from
the primeval slime. Those who so assert, Mr. Noyes
compels backward to that primeval nothingness out
of which, they tell us, man, and Christ, and God's
wonder-world of miracle and mystery eventually
evolved :

" Out of this Nothingness arose our thought ?
This black abysmal Nought
Woke, and brought forth that lighted City street,
Those towers, and that great fleet.

When you have seen those vacant primal skies
Beyond the centuries,
Watched the pale mists across their darkness flow,
(As in a lantern show !)
Watched the great hills like cloud arise, and set,
And one named Olivet ;
When you have seen as a shadow passing away
One child clasp hands and pray ;
When you have seen emerge from that dark mire
One martyr, ringed with fire ;
Or from that Nothingness, by special grace,
One woman's love-lit face. . . ."

When those with such views on the origin of life have seen and have admitted—as they in honesty must—all this and more, will they then, Mr. Noyes asks, have the courage to deny that—

> " You found on that dark road you trod,
> *In the beginning—God*" >

The Cottage of the Kindly Light

The Cottage of the Kindly Light, filling eight pages as it does, is too long to quote in full, so I must outline it only in brief extracts. It is the old, old story so often told in beautiful Bible words, of one, " the only son of his mother, and she was a widow." The scene is laid in a tiny sea-facing cottage, built on a cliff, and looking down, possibly, on the landward side to where—

> " The cottage-clustered valleys held the lilac-last of night,"

and where—

> " Alone she lived and moved and breathed,
> Having no other thought but *This is home,*
> *My part in God's eternity.*"

Here the widow remained, watching over her boy, till he grew to man's estate :

> " and old adventures filled his heart,
> And he forgot, as all of us forget,
> The imperishable and infinite desire
> Of the vacant arms and bosom that still yearn
> For the little vanished children, still, still ache
> To keep their children little. He grew wroth
> At aught that savoured of such fostering care
> As mothers long to lavish, aught that seemed
> To rob him of his manhood, his free will :
> And she—she understood and she was dumb."

Then :

> " One eve in May his mother wandered down
> The hill to await his coming, wistfully

Wandered, touching with vague and dreaming hands
The uncrumpling fronds of fern and budding roses
As if she thought them but the ghosts of spring.
From far below the golden breezes brought
A mellow music from the village church
Which o'er the fragrant fir-wood she could see
Pointing a sky-blue spire to heaven : she knew
That music, her most heart-remembered song—
' *Sun of my soul, Thou Saviour dear,*
   It is not night if Thou be near ! '

And as the music made her one with all
That soft transfigured world of eventide,
One with the flame that sanctified the West,
One with the golden sabbath of the sea,
One with the sweet responses of the woods,
One with the kneeling mountains, there she saw
In a tangle of ferns and roses and wild light
Shot from the sunset through a glade of fir,
Her boy and some young rival in his arms,
A girl of seventeen summers, dusky-haired,
Grey-eyed, and breasted like a crescent moon,
Lifting her red lips in a dream of love
Up to the red lips of her only son.
Jealousy numbed the mother's lonely soul,
And sickening at the heart, she stole away."

Wisely she waits till the boy himself tells her of
his love and his hopes, but every night when he is at
sea :

" She placed a little lamp
In the cottage window, that if e'er he gazed
Homeward by night across the heaving sea
He might be touched to memory. But she said
Nothing. The lamp was like the liquid light
In some dumb creature's eyes, that can but wait
Until its master chance to see its love
And deign to touch its brow.

Now in those days
There went a preacher through the country-side
Filling men's hearts with fire ; and out at sea
The sailors sang great hymns to God ; and one
Stood up one night, among the gleaming nets
Astream with silver herring in the moon,

And pointed to the lamp that burned afar
And said, ' *Such is that Kindly Light* we sing! '
And ever afterwards the widow's house
Was called *The Cottage of the Kindly Light.*"

One night the boy does not return, but she is
steadfast in hope :

" ' Lost ? My boy lost ? ' she smiled. ' Nay, he will come
To-morrow, or the next day, or the next,
The Kindly Light will bring him home again.'
 .   .   .   .

                              She had not wept,
And ere that week was over, came the girl
Her boy had loved. With tears and a white face
And garbed in black, she came, and when she neared
The gate, his mother, proud and white with scorn,
Bade her return and put away that garb
Of mourning : and the girl saw, shrinking back,
The boy's own mother wore no sign of grief,
But all in white she stood ; and like a flash
The girl thought, ' God, she wears her wedding dress !
Her grief has made her mad ! '
 .   .   .   .   .   .

                              The year passed ;
And on an eve in May her boy's love climbed
The hill once more, and as the stars came out
And the dusk gathered round her tenderly,
And the last boats came stealing o'er the bar,
And the immeasurable sea lay bright and bare
And beautiful to all infinity
Beneath the last faint colours of the sun
And the increasing kisses of the moon,
A hymn came on a waft of evening wind
Along the valley from the village church
And thrilled her with a new significance
Unfelt before. It was the hymn they heard
On that sweet night among the rose-lit fern—
Sun of my soul ; and as she climbed the hill,
She wondered, for she saw no Kindly Light
Glimmering from the window, and she thought,
' Perhaps the madness leaves her.' There the hymn,
Like one great upward flight of angels, rose
All round her, mingling with the sea's own voice—

' Come near and bless us when we wake,
Ere through the world our way we take,
Till, in the ocean of Thy love,
We lose ourselves in heaven above.'

And when she passed the pink thrift by the gate,
And the rough wallflowers by the white-washed wall,
And entered, she beheld the widow kneeling,
In black beside the unlit *Kindly Light*;
And near her dead cold hand upon the floor
A fallen taper, for with her last strength
She had striven to light it and, so failing, died."

The whole poem is as fragrant with simple faith as the white and perfumed linen, which our mothers smoothed and stored so carefully away in linen-chest or cupboard, was fragrant with the scent of sweetbriar and lavender.

The Old Sceptic

In *The Old Sceptic*, the picture of the tired thought-worn man turning wearily away, with heart and soul empty and unsatisfied, from the sophistries and the false gods of scepticism to the pitiful arms of the Christ is strangely moving ; it shall be my concluding quotation :

" I will go back to my home and look at the wayside flowers,
  And hear from the wayside cabins the kind old hymns again,
Where Christ holds out His arms in the quiet evening hours,
  And the light of the chapel porches broods on the peaceful lane.

And there I shall hear men praying the deep old foolish prayers,
  And there I shall see, once more, the fond old faith confessed,
And the strange old light on their faces who hear as a blind man hears—
  Come unto Me, ye weary, and I will give you rest."

John Drinkwater

John Drinkwater

IF I may filch an adjective from Christopher Smart's reference to a certain fruit as " the sharp, peculiar quince," I should say that Mr. John Drinkwater's work is peculiar, in the sense that, like the quince, it has savour and colouring entirely its own. Apart from the plays, with which I am not dealing here, there are no great canvases in his studio. His touch is as sure, his art as fault-less, as in the work of other living poets, but, in the minuteness and the exactness with which he fills in details, and in the careful alternation of light and shade, Mr. Drinkwater's poems remind us not a little of " interiors " by painters of the Dutch school. Here is an example :

> " Comes back an afternoon
> Of a June
> Sunday at Elsfield, that is up on a green
> Hill, and there,
> Through a little farm parlour door,
> A floor
> Of red tiles and blue,
> And the air
> Sweet with the hot June sun, cascading through
> The vine leaves under the glass, and a scarlet fume
> Of geranium flower, and soft and yellow bloom
> Of musk, and stains of scarlet and yellow glass."

The uncommon word " fume " (a halving of per-fume), suggestive as it is of the faint and floating

scent-memory rather than of scent—of scent atmosphere rather than of actual aroma—of which we
are conscious in still cathedral aisles or cloistered
cells where incense has glowed and smouldered in a
censer, is admirable as applied to the musky odour
of the flame-coloured geranium.

A poet once said in my presence that the geranium,
if only because of its scarlet jersey and its unconquerable cheerfulness, should be the chosen flower of
the Salvation Army.

Another poet, a Roman Catholic, replied :
" Oh, no ! Cardinal is the colour of the princes
of my Church. Your geranium always seems to me
a red-cassocked acolyte, standing with glowing
censer to offer incense of praise and thanksgiving
before the high altar of the sun."

Being neither a Salvationist nor a Roman Catholic,
I refrain from a casting vote in the matter of this
pretty flower-imagery quarrel. Instead, let me call
attention to a daring and Drinkwateresque inno-
vation in the lines I have quoted.

In our Gothic churches the rich tints of old stained-
glass windows (toned to a colour-symphony, exquisite
and softened as the iridescence of a shell) are as
entirely in harmony with the architecture as the
coloured squares of red and yellow glass, set by a
jerry builder in the conservatory of a suburban villa,
seem sadly out of place among flowers and ferns—
reminding us as the glass squares do, of the cheap
chromo and the oleographic print. I have even
heard these squares of red and yellow glass described
as vulgar. Mr. Drinkwater is probably the very
first poet of distinction who has dared to inset, as
one insets jewels in a ring, these cheap kaleidoscope
effects of crudely-coloured glass into a poem, and
so to tone them in with the picture, that one is
conscious not of a jar or clash but of fitness and
harmony.

"History"

The poem in which these lines I have quoted occur is entitled *History*, and closes thus :

"Such are the things remain
Quietly, and for ever in the brain,
And the things that they choose for history-making pass."

This is a predominant note in Mr. Drinkwater's poems. I will not say that we personify History as the Recorder of the Centuries, for the duties of the Recorder of London and of other cities, judging by what one reads in the papers, seem to deal more with magisterial matters than with records. Perhaps I may say that we personify History, capped and robed like Portia, as a sort of Woman Clerk to the Great Assizes of the Centuries. She sifts and sorts the facts and the evidence before the court, so as to set down in her records only what is tested and true.

That is not Mr. Drinkwater's conception of History. She is to him no cold and far-off Recording Angel, but the living woman (lover or wife as the case may be) who was with us but a moment ago. We see history in the making, and engraved a word or two at a time, in the slow passing of years. He sees it as either written beforehand, and much of it mere repetition of what has already been, or else as already made, and become History in the tick of a clock. To him it is like the sheet of apparently blank paper, upon which, when held to the fire, written words of meaning, even of menace, appear. The message, the history was already recorded there, but in invisible ink, which the fire of adversity, sorrow, anger, love, or other human passion, or experience, makes visible.

Mr. Drinkwater is right in seeing in true perspective what makes or does not make history. He holds that it is not a matter of Kings, Courts, Popes, Princes, Armies, Navies, and Politics only, but is spiritual, psychological, individual ; that it is more nearly concerned with the people, perhaps with the reader's and my own seemingly petty and little life, than with many so-called historical events which are chronicled in Haydn's *Dictionary of Dates*. A Drinkwater's Dictionary of Dates would afford us informing and illuminating reading.

The frank and sunny smile, a smile which comes from the heart before it is seen upon the face, the modesty and the manliness of bearing ; the power of winning instant loyalty and devotion to his own person of that most princely of soldiers and most soldierly of princes, our future King, will play a great part in the making of history, but unrecorded in Haydn's Dictionary. A dictionary edited by John Drinkwater would not inform us when Mr. St. John Brodrick, now Lord Midleton, issued, as Secretary of State for War, the order that our soldiers should appear on parade in peakless caps, such as are still worn by Royal Marines ; but it *would* tell us when and where to look for battalions of coltsfoot, helmeted in burnished gold, and standing stiffly at attention upon their leafless stalks. Drinkwater's Dictionary of Dates would chronicle the great events of history, but would not exclude Natural History. That he is a student of history, his historical plays, *Cromwell and Abraham Lincoln*, prove ; but for the doings of fussy politicians, who flatter themselves *they* are making history, we should look in vain. From the poem *Politics*, included in *Tides*, one gathers that the tides of Mr. Drinkwater's interests are not greatly swayed by the moonshine of politics.

" You say a thousand things
    Persuasively,
And with strange passion hotly I agree,

And praise your zest,
And then
A blackbird sings
On April lilac, or field-faring men,
Ghost-like with loaded wain,
Come down the twilit lane
To rest,
And what is all your argument to me ?
Oh, yes—I know, I know,
It must be so—
You must devise
Your myriad policies,
For we are little wise,
And must be led and marshalled, lest we keep
Too fast a sleep
Far from the central world's realities.
Yes, we must heed—
For surely you reveal
Life's very heart ; surely with flaming zeal
You search our folly and our secret need ;
And surely it is wrong
To count my blackbird's song,
My cones of lilac, and my wagon team,
More than a world of dream.
But still
A voice calls from the hill—
I must away—
I cannot hear your argument to-day."

The Wisdom of
the Mad

Is it because, as we are told, genius and madness
are near allied, that two living poets—Mr. Noyes in
The Universalist, Mr. Drinkwater in *Mad Tom
Tatterman*—have the genius to show us that the
random talk of a madman can come nearer to
heavenly sense than some of the considered wisdom
of the wise ?

" Mad Tom Tatterman, that is how they call me.
  Oh, they know so much, so much, all so neatly dressed ;
  I've a tale to tell you—come and listen, will you ?—
  One as ragged as the twigs that make a magpie's nest.

Ragged, oh, but very wise.   You and this and that man,
All of you are making things that none of you would lack,
And so your eyes grow dusty, and so your limbs grow
        rusty—
But mad Tom Tatterman puts nothing in his sack.

Nothing in my sack, sirs, but the Sea of Galilee
Was walked for mad Tom Tatterman, and when I go to sleep
They'll all know that I've driven through the acres of broad
        heaven
Flocks are whiter than the flocks that all your shepherds keep."

Of the poem *Mamble* I feel as a certain Canadian
soldier told me he felt about fate.   " I don't worry
about what's coming to me," he said.   " If it is down
in the book of fate that I'm to be hit—hit I shall be,
and if it isn't so down, I shan't be hit, so why
worry ? "   And so of *Mamble*.   It had to be.   It
was preordained.   I admit that before I had read
the poem, I did not know where Mamble was, nor
that any place there was of that name.   But I am
convinced that Fate placed Mamble where it is,
gave it the name (there is predestined laziness in a
name that rhymes with " amble " and " shamble ")
and the indolent character it bears—for the one and
only reason that Mr. Drinkwater should thereafter
write a poem about it.

> " I never went to Mamble
>   That lies above the Teme,
> So I wonder who's in Mamble,
>   And whether people seem
> Who breed and brew along there
>   As lazy as the name."

Mr. Drinkwater is wise not to go to Mamble, even
though Worcestershire be his Warwickshire's near-
by and neighbouring county.   Like the knight who
fell in love with a maiden, only from once hearing
her lovely voice, and without so much as seeing her
face—Mr. Drinkwater's dream of Mamble, so long

Photo
Claude Harris

John Drinkwater

as he go not there, remains. Not to dig for hidden gold where the rainbow seems to dip is wise. It is good news to those of us who love as I do, Mr. Drinkwater's splendid " fling " for a new adventure, to know that for him, and so for us, perhaps the greatest adventure of all, the " find " of his life, may be awaiting him and us—in Mamble.

His Self-Consciousness

In the course of this article I shall have occasion to speak of the self-conscious note which Mr. Drinkwater sometimes strikes. I attribute this self-consciousness, so far as it affects his poetry, to certain views of his upon the subject of " Art," and to illustrate my point of view, I may, perhaps, be permitted a reminiscence.

Among my earliest friends in the days when he and I were, as the Americans say, " beginning author " together, was Mr. Jerome K. Jerome, who has now come, as even in those days I was convinced he would come, to high and deserved honour. One evening, over a pipe, he spoke of a writer, whether imagined, fable-wise, or known personally to Mr. Jerome does not matter. As a young fellow, this man started life with high and noble ideals, and with a passionate longing to be of service to his day and generation. So, out of his heart's thoughts, and with all the literary skill at his command, he wrote books which moved the world, and fired others to like nobleness. Then some sort of Job's comforter of a friend, one of those superior persons who, whenever a man strikes out his own line in life, and succeeds in it, invariably asks why he did not do something quite different (the reader will possibly number comforters of the sort among her or his own friends or relatives), said that this man's work was well enough in its way, " but was it literature ? "

P

As a matter of fact it was, for the young man in question not only had brains, but was educated, and had a natural gift for expression.

He had what Mr. Drinkwater, in five consecutive pages of *Prose Papers* (see pages 229 to 233) speaks of as " style," but which, since I heard a young man who had written an able, but rather nasty, book remark : " But for the fact that some three or four of us are stylists, one might say that literature was a dead letter in England," I prefer to call distinction or character.

Mr. Jerome's author-friend had personality. In his books he expressed that personality naturally and unaffectedly, and so with ease, as well as with grace, for, in literature as in life, the essence of all fine breeding is ease, and where ease and naturalness are, there too is generally grace.

But he took his friend's talk about " literature " very much to heart. In schoolboy slang, he " fugged up " the books which instruct in the attainment of " style," as well as the books by authors who were instanced as possessing a " style." Worse, he set sedulously to imitate these authors—with the result that his own books may or may not have improved in " art " and in " style," but lost naturalness and ease, became stilted and self-conscious, and ceased to be read.

Mr. Drinkwater reminds me just a little of that young man, not as ceasing to be read, but because there was an appeal in his earlier work, if only because of the ease, directness, simplicity, beauty, and strength, which, in these days, he is in danger of losing by becoming self-consciously an artist and a poet of the school of Mr. Thomas Hardy.

Self-consciousness, like ivy fastening on the bole of a sturdy oak, may cramp, but cannot greatly retard either Mr. Drinkwater's own intellectual growth, or the increase in the number of his readers.

But could he, would he, cut away the strangling coils, we should see the tree—bole and branches and foliage—in all its grandeur, and his circle of readers would widen with his widening powers.

I did not intend here to touch upon Mr. Drinkwater's prose, but as the first four articles in the book *Prose Papers* are concerned with the principles of poetry—crystallize, indeed, his theories of poetic art into a creed—some mention of the matter is necessary.

His Theories of Poetry Art

In the essay *The Poet and His Vision*, he says : " The poet is to hold the mirror up to Nature, and the mirror is his own temperament." Even so, if the poet have pinned up, at his desk's side, a " Lest we forget " paper, setting forth the standards of art, on which one eye must self-consciously be kept, while the other is on the mirror, he will miss something which he ought to see and to record. Elsewhere in the same essay Mr. Drinkwater says : " The poet's business is not to express his age, but to express himself."

Of course, it is true that every writer unconsciously reveals himself in his work, but, self-consciously, to sit down, pen in hand, with the intention of such revelation, seems to me, if I may be pardoned army slang, to "cramp one's style," still more, to cramp, if not to darken, one's vision. The artist may work subconsciously, but never self-consciously. Just as a skilled musician keeps his eyes upon the " score "—knowing well that his hands, highly trained as he is in his art, will instinctively light upon the right notes—so the artist has eyes only for his vision while creating. So far from being self-conscious, he is scarcely conscious of self, of time, of place, of art—even, it may be of his own name when he is at work, and lost in his work.

Of a soldier one sometimes hears the phrase : " He is a book-bound man," so I take another illustration this time from army life. Here is a young fellow who proposes to become an officer, and so must concentrate himself upon the art of war. First of all he must be drilled and trained to the point when it becomes, as it were, unnecessary to think. Were he, when an order is given, to stop to think, he might become self-conscious and so, confused ; but he is trained to his work, until his work has become second nature. Automatically, mechanically, he does what there is to do, and does it aright. Next he must study his red books, his manuals, until he has them, in spirit, if not in letter, by heart. He must perfect himself in Strategy and Tactics, must master the principles of Attack and Defence, and read widely in military history.

Thus far, the art of war has been his master, but there comes a time when he is master of his art. Hitherto he has done its bidding : now it must do his. His art, in exact proportion to the perfection of his training, and of his abilities, still acts in and through him, for drill and training and manuals are in his brain and of his blood. But on the battle-field he has no conscious, nor even subconscious, thought of drill and manual. He decides and acts now on his own initiative.

This is equally true of the artist. He is so perfectly trained in his art that, in the act of creating, he is unconscious of art, for though in a sense he is still art's son and servant—yet none the less he is faithfully served by his art, as a master is served by an obedient servant.

Mr. Drinkwater is not as yet entirely emancipated from art's thraldom. He is still something of a " book-bound soldier," and afraid entirely to trust to his own initiative, which, in a poet, may be likened to trained inspiration.

Great imagery and golden words come naturally to trained inspiration. They do not come by self-conscious seeking and selection. The imagery, if it be not seen in an instant, as by a lightning-flash, may not be discovered, though one rack each convolution of the brain, as it were, candle in hand, or even sweep, as with a searchlight, the known heavens and earth. Mr. Drinkwater does seem so to rack his brain, does seem so to sweep the heavens and earth with the searchlight of imagination—the result being that when his imagery is found and set in his pages, it may and does shine there as a jewel, a priceless gem of art, but not always as a star or a flower. For poetry is living and sentient as a flower. If in transplanting a flower of poetry from the unseen garden of the imagination, to set it in the invisible garden of art, we fail of sacramental reverence—if if be over-handled, the virginal glory is gone. Even a single word, reborn as it were, and so newly, into the new world of a poem—even a word may bear signs of the brain-labour, the thought-travail with which it was brought to birth. Let me instance Mr. Drinkwater's poem *To Alice Meynell*, whom all that know her personally revere, all who know her only by her poems, count as the peer of Emily Brontë, Mrs. Browning, and Christina Rossetti.

> " I too have known my mutinies,
>   Played with improvident desires,
> Gone indolently vain as these
>   Whose lips from undistinguished choirs
>   Mock at the music of our sires.
>
> I too have erred in thought. In hours
>   When needy life forbade me bring
> To song the brain's unravished powers,
>   Then had it been a temperate thing
>   Loosely to pluck an easy string.

> Yet thought has been, poor profligate,
>   Sin's period.   Through dear and long
> Obedience I learn to hate
>   Unhappy lethargies that wrong
>   The larger loyalties of song.
>
> And you upon your slender reed,
>   Most exquisitely tuned, have made
> For every singing heart a creed.
>   And I have heard, and I have played
>   My lonely music unafraid.
>
> Knowing that still a friendly few,
>   Turning aside from turbulence,
> Cherish the difficult phrase, the due
>   Bridals of disembodied sense
>   With the new word's magnificence."

This is finely chiselled, admirably phrased, though, incidentally, it tells us more—we do not complain for his is a fascinating personality—of Mr. Drinkwater than of Mrs. Meynell to whom the poem is addressed.   But take the passage :

> " Yet thought has been, poor profligate,
>   Sin's period."

Is this the free and liquid nightingale note of poetry, or is it an unmelodious thought, caught, birdwise, after much chasing, and prisoned in a poem, as in a cage ?

"Pregnant and living words, pregnant and living, for here is the secret of poetry," writes Mr. Drinkwater elsewhere. I agree, and taking the poem to Mrs. Meynell as a whole, it resolutely fulfills Mr. Drinkwater's own ideals. Most of his words are pregnant, living, and new ; for he attains what in his last line he calls :

> " the new word's magnificence."

It is as I say finely phrased, but thus to pride one-

self in print as if by a pointing finger, on one's
selection of words, seems to me to suggest word-
laying rather than building the lofty rhyme.   It
reminds one of Sir William Watson's line :

" And little masters make a toy of song—"

rather than of the " songsmith " of whom the same
poet speaks. Of Swinburne I once wrote as stealing
into the room, noiseless in his movements, even when
excited, to chant to us some new and noble poem,
carried like an uncooled bar of glowing iron, direct
from the smithy of his brain, and still vibrating with,
still intoning the deep bass of the hammer on the
anvil, still singing the red fire-song of the furnace
whence it came. This is precisely what I miss in
Mr. Drinkwater's work. A poet-friend of mine once
said of some one known to him : " Of all men I have
ever met, he, more than any other, has what I may
call the gift of ' glow.' In a room, his eager, vivid
personality seems to radiate light and warmth. To
take up a book of his is like falling into the company
of some one just in from a winter walk, and ruddy
with exercise, health and high spirits."

As revealed in his poems, this gift of " glow " has
apparently been denied to Mr. Drinkwater, unless we
except a certain brain phosphorescence, cold as the
light of a glow-worm. He speculates, meditates,
ruminates, but only rarely illuminates—other than
as the glow-worm illuminates himself, and his own
surroundings. I attribute this fact to Mr. Drinkwater's self-consciousness.

Mr. Drinkwater is unknown to me personally.
Were I acquainted with him, I might think otherwise,
but not many of his poems give me the impression
of being penned, as Swinburne's were, in moments
of exultation. He pens his line more often, I
imagine, in the cold ink of thought, than in the red
blood of a fired brain.   He is more of a mosaic maker

than a wonder worker. Rarely is there a catch of the breath in reading him. He is thought-suggestive, thought-stimulating, but sets no kindling spark either to the imagination or to passion. In his quest of the new word, he loses something of inspiration. Blanco White won a great reputation by a single sonnet, *To Night*, so a poet may yet be born who will be remembered by the magnificence of a " new word." But the word must shine out as naturally and as spontaneously as, with the passing of a cloud, a star shines out in the heavens. If we do not feel that the word was born with the poem—was a single star in the poem even before the poem has risen above our horizon, just as, when the cloud passes, the star is seen to be part of a constellation—if this be not so, not all the " magnificence " of the new word will make of the poem a constellation in the skies of poetry. Nor will the poet attain to the vision splendid, perfect as his poem may be as a work of art.

In the admirable essay on Theodore Watts-Dunton, Mr. Drinkwater says : " The measure of a poet's greatness is not the contents of his art, but his art itself ; by the perfect shaping of his vision, and not by the nature of his vision is he admirable."

I join issue with Mr. Drinkwater here. To say either that it is not the vision but the shaping of the vision which makes admirable poetry, or to say that it is not the shaping but only the vision which makes poetry admirable, is to state only half a truth. The whole truth is that poetry is neither vision nor art, but the perfect mating of the two in happy wedlock. As well call that a marriage to which there goes only a bridegroom and no bride, or only a bride and no bridegroom, as call that great poetry where there is either only art, and imperfect vision, or only vision, and imperfect art.

Poetry is the perfect and beautiful body (and so of the senses) in which a perfect and beautiful thought or vision (and so of the soul) are divinely mated and made one.

When a poet of Mr. Drinkwater's distinction directly lays down the law on his own art, one is conscious of no little presumption in challenging what is said. But if, as we are told, a lie which is only half a lie is ever the worst of lies—a truth which is only half a truth is not without its danger. This particular half-truth may—indeed must—lead to some misapprehension in regard to the true nature of poetry, as may another statement by Mr. Drinkwater in the same volume, *Prose Papers*.

In dedicating the book to Mr. Rothenstein, he says :

" We artists have the world to fight. Prejudice, indifference, positive hostility, misrepresentation, a total failure to understand the purposes and the power of art, beset us on every side. Nevertheless if the world is to be renewed, it will be renewed by us." That is to say that Statesmen, Men of Science, Leaders of Thought and of work in other realms, including of course religion—I need not extend the list—do not appear to come within Mr. Drinkwater's sphere of vision, as sharing in the renewal of the world. .

All of us look to Art to take her part, a great part, in such renewal. All of us deplore with Mr. Drinkwater that Art, Science, Literature, go, officially at least, so often neglected in England, but to plump for the artist as the Superman and the superfactor in the work of reconstruction, without so much as a mention of those who follow other callings, is scarcely, in Matthew Arnold's words, to see " life steadily, and see it whole."

I do not question Mr. Drinkwater's sincerity, but

I do question his sense of perspective and his sense of humour, especially when he writes :

" It is time that we who care for art, and understand its character, insisted roundly and in every season that we are the strictly practical people, that we are the people who have our eyes set straight, not squinting, and so can see beyond our noses. And the supreme hope of the world is that in nearly every one of us lies the capacity for the understanding of art."

So this, then, is the " supreme hope " of a war-broken and bleeding world. Mr. Drinkwater proclaims, it will be seen, the carrying of a fiery cross of art to the world. He preaches—as seriously as if he were a new and heaven-sent John Baptist of art, a voice crying aloud in a wilderness that is formless and void and without art—a new crusade. " Here," he says (and while the world was still at war), " is the new crusade." His artist friends are, it seems, to go out into the highways and byways, preaching salvation by art. He proposes to conquer the world by and for Art—and for Art the sequel would be disastrous. At first, and while the novelty lasted, amused—the people of this country would soon become badly bored, and to be bored, the people of this country will not for long endure. Lord Roberts once said to me, half sadly, half smilingly, that he believed the British people would rather lose a war than be bored beforehand by warnings of coming war. Lord Roberts at least spoke like a soldier in delivering his warning. Mr. Drinkwater does not even write like an artist when, in his rôle of a new Noah, warning the world that only within his Ark of Art is there safety, he charges his brother artists to go abroad " roundly, and in every season insisting that we are the people who have our eyes set straight, not squinting, and so can see beyond our noses."

Art achieves its effects by means of fine balances, not by extravagance and exaggeration. Those who climb the pulpit stairs to preach the gospel of art, will make no converts by cushion-thumping. Art's conquests are for the most part made silently, and by the compelling power of beauty, whether it be beauty as bodied forth by the imagination in marble, in a picture, or by the beauty of the written word.

And all the time Mr. Drinkwater's new nostrum for the healing of the nations is neither his own discovery, nor even new. Most, if not all of it, was more wisely and more persuasively (because wittily and less immoderately) said, by the unhappy Oscar Wilde, of whom Mr. Drinkwater elsewhere finely speaks as

" Misfortune's moth, and laughter's new wing-feather."

Rightly or wrongly, I attribute to these theories, and to this tendency to exaggerate the letter of art, at the expense of the spirit, the limitations, as I count them, of Mr. Drinkwater's work. No one has striven more honourably or more greatly than he to perfect himself in his art. If the definition of genius as the power of taking pains be accepted, a genius, in that sense, he undoubtedly is. I imagine that, as was said of Sir Walter Raleigh, " he can toil terribly." Possibly he toils too terribly. Now and again he reminds me of an over-anxious passenger who is so fussed about the importance to himself and to others in the matter of the exactness of the wording inscribed on his luggage, that, in satisfying himself that the labelling is punctiliously perfect to the last word—he contrives to miss the train.

In the poem *Reverie*, Drinkwater pours scorn on those

" who have not learned to be
Lords of the word."

Quite so. But paradoxical as it may seem to say so of one who claims to be a Lord of the word, Mr. Drinkwater is in some danger of being over-lorded by words, just as the passenger to whom I have likened him may be overloaded with anxious thoughts about his luggage.

When Mr. Drinkwater forgets, as fortunately for us, his admirers, he not unfrequently does forget, himself and his art, he writes his greatest poetry. Not even our Sussex-born and Sussex-true poets have painted a more perfect picture than this *Of Greatham*.

. . . .

" And peace upon your pasture lands I found,
    Where grazing flocks drift on continually,
As little clouds that travel with no sound
    Across a windless sky.

Out of your oaks the birds call to their mates
    That brood among the pines, where hidden deep
From curious eyes a world's adventure waits
    In columned choirs of sleep.

Under the calm ascension of the night
    We heard the mellow lapsing and return
Of night owls purring in their grounding flight
    Through lanes of darkling fern.

Unbroken peace where all the stars were drawn
    Back to their lairs of light, and ranked along
From shire to shire the downs out of the dawn
    Were risen in golden song."

" Out of the dawn," the downs have indeed in these perfect lines arisen " in golden song," and in imperishable song. I can liken the poem only to a picture by Claude Lorraine, whom as a landscape painter I esteem most of all. Before such pictures as the Botticellis, the Fra Angelicos and the Leonardo of the National Gallery, I stand, to quote Mr. Drink-water's words of poetry :

" Stilling my mind from tribulation
Of life half-seen, half-heard,
With images made in the brain's quietness,
And the leaping of a word."

To some of us the " word," the only possible word,
which comes to our lips in the contemplation of
such pictures, is a word of reverent thanksgiving and
prayer. We are "subdued by muted praise," as
the poet of whom I am writing has it, we feel with
him that " art is holy," and we know in his own
exquisite words :

" Such peace as bids at eventide
The happy shepherd from the fold."

It is for that reason that I leave to the last a certain
Claude Lorraine picture, over the liquid and league-
clear atmosphere of which broods a benediction like
that following after prayer. With that picture in
my thoughts, I pass out, as though I had indeed
heard the beautiful benediction of the Church from
the lips of God's minister. Nor though, outside
again in the noisy London streets, it be raining, and
the hurtling motor omnibuses splash mud abroad
as they pass, can mud or noise mar the perfect
memory of the picture ; for that memory is, in Mr.
Drinkwater's words :

" as a pearl unsoiled,
Nay, rather washed to lonelier chastity,
In gritty mud,"

and,

" wonder has come down
From alien skies upon the midst of us ;
The sparkling hedgerow and the clamorous town
Have grown miraculous."

Now, to show what " far rangers " are the poet's
moods, let me quote three stanzas in which, not art
but happy laughter is held to symbolize what is

spiritual and holy.   It has the child-heart of Stevenson's *Child's Garden of Verse*, and is entitled *Holiness* :

" If all the carts were painted gay,
    And all the streets swept clean,
And all the children came to play
    By hollyhocks, with green
    Grasses to grow between,

If all the houses looked as though
    Some heart were in their stones,
If all the people that we knew
    Were dressed in scarlet gowns,
    With feathers in their crowns,

I think this gaiety would make
    A spiritual land.
I think that holiness would take
    This laughter by the hand,
    Till both should understand."

And here, from the same volume *Olton Pools* is another poem in which as indicated by the title, *Invocation*, the poet invokes the Spirit of Happiness, no less than the Spirit of Wisdom, to sing through his moods and upon his lips :

" As pools beneath stone arches take
    Darkly within their deeps again
Shapes of the flowing stone, and make
    Stories anew of passing men,

So let the living thoughts that keep,
    Morning and evening, in their kind,
Eternal change in height and deep,
    Be mirrored in my happy mind.

Beat, world, upon this heart, be loud
    Your marvel chanted in my blood,
Come forth, O sun, through cloud on cloud
    To shine upon my stubborn mood.

> Great hills that fold above the sea,
>   Ecstatic airs and sparkling skies,
> Sing out your words to master me,
>   Make me immoderately wise."

In *Reciprocity*, which I take from the volume *Tides*, Mr. Drinkwater rings the changes upon his own moods—this time more tranquil. Again Nature is " the immense shadow of man " and the mirror of man's mind :

> " I do not think that skies and meadows are
> Moral, or that the fixture of a star
> Comes of a quiet spirit, or that trees
> Have wisdom in their windless silences.
> Yet these are things invested in my mood
> With constancy, and peace, and fortitude,
> That in my troubled season I can cry
> Upon the wide composure of the sky,
> And envy fields, and wish that I might be
> As little daunted as a star or tree."

While speaking of John Drinkwater's Nature poems, I must not forget, perhaps, the most original and distinctive of all, *Crocuses*.

> " Desires,
>   Little determined desires,
>   Gripped by the mould,
>   Moving so hardly among
> The earth, of whose heart they were bred,
> That is old ; it is old,
> Not gracious to little desires such as these,
> But apter for work on the bases of trees,
>   Whose branches are hung
>   Overhead,
> Very mightily there, overhead.
>
> Through the summer they stirred,
> They strove to the bulbs after May,
> Until harvest and song of the bird
> Went together away ;

And ever till coming of snows
They worked in the mould, for undaunted were those
Swift little determined desires, in the earth
Without sign, any day,
Ever shaping to marvels of birth,
Far away.

And we went
Without heed
On our way,
Never knowing what virtue was spent,
Day by day,
By those little desires that were gallant to breed
Such beauty as fortitude may.
Not once in our mind
Was that corner of earth under trees,
Very mighty and tall,
As we travelled the roads and the seas,
And gathered the wage of our kind,
And were laggard or trim to the call
Of the duties that lengthen the hours
Into seasons that flourish and fall.

And blind,
In the womb of the flowers,
Unresting they wrought,
In the bulbs, in the depth of the year,
Buried far from our thought ;
Till one day, when the thrushes were clear
In their note it was spring—and they know—
Unheeding we came into sight
Of that corner forgotten, and lo,
They had won through the meshes of mould,
And treasuries lay in the light,
Of ivory, purple, and gold."

His Use of Irregular Lines

This last quotation is in lines of irregular length—
perhaps I should say they are irregular of alignment.
Possibly Mr. Drinkwater's preference for lines of
irregular length is that he finds that the stanza and
the rhymed quatrain necessitate either the incom-

pletion by curtailment, or the expansion by unrequired words, of the thought he has in mind ; and so he adopts the uneven line form, preferring, in this case, that thought should mould form, rather than form, thought.

Whatever the cause, the result is ease, spontaneity, and natural directness of expression. Here is another and very beautiful instance, the title of which is *To One I Love* :

" As I walked along the passage, in the night, beyond the stairs
In the dark,
I was afraid,
Suddenly,
As will happen you know, my dear, it will often happen.
I knew the walls at my side,
Knew the drawings hanging there, the order of their placing,
And the door where my bed lay beyond,
And the window on the landing—
There was even a little ray of moonlight through it—
All was known, familiar, my comfortable home ;
And yet I was afraid,
Suddenly,
In the dark, like a child, of nothing,
Of vastness, of eternity, of the queer pains of thought,
Such as used to trouble me when I heard,
When I was little, the people talk
On Sundays of ' As it was in the Beginning,
Is Now, and Ever Shall Be. . . .'
I am thirty-six years old,
And folk are friendly to me,
And there are no ghosts which should have reason to haunt
    me,
And I have tempted no magical happenings,
By forsaking the clear noons of thought
For the wizardries that the credulous take
To be golden roads to revelation.
I knew all was simplicity there,
Without conspiracy, without antagonism,
And yet I was afraid,
Suddenly,
A child in the dark, forlorn. . . .
And then, as suddenly,
I was aware of a profound, a miraculous understanding,

Knowledge that comes to a man
But once or twice as a bird's note
In the still depth of the night
Striking upon the silence. . . .
I stood at the door, and there
Was mellow candle light,
And companionship, and comfort,
And I knew
That it was even so,
That it must be even so
With death.
I knew
That no harm could have touched me out of my fear,
Because I had no grudge against anything,
Because I had desired
In the darkness, when fear came,
Love only, and pity, and fellowship,
And it would have been a thing monstrous,
Something defying nature
And all the simple universal fitness
For any force there to have come evilly
Upon me who had no evil in my heart,
But only trust and tenderness
For every presence about me in the air,
For the very shadow about me,
Being a little child for no one's envy.
And I knew that God
Must understand that we go
To death as little children,
Desiring love so simply, and love's defence,
And that He would be a barren God, without humour,
To cheat so little, so wistful a desire,
That He created
In us, in our childishness. . . .
And I may never again be sure of this,
But there, for a moment,
In the candle light,
Standing at the door,
I knew."

The form, here and elsewhere, is that most often
adopted by Emerson, who, by the way, never once,
so far as I know, attempted the sonnet, a form which
does not appear to attract Mr. Drinkwater greatly,

for his sonnets, though excellent, are comparatively few.

Why I mention Emerson in this connexion is that, except for the fact that he was the most happy-go-lucky, hit-or-miss mortal who ever essayed to wing thoughts in verse, taking his chances whether the shaft found the target of poetry, or went so wide of the mark as to find no target at all, unless that which Hood called " Prose—and Worse," and that Mr. Drinkwater never so much as draws arrow to bow with any other target than perfection, the younger poet often reminds one of the older.

Emerson chanced sometimes to centre on Art's target with such lines as :

> " Still on the seeds of all He made
> The rose of beauty burns ;
> Through times that wear, and forms that fade,
> Immortal youth returns."

At other times he stampeded us out of sound or sight of his shooting lest we, as well as poetry, be wounded to the heart by a shaft poisoned with such execrable stuff as this :

> " Hear you, then, celestial fellows ;
> Fits not to be over zealous ;
> Steads not to work on the clean jump,
> Nor wine nor brains perpetual pump."

Yet though Mr. Drinkwater faithfully and perfectly serves, and the other comes nigh to assassinating, Art, the two men have much in common, and between their work there is often a strange resemblance. Asked who penned

> " And my communion with them
> Ails not in the mind's strategem,"

nine out of ten who know the Emerson manner of expression and the Emerson turn of thought would

reply that it was unmistakably by him, whereas it is
by Mr. Drinkwater. On the other hand, Mr. Drinkwater himself might have written of that "yellow
breeched philosopher," that "rover of the under-
woods," the humble bee, who

> " The green silence dost displace
> With thy mellow breezy bass."

The couplet, as it happens, is Emerson's, but here
is a quatrain by Mr. Drinkwater which might easily
be attributed to Emerson :

> " Though, heart, you measure
> But one proud rhyme,
> You build a treasure
> Confounding time."

Had Emerson been a Cotswold man, he too would
have said :

> " And no theologies have made
> So quick a Paradise
> As this, my Cotswold corner laid
> Under the Cotswold skies."

To his wife, Emerson would have written as Mr.
Drinkwater writes to his :

> " I think what miracle has been
> That you whose love among this green
> Delightful solitude is still
> The stay and substance of my will,
> The dear custodian of my song,
> My thrifty counsellor and strong,
> Should take the time of all time's tide
> That was my season, to abide
> On earth also ; that we should be
> Charted across eternity
> To one elect and happy day
> Of yellow primroses in May."

The imagery is so happy that my readers will
forgive me if I extend my quotations, thereby

gathering, as it were into a jewel tray, scattered gems which otherwise might have gone unnoticed. Here is a picture of sleepers, awakening to find themselves in June woods :

> " One by one they woke, their faces
> Still with some new wonder,
> As when in quiet shadowy places
> Wandering hands may move asunder
> Secret foliage, and intrude
> On the ancestral solitude
> Of some untutored forest thing—
> Neither doubt nor fear they bring,
> But just a strange new wonder."

Mr. Drinkwater knows birds, as Emerson knew them. Here is a glimpse of the crow :

> " In the boughs where the gloom
> Is a part of his plume."

And here is a picture of the blackbird :

> " He comes on chosen evenings,
> My blackbird bountiful, and sings
> Over the gardens of the town
> Just at the hour the sun goes down.
> His flight across the chimneys thick,
> By some divine arithmetic."

That " divine arithmetic " is very Emersonian. So, too, is the following :

> " When to one field that crowns a hill,
> With but the sky for neighbourhood,
> The crowding counties of my brain
> Give all their riches, lake and plain,
> Cornland and fell and pillared wood.
>
> . . . .
>
> When in a furrowed hill we see
> All beauty in epitome—
> Those hours are best, for they belong
> To the lucidity of song."

Many other instances of resemblance to Emerson could be adduced, especially in regard to lines which, in geological terms, might be described as poetry in granulated form, rather than in strata. I do not for a moment imply that Mr. Drinkwater has in any way formed himself upon Emerson, whose poems, if only because of their frequent uncouthness, Mr. Drinkwater may never have studied nor even read.

Among Mr. Drinkwater's greatest poems I count *Uncrowned*. Elsewhere he speaks of women who

> " turn, and go,
> Unweaponed, towards the world's untried abyss."

In *Uncrowned* he lays bare the soul of one of those beautiful but tragic women who make shipwreck of life, less from evil in themselves, than because it is their unhappy fate to win all men's worship for their beauty, but to win no man's honourable love for, and understanding of, the deep woman-soul within. His poem is so supremely done that even to preface my extracts (it is too long to quote entire) with these few words is an impertinence.

> " Men came, a courtly crowd, to her,
> And spoke of love aloud to her,
> Day-long, day-long, they flattered her,
> And called her beauty good,
> But no man came with secret flame
> To cover her and lend her name
> A glory that should leaven all
> Her holy womanhood—
> Her hungry womanhood.
>
> She watched the other women go
> With quiet mates, the women so
> Far set below her in the things
> That make a woman fair.
> And now she leant across the night,
> Breast open to the soft moonlight,
> And silver arrows of the moon
> Were splintered in her hair.

' O God of all the yellow fields
Of stubble, God of stars,
Why should the woman that is me
Be prisoned in the bars
Fashioned by men because their eyes
Are sealed, their sweet souls dead—
Why should my armoured pride so make
Uncomraded my bed ?

    .   .   .   .   .   .

' My name is heard throughout the land,
Men sing my body's praise,
They listen when I laugh, my words
Are coveted, my days
Are rich in tribute, yet I find
No man that dares to be
Lord of the secret heart I bear,
The woman that is me.

'How shall I speak ?   How, being proud,
Shall I cry out that this
Woman they praise is hungering
For one unfettered kiss,
That she they make a song-burden
Is starving while they sing.
Starving among them all, O God,
How shall I cry this thing ?

' Hidden within my Body's flame
And flames which are my soul
A secret beauty lies.   Until
One rides to make it whole,
To set it on his brow, to make
It free, yet never free,
Crying for birth goes wandering
The woman that is me.

' And while I wait I have no joy
Of homage nor the things
That make the season beautiful,
And folded are the wings
Whereon—ah, well, night moves apace,
Anew the dawn-tide runs—
Day and the little light that is
The shadow of Thy Suns.'

She curtained out the moonlight, pale
In marriage with the day.
As golden nets her golden hair
Along the pillows lay ;
And the wind stirred among the leaves,
And God's work went its way."

In all that has been written upon the subject by contemporary poets, is there, for beauty, insight, truth, tenderness, humanity, anything comparable to this ?   I am not sure that there is anything comparable to it in literature, unless it be Hood's *Bridge of Sighs* and Rossetti's *Jenny*.

The last stanza recalls Rossetti, even in metre, as will be seen by a comparison with the following lines from *The Blessed Damosel* :

" Her robe, ungirt from clasp to hem,
No wrought flowers did adorn ;
But a white robe of Mary's gift,
For service meetly worn ;
Her hair, that lay along her back,
Was yellow like ripe corn."

In this particular poem, the influence of Rossetti seems unmistakable, for we have not only subject but also metrical similarity.   It is, however, only fair to Mr. Drinkwater to say here, as elsewhere I shall more fully say in this article, that one great characteristic of his work in poetry is its individuality. The only poet whose influence is discernible is Mr. Hardy.   Of all living poets none is less an echo of those who have gone before than John Drinkwater. And of the two poems, *Jenny* and *Uncrowned*, I count the latter the more profound in insight, the more perfect in imagery.   Comparing, as I have just compared, *Uncrowned* with *Jenny*, there is here and there a passage in Rossetti's which (I admit only since reading Mr. Drinkwater's poem) gives me the impression of being less delicate and restrained than

I had hitherto thought it to be. In Mr. Drinkwater's poems, as indeed in almost everything he writes, there is no single unnecessary word. Fine restraint, exquisite reserve are the very signature of his work as an artist. One, and one only exception there is with which I will now deal. The volume *Olton Pools* contains some verses entitled *To the Defilers*. Mr. Drinkwater has in mind, of course, the vandals who either erect advertisement hoardings among lovely scenery, or defile the face of nature by leaving behind them scraps of broken food and bottles, greasy sandwich papers and banana skins.

> " Go, thieves, and take your riches, creep
>   To corners out of honest sight ;
> We shall not be so poor to keep
>   One thought of envy or despite.
>
> But know that in sad surety when
>   Your sullen will betrays this earth,
> To sorrows of contagion, then
>   Beelzebub renews his birth.
>
> When you defile the pleasant streams
>   And the wild bird's abiding place,
> You massacre a million dreams
>   And cast your spittle in God's face."

I am no Bowdlerizer for the whittling away, lest one offend the squeamish, of that which makes for directness and strength in literature. Had I to choose between frank outspokenness and veiled suggestiveness, I should choose the former as infinitely less harmful. But shrillness and stridency are not strength, violence of word and imagery is not vigour. No gardener mistakes an unsightly excrescence for young and lusty growth. The young and lusty growth he leaves, the ugly excrescence he

prunes away.   Mr. Drinkwater's last line is painful
alike to one's sense of taste, and to reverence.   He
cannot altogether be acquitted of the very offence he
condemns, for soilure of scenery is counterparted by
this soilure of poetry.   I earnestly hope he will
expunge the passage from his next edition.

Patriotic
Poems

Mr. Drinkwater has written not a few patriotic
poems, as witness, *Inscription for a War-Memorial
Fountain, We willed it not, The Cause, Rebuke, On the
Dead, Gathering Song, England to Belgium,* and *The
Poet to the Heroes.*   These are faultless in form and
admirable in spirit.   I question whether, in all the
literature of the war, a nobler and more beautiful
tribute to the fallen has been written than the last
named.   It is as if, for a Great Dead March, by
Chopin or Handel, fitting words had at last been
found.   Anguish there is in the music, yet true
serenity ;   gentle sweetness, yet strength.   War-
poem though it is, we think of the battlefield as one
whereon the angel of darkness and slaughter lies
broken of wing, and with his life-blood spilling, while
overhead, on calm pinion, broods the angel of God's
peace.   Only by quoting *The Poet to the Heroes* in
its entirety—nine stanzas each of six lines, and
occupying three pages—could justice be done to the
poem, so I refer the reader to pages 54, 55, 56 of
Swords and Ploughshares.
England to Belgium is another noble work, of
which I quote the last stanza :

> " For all things clean, for all things brave,
>   For peace, for spiritual light,
> To keep love's body whole, to save
>   The hills of intellectual sight,

Girt at your Belgian gate we stand
  Our trampled faith undaunted still,
With heart unseared and iron hand,
  And old indomitable will."

With the exception of *Gathering Song*, beginning,
" A word for you of the Prussian boast," which
makes time to the drum-tap and to the marching
of multitudes, the remainder of Mr. Drinkwater's
patriotic poems do not greatly stir. Some are
scornful or rebukeful of Germany. Two or three—
Nineteen-Fifteen, for instance—are protests against
the civilization which permits anything so uncivilized,
so inhuman, and so devilish as war.

" On a ploughland hill against the sky,
  Over the barley, over the rye,
  Time, which is now a black pine tree,
  Holds out his arms and mocks at me—

In the year of your Lord nineteen-fifteen
  The acres are ploughed and the acres are green,
  And the calves and the lambs and the foals are born,
  But man the angel is all forlorn.

The cropping cattle, the swallow's wing,
  The wagon team and the pasture spring,
  Most in their seasons and are most wise,
  But man, whose image is in the skies,

Who is master of all, whose hand achieves
  The church and the barn and the homestead eaves—
  How are the works of his wisdom seen
  In the year of your Lord nineteen-fifteen ? "

I question whether, in 1915, anyone in England
needed reminding of the horrors and the inhumanities
of war. The weaker of us did sometimes need
reminding of England's desperate efforts, at every
cost save that of honour, to avert war. From that
memory came courage, faith in God and in righteousness ; and so the will to endure ; from the contem-

plation of war's inhumanities came only anguish and
horror. His own views on war, Mr. Drinkwater has
more explicitly expressed in *The Patriot*:

" Scarce is my life more dear to me.
    Brief tutor of oblivion,
Than fields below the rookery
    That comfortably looks upon
    The little streets of Piddington.

I never think of Avon's meadows,
    Ryton woods or Rydal mere,
Or moontide moulding Cotswold shadows,
    But I know that half the fear
    Of death's indifference is here.

I love my land. No heart can know
    The patriot's mystery, until
It aches as mine for woods ablow
    In Gloucestershire with daffodil,
    Or Bicester brakes that violets fill.

No man can tell what passion surges
    For the house of his nativity
In the patriot's blood, until he purges
    His grosser mood of jealousy,
    And comes to meditate with me.

Of gifts of earth that stamp his brain
    As mine the pools of Ludlow mill,
The hazels fencing Trilly's Lane,
    And forty acres under Brill,
    The ferry under Elsfield hill.

These are what England is to me,
    Not Empire, nor the name of her,
Ranging from pole to tropic sea.
    These are the soil in which I bear
    All that I have of character.

That men my fellows near and far
    May live in like communion,
Is all I pray; all pastures are
    The best beloved beneath the sun;
    I have my own; I envy none."

Here I had better say that I am not in sympathy with the poet. Perhaps the fact that I had the honour to hold, first, His Majesty King Edward's commission as an officer in the Territorial Army, and later to be recommissioned by His Majesty King George, makes it difficult for me to see the matter from so detached a standpoint. Speaking frankly, for a poem written in war-time, *The Patriot* seems to me to have a certain self-centred, almost selfish, meditativeness, and to be local of outlook. Comfort of sorts it may have brought to him who

> " comfortably looks upon
> The little streets of Piddington,"

but the poem strikes one as more inspired by love of Piddington than by love of the England of Kipling, Noyes, Newbolt, Maurice Baring and Rupert Brooke. I very much prefer the conception of patriotism given us by the last-named poet to Mr. Drinkwater's. Every reader knows Rupert Brooke's lines, but remembering that the writer was proud and ready to give—did give his glad young life for his country, I may be pardoned for quoting the sonnet once again :

> " If I should die, think only this of me :
>   That there's some corner of a foreign field
> That is for ever England. There shall be
>   In that rich earth a richer dust concealed ;
> A dust whom England bore, shaped, made aware,
>   Gave, once, her flowers to love, her ways to roam,
> A body of England's breathing English air,
>   Washed by the rivers, blest by suns of home.
>
> And think, this heart, all evil shed away,
>   A pulse in the eternal mind, no less
> Gives somewhere back the thoughts by England given ;
> Her sights and sounds ; dreams happy as her day ;
>   And laughter, learnt of friends ; and gentleness,
>   In hearts at peace, under an English heaven."

In another war-time poem, Mr. Drinkwater seems not a little concerned because the war came between him and the making of poetry :

"Because a million voices call
    Across the earth distractedly,
Because the thrones of reason fall
    And beautiful battalions die,
My mind is like a madrigal
    Played on a lute long since put by.

In common use my mind is still
    Eager for every lovely thing—
The solitudes of tarn and hill,
    Bright birds with honesty to sing,
Bluebells and primroses that spill
    Cascades of colour on the spring.

But now my mind that gave to these
    Gesture and shape, colour and song,
Goes hesitant and ill at ease,
    And the old touch is truant long,
Because the continents and seas
    Are loud with lamentable wrong."

Here the poet expresses what all of us feel. "Nature forgets not soon, 'tis we forget," says Sir William Watson, but, in war-time, Nature forgets while we remember. Of all the war-neutrality, Nature's seemed the most unnatural. Had the sun been darkened at noon, had the moon glowed blood-red at night, in the time of Armageddon when we could almost believe that God and Satan were contending in heaven for spiritual mastery, even as the powers of Right and of Might were contending on earth, we should scarcely have wondered. That while the lovely body of Nature was being desecrated and destroyed in France and Belgium, even as the fair bodies of men made in the image of God were being torn asunder or rent into fragments—the fact that here in England, Nature should go on her way smiling, unconcerned, unchanged, and rejoicing, seemed to make of her, not the Nature that we knew and loved, but something alien, strange, and heartless as a wanton. Here, then, we are at one with Mr. Drinkwater in feeling that those years of war were— for all the difference that the coming of spring and summer meant to us—dead years of dust and ashes ; were like a limb severed from the beautiful body of human life. The very sunlight seemed a mockery, the scent of hay or of the spring flowers, even the laughter of children, were unbearable when we remembered that the mine or the submarine, at sea, and every devil-invented ingenuity, on land, might at that moment be hurling those of our flesh and blood, our fellow-countrymen, to the most horrible of deaths.

Mr. Drinkwater, it will be seen, abhors war as we all do, but I am not sure that he altogether realizes the horrors of war. To realize his own mood seems to him to be the more important. In a very original volume which should interest all students of contemporary poetry, *Criticism at a Venture* (Erskine Macdonald), Miss Geraldine Hodgson, Vice-Principal of Ripon Training College, says of one of Mr. Drinkwater's poems : " Even here there is the modern element of ' self-expression ' rather than of the self-abnegation of those eager craftsmen of the twelfth and immediately following centuries, who wrought in stone and wood and glass for Worship and not for their own credit." This point of view is supported by the fact that Mr. Drinkwater thinks it necessary, as in the following lines, to write :

> " Because the thrones of reason fall
>   And beautiful battalions die,
> My mind is like a madrigal
>   Played on a lute long since put by,"

and that " the old touch " in his work is " truant long "

> " Because the continents and seas
>   Are loud with lamentable wrong."

Thus to set the one against the other—the one as an explanation of the other, and as if both were tragic—the two facts that " beautiful battalions die," and that, in consequence, Mr. Drinkwater finds it difficult to write poetry, implies a strange sense of what artists call " values."

Next I take the poem *The Soldier* which, though included in a volume published in 1917, was written, it is only fair to Mr. Drinkwater to remember, before the war :

> " The large report of fame I lack,
>   And shining clasps and crimson scars,
> For I have held my bivouac
>   Alone amid the untroubled stars.
>
> My battlefield has known no dawn
>   Beclouded by a thousand spears,
> I've been no mounting tyrant's pawn
>   To buy his glory with my tears.
>
> It never seemed a noble thing
>   Some little leagues of land to gain
> From broken men, nor yet to fling
>   Abroad the thunderbolts of pain.
>
> Yet I have felt the quickening breath
>   As peril, heavy peril kissed—
> My weapon was a little faith,
>   And fear was my antagonist.
>
> Not a brief hour of cannonade,
>   But many days of bitter strife,
> Till God of His great pity laid
>   Across my brow the leaves of life."

Mr. Drinkwater has, in two poems, *Thomas Yarnton of Tarlton* and *At an Earthworks*, indicated that he comes of the sturdy yeoman stock which has given us some of our greatest Englishmen.   The lines just quoted give cause for wonder whether he have not also some Quaker blood in his veins, for something there is of quiet Quaker-like dignity and sincerity in other poems of his writing. If a Quaker by ancestry and upbringing he be, his standpoint in the two poems *The Patriot* and *The Soldier* is explained. Whether accepting or not accepting Quaker views, for those views one has only respect. That, these views notwithstanding, not a few of Quaker upbringing felt called upon, in the war, to take up arms—many died —for their country we all know ; but that apart, the Quakers and the pioneers of the Salvation Army have faithfully striven to observe, and to preserve, pure and inviolate, the primal precepts, the self-sacrificing and lovely life, first enjoined on us by Christianity. These ideals even we who are not Quakers long and hope to see realized ; for with the men and women who think that the war has indefinitely postponed, or demonstrated the hopelessness of the attainment of such ideals, we cannot agree. On the contrary, the war has demonstrated that, for Christendom at least—one dare not dogmatize about non-Christian nations whether white or coloured—unless such ideals be not only attainable, but attained, Christendom (I do not say Christianity) will perish. I am assured by some friends that the League of Nations, by others that the Brotherhood Movement, will for ever make an end of war. They find more comfort in comforting new names than I do. The tendency, to-day, is to advertise new panaceas for present evils by proffering old gospels as new discoveries, under a fine-sounding new name. To Christianity I am old-fashioned enough to prefer frankly to ascribe the Gospel of Love which has its origin in Christianity. For, call it by what new name you will (and Christianity surely means Brotherhood, and more) ; call it, if you so choose, a League of Nations (which is but constraining the nations to act towards each other in the same

R

loving and peace-loving spirit of mutual forbearance, forgiveness and justice which was enjoined upon us by our Lord)—it is to Christianity and to Christianity only that we can look to end, for all time, the devilries of war.   When the majority at least of men and women—one scarcely dares to say when every one—in each country is humbly seeking to follow in the footsteps of Christ, then, and not before then, will war be no more.

Just as Mr. Drinkwater sees history in everyday events, so in everyday events, in trivial happenings, he sees symbolized what is heroic, marvellous, even what is holy and sacramental. There is he indeed in the apostolical succession of poets, then dawns for him a poet's day of pentecost. The reader will remember W. E. Henley's *Ballad of Dead Actors*, each stanza of which closes : " Into the night go one and all."   Compared with Mr. Drinkwater's *Epilogue for a Masque*, Henley's much-quoted Ballad is stagey and spectacular. Speaking of those once admired dead actors, Mr. Drinkwater adds :

" And now their dust is on a thousand hills.

We dream of them, as men unborn shall dream
Of us, who strive a little with the stream
Before we too go out beyond the day,
And are as much a memory as they.

And Death, so coming, shall not seem a thing
Of any fear, nor terrible his wing.
We, too, shall be a tale on earth, and time
Shall shape our pilgrimage into a rhyme."

Young man, comparatively, as Mr. Drinkwater is, he has already written some poems over which " men unborn shall dream " of him, as he now dreams of these dead actors.

In *Poems*, 1908-1914, Mr. Drinkwater has collected the non-dramatic poems, published before the latter date, by which he hopes to be remembered. It is thus his most representative volume, and there is significance in the fact that the opening poem is entitled *Symbols*. Under that title all Mr. Drinkwater's work might come. For those readers who expect a poet's meaning to leap to the eye, who, in fact, read superficially, Mr. Drinkwater's work will have as small attraction as the music of some composers has for the public which demands music "with a tune in it." You must look into the heart of his poems, not upon the surface, for the meaning, and then must read that meaning symbolically.

The Building is characteristically Drinkwateresque, though in this case the symbolism is apparent. Here are some extracts. In the hush of early morning, while the great city is still a city of sleep, the poet sees builders already at work.

    · · · · · · ·

"Swart men bearing bricks of bright red clay
In laden hods; and ever the thin noise
Of trowels deftly fashioning the clean
Long lines that are the shaping of proud thought.
Ghostlike they move between the day and day,
These men whose labour strictly shall be wrought
Into the captive image of a dream.
Their sinews weary not, the plummet falls
To measured use from steadfast hands apace,
And momently the moist and levelled seam
Knits brick to brick and momently the walls
Bestow the wonder of form on formless space.

    · · · · · ·

          When he came,
God upon chaos, crying in the name
Of all adventurous vision that the void
Should yield up man, and man, created rose
Out of the deep, the marvel of all things made,
Then in immortal wonder was destroyed
All worth of trivial knowledge, and the close
Of man's most urgent meditation stayed
Even as his first thought—'Whence am I sprung?'"

What proud ecstatic mystery was pent
In that first act for man's astonishment,
From age to unconfessing age, among
His manifold travel.   And in all I see
Of common daily usage is renewed
This primal and ecstatic mystery
Of chaos bidden into many-hued
Wonders of form, life in the void create,
And monstrous silence made articulate.

Not the first word of God upon the deep
Nor the first pulse of life along the day
More marvellous than these new walls that sweep
Starward, these lines that discipline the clay,
These lamps swung in the wind that send their light
On swart men climbing ladders in the night.
No trowel-tap but sings anew for men
The rapture of quickening water and continent,
No mortared line but witnesses again
Chaos transfigured into lineament."

Rhetoric, I imagine, John Drinkwater abhors.   In
saying this I am not belittling noble rhetorical utterance, for under the sneer, " This is merely rhetoric,"
some of the most treasured passages in literature, some
of the most memorable deliverances in the language,
would come.   I mean no more than that of the rhetoric of which great poets and great orators have on
occasion made great use, you find no trace in Mr.
Drinkwater's work.   As I have said, he sees everything in life symbolically.   In the poem *Symbols*, he
sees " history in a poet's song," " in a crown of
thorns : in a daffodil," and just as he sees

" the glory of all dead men
In the shadow that went by the side of me,"

so, in the woman he loves, he sees the glory of all
women glorified :

" The stars were tangled in your hair,
And all your limbs were praise,
And all your movements as a lyric prayer."

That is why, not only

> " along the bases
> Of lands that set their wide
> Frank brows to God,"

he thanks God for the gift of life, but can see, even
in a greengrocer's shop in a dingy Birmingham street,
the glory and the wealth of colour in search of which
poets and artists have gone afar to Southern climes
and Eastern bazaars :

> " All day long the traffic goes
> In Lady Street by dingy rows
> Of sloven houses, tattered shops—
> Fried fish, old clothes, and fortune-tellers—
> Tall trams on silver-shining rails,
> With grinding wheels and swaying tops,
> And lorries with their corded bales,
> And screeching cars. ' Buy, buy ! ' the sellers
> Of rags and bones and sickening meat
> Cry all day long in Lady Street.
>
> . . . . . .
>
> Yet one grey man in Lady Street
> Looks for the sun. He never bent
> Life to his will, his travelling feet
> Have scaled no cloudy continent,
> Nor has the sickle-hand been strong.
> He lives in Lady Street ; a bed
> Four cobwebbed walls.
>   But all day long
> A time is singing in his head
> Of youth in Gloucester lanes. He hears
> The wind among the barley blades,
> The tapping of the woodpeckers
> On the smooth beeches, thistle-spades
> Slicing the sinewy roots ; he sees
> The hooded filberts in the copse
> Beyond the loaded orchard trees,
> The netted avenues of hops :
> He smells the honeysuckle thrown
> Along the hedge. He lives alone,
> Alone—yet not alone, for sweet
> Are Gloucester lanes in Lady Street.

Aye Gloucester lanes. For down below
The cobwebbed room this grey man plies
A trade, a coloured trade. A show
Of many-coloured merchandise
Is in his shop. Brown filberts there,
And apples red with Gloucester air,
And cauliflowers he keeps, and round
Smooth marrows grown on Gloucester ground,
Fat cabbages and yellow plums,
And gaudy brave chrysanthemums.
And times a glossy pheasant lies
Among his stores, not Tyrian dyes
More rich than are the neck-feathers ;
And times a prize of violets,
Or dewy mushrooms satin-skinned,
And times an unfamiliar wind
Robbed of its woodland favour stirs
Gay daffodils this grey man sets
Among his treasure.
                            All day long
In Lady Street the traffic goes
By dingy houses, desolate rows
Of shops that stare like hopeless eyes,
Day long the sellers cry their cries.

        .   .   .   .   .   .

But this grey man heeds not at all
The hell of Lady Street. His stall
Of many-coloured merchandise
He makes a shining paradise,
As all day long chrysanthemums
He sells, and red and yellow plums
And cauliflowers. In that one spot
Of Lady Street the sun is not
Ashamed to shine and send a rare
Shower of colour through the air ;
The grey man says the sun is sweet
On Gloucester lanes in Lady Street."

It is when Mr. Drinkwater, as in this typical
poem :
        " Makes rough ways smooth and dark ways plain,
           Till, holpen, we take heart again,"

and when he writes thus in quiet, still, often subdued,

but subtly-phrased, subtly-chosen and pregnant words, the very salt of expression, waiting as at a Quaker meeting, the coming of the spirit, that he is at his best. The more closely we read such work as this, the more it " grows " upon us, and the more grateful we are to him. Of cities and towns he has written as finely as any living poet. Witness first these lines on *Oxford* :

" Long have we laboured in the great cities, where all things lovely
Sicken and cease ;
Daughter of dreaming, lady of learning, mother of wisdom,
Lend us thy peace."

Next of *London at Night* :

" And the shadow of night that covers the meadows with peace,
But covers thy terrible beauty with infinite awe."

Lastly of his own Birmingham :

" Once Athens worked and went to see the play,
And Thomas Atkins kissed the girls of Rome,
In council in Victoria Square to-day
Are grey-beard Nazarenes, with shop and home
And counting-house and all the friendly cares
That Joseph knew ; in Bull-Ring markets meet
Gossips as once in Babylonian fairs,
And Helen walks in Corporation Street.

Now Troy is Homer ; and of Nazareth
Grave histories are of one love that was strong ;
Athens is beauty ; Rome an immortal death ;
And Babylon immortal in a song. . . .
Perplexed as ours these cities were of old ;
And shall our name greatly as these be told ? "

Nature and the Past

To go abroad with Mr. Drinkwater in cities and towns by means of his books is fascinating, for though in cities and towns he is never at home, he makes us see with new eyes, and as if for that " first time which never comes back." But to go abroad with John Drinkwater among the Cotswold hills and vales must be a joy, for when he is with us Nature herself is sure to be of the company, not as a high priestess, a goddess, a personification of all that we call by her name, but a gracious and lovely woman, the dear companion of our walk, who, since we are with him, as his friend, withholds nothing from us, but shares her secrets with us, as with him. Though Mr. Drinkwater has in his books given only of his best, I have the feeling that John Drinkwater the man would be better company even than his books. He has such joy of life, is so tinglingly alive, above all, has such boyish and buoyant zest for adventure. It is this zest for new experience, new adventure, and his readiness to

> " Hail the advent of each dangerous day,
> And meet the last adventure with a song,"

which most attracts me to him. Here is his last word on the subject, his message, in the *Epilogue* to his Collected Poems, to the reader :

> " If the grey dust is over all,
> And stars and leaves and wings forgot,
> And your blood holds no festival—
> Go out from us ; we need you not.
>
> But if you are immoderate men,
> Zealots of joy, the salt and sting
> And savour of life upon you—then
> We call you to our counselling.
>
> And we will hew the holy boughs
> To make us level rows of oars,
> And we will set our shining prows
> For strange and unadventured shores.
>
> Where the great tideways swiftliest run
> We will be stronger than the strong,
> And sack the cities of the sun,
> And spend our booty in a song."

Religious Poems

Of four of the poets of whom I have in this series written, I had occasion to mention that each was a man of religious faith. Not to say as much of Mr. Drinkwater might imply the contrary, and though it is with poetry, not with religion, that I am dealing, I may be permitted briefly to touch upon the subject here.

" A wise and deep understanding of character," writes Mr. Drinkwater in his *Prose Papers*, " is one of the rarest, as it is one of the most precious, of man's possessions." Poetry has, to use a favourite word of his, the " signature " of character ; and as in most of us character and conviction act and react, the one upon the other, some knowledge of a poet's religious convictions may assist towards the interpretation of his poetry. I need hardly add that to belittle or to over-extol a man's poetry, as poetry, because of his views on religion, or on any other matter, would be as mean as it would be dishonest and immoral. Belief and faith in God Mr. Drinkwater has in no small measure. He has the intense reverence which is born of the sense of life's miracle and wonder, and is, in most of us, the beginning of worship. This sense is manifest in *Mystery*, a poem which, to the shallow and to the superficial, may seem in no way religious. Read by those who can divine the inner meaning and symbolism, it will seem profoundly if suggestively so. It conveys in poetry what G. F. Watts, with seer-like vision, strove to convey on canvas. It erects no shrine at which to kneel in worship, it interposes, rather than draws aside, a veil between us and the heavens, but behind that veil lies eternity, and beyond eternity—God.

" Think not that mystery has place
In the obscure and veilèd face,

Or when the midnight watches are
Uncompanied of moon or star,
Or where the fields and forests lie
Enfolded from the loving eye
By fogs rebellious to the sun,
Or when the poet's rhymes are spun
From dreams that even in his own
Imagining are half unknown.

These are not mystery, but mere
Conditions that deny the clear
Reality that lies behind
The weak unspeculative mind,
Behind contagions of the air
And screens of beauty everywhere,
The brooding and tormented sky,
The hesitation of an eye.

Look rather when the landscapes glow
Through crystal distances as though
The forty shires of England spread
Into one vision harvested,
Or when the moonlit waters lie
In silver cold lucidity ;
Those countenances search that bear
Witness to every character,
And listen to the song that weighs
A life's adventure in a phrase—
These are the founts of wonder, these
The plainer miracles to please
The brain that reads the world aright ;
Here is the mystery of light."

Of directly religious poems, *Petition* affords a
beautiful instance. Like charity in the proverb it
begins at home with the one the poet loves best, but
does not end there. It is a poet's, an artist's, a
beauty lover's prayer for a soul purified by fire, a
body " clean as clover dew " ; but it does not
forget friendship, nor even the writer's life's task,
in making petition :

" O Lord I pray : that for each happiness
My housemate brings I may give back no less
Than all my fertile will ;

That I may take from friends but as the stream
Creates against the hawthorn bloom adream
   Above the river sill ;

That I may see the spurge upon the wall,
And hear the nesting birds give call to call,
   Keeping my wonder new.

That I may have a body fit to mate
With the green fields, and stars, and streams in spate,
   And clean as clover dew ;

   .   .   .   .   .

That I may know all strict and sinewy art
As that in man which is the counterpart,
   Lord, of Thy fiercest pride ;

That somehow this beloved earth may wear
A later grace for all the love I bear,
   For some song that I sing ;

That when I die, this word may stand for me—
He had a heart to praise, an eye to see,
   And beauty was his king."

In speaking of Mr. Drinkwater's religious poems, *The Fires of God* must have place, for, though, like *Mystery*, only indirectly religious, it is profoundly so in intention. No one could mistake it for the work of any other poet than John Drinkwater, for it is almost morbidly, painfully, introspective and self-analytic. I read recently in the papers of a man so devoted to science, that, in his will, he expressly left his body to be dissected in the interests of Science. A poet may write for posterity, as Mr. Drinkwater does, for there are passages in his poems which imply that his poems will survive the poet :

   " And you shall walk with Julius at Rome,
   And Paul shall be my fellow in the Strand ;
   There in the midst of all those words shall be
   Our names, our ghosts, our immortality,"

but if a poet's soul is to be dissected for the benefit of

his contemporaries or of posterity, it must be done while the poet lives. *The Fires of God* is such a dissection.   It is the story of a soul in the making, a soul which, at first, is shown as a soul in thrall to mean despairs, a soul of narrow outlook, mean of belief, mean of love and of hope, and given over to self-pity :

> " Along that little span my unbelief
> Had fashioned in my vision as all life.
> Now even this so little virtue waned,
> For I became caught up into the strife
> That I had pitied, and my soul was stained
> At last by the most venemous despair,
> Self-pity."

Upon that soul fell the fierce Fires of God :

> " And now my pride had perished in the flame.
> I cried for succour as a little child
> Might supplicate whose days are undefiled,—
> For tutored pride and innocence are one."

Then there comes into the refrain, on which the earlier stanzas close, the first gleam of hope :

> " To the gloom has won
> A gleam of the sun
> And into the barren desolate ways
> A scent is blown
> As of meadows mown
> By cooling rivers in clover days."

Only by continuous and lengthy quotation could justice be done to one of the most remarkable—if only because of the relentlessness and honesty of the self-analysis—poems of our time.   There are, however, twelve pages, and I must do no more than quote a few lines.   Beyond the clash and discord, a new and great music, the music, now, of God's making is heard :

> " Full throated, fierce, and rhythmic with the wide
> Beat of the pilgrim winds and labouring seas,"

music which is at one with

> " the inscrutable wonder of the stars
> Flung out along the reaches of the night."

At last the poet can truly say of himself and of those who have trodden the path of so bitter a soul :

> " In sorrow we have grown to be
> The masters of adversity."

Only once in Mr. Drinkwater's work is the note of agnosticism which is heard in so many poems by Georgian poets sounded, and then only as an echo, possibly as the recollection, of a mood :

> " Although beyond the track of unseen stars
> Imagination strove in weariless might,
> Yet loomed at last inviolable bars
> That bound my farthest flight.
>
> And when some plain old carol in the street
> Quickening a shining angel in my brain,
> I knew that even his passionate wings should beat
> Upon those bars in vain.
>
> And then I asked if God omnipotent
> Himself was caught within the snare, or free,
> And would the bars at His command relent,—
> And none could answer me."

Of Mr. Drinkwater's view on Christianity, I cannot presume to speak for, as in the poem just quoted, he commits himself to no statement of belief ; and only in two or three poems do I recall more than a passing reference to Christianity's Divine Founder. The first is a war-poem, *Eclipse*, which I quote in full :

> " A man is dead . . . another dead . . .
> God ! can you count the companies
> Of stars across dear heaven spread ?
> They are numbered even as these.

Blind brain of the world! And is the day
   Moving about its Christmas bells?
Poor spinning brain, and wellaway . . .
   Christ . . . Christ? But no man tells.

The thoughts of men are kings. They keep
   The crown, the sepulchre, the song.
The thoughts of men are kings. They sleep . . .
   The thrones are empty overlong.

So rebel death a million-fold
   Of lamentable service takes.
The prophesying heart is cold . . .
   Is cold . . . or breaks.

What now were best? Some little thing?
   To trim the dock-weed, cleanse the floor,
To die, to grieve on death, to bring
   The pitcher to the door?

Dig deep the grave, hew down the tree,
   Shatter the millstones, break the plough.
And was there once a Calvary?
   And thorns upon His brow?"

By the title, *Eclipse*, and by the last line, I take
the poet's meaning to be that the sufferings of the
Crucified One on Calvary have been eclipsed by
the sufferings of soldiers in war. My only comment
is that the anguish of soul which brought sweat of
blood to the brow of Him who prayed in Gethsemane,
was possibly infinitely more agonizing than the
physical tortures of Calvary.

The other poem which centres around the figure of
the Saviour is entitled *A Christmas Night*:

" Christ for a dream was given from the dead
   To walk one Christmas night on earth again,
Among the snow, among the Christmas bells.
He heard the hymns that are His praise; *Noel*
And *Christ is Born*, and *Babe of Bethlehem*.

He saw the travelling crowds happy for home,
The gathering and the welcome, and the set

Feast and the gifts, because He once was born,
Because He once was steward of a word.
And so He thought, ' The spirit has been kind ;
So well the peoples might have fallen from Me,
My way of life being difficult and spare.
It is beautiful that a dream in Galilee
Should prosper so. They crucified Me once,
And now My name is spoken through the world,
And bells are rung for Me and candles burnt.
They might have crucified My dream who used
My body ill ; they might have spat on Me
Always as in one hour on Golgotha.' . . .
And the snow fell, and the last bell was still,
And the poor Christ again was with the dead."

From a poem describing either an actual or an imagined dream, no construction in regard to the writer's religious belief can be drawn. The two poems, the only two, so far as I am aware, which touch directly upon the subject of Christianity, are quoted here, so that Mr. Drinkwater may speak for himself, and the reader draw his or her own construction, without comment of mine.

The Poet's Frequent Note
of Thanksgiving

Where Mr. Drinkwater never fails is in thanksgiving. Again and again the same glad and grateful note is sounded. I must quote only one of many instances :

" Thank God for sleep in the long quiet night,
    For the clear day calling through the little leaded panes.
For the shining well water and the warm golden light,
    And the paths washed white by singing rains.

    .   .   .   .   .   .

Thank God for good bread, for the honey in the comb,
    For the brown-shelled eggs, for the clustered blossoms set
Beyond the open window in a pink and cloudy form,
    For the laughing loves among the branches met.

For the kind-faced women we bring our thanks to Thee,
    With shapely mothering arms and grave eyes clear and blithe,
For the tall young men, strong-thewed as men may be,
    For the old man bent above his scythe.

For earth's little secret and innumerable ways,
    For the carol and the colour, Lord, we bring
What things may be of thanks, and what Thou has lent our
    days
    Eyes to see and ears to hear and lips to sing."

I have spoken of Mr. Drinkwater's self-consciousness, but it is chiefly in his later writings that he shows a passion for theorizing about art, and for holding, as it were, ante-mortem examinations upon the psychology of his own soul. In his earlier work his self-consciousness is not apparent. The earliest book of his in my possession is *Poems of Men and Hours*, published in 1911, whereas *Tides* from which the poem *To Alice Meynell* is taken was issued in 1917. In this first book not a few of my quotations will be found. Here is his noble poem *A Prayer*. Could anything be simpler, stronger or more direct than these concluding stanzas ?—

" Grant us the will to fashion as we feel,
    Grant us the strength to labour as we know,
    Grant us the purpose, ribbed and edged with steel,
    To strike the blow.

Knowledge we ask not—knowledge Thou hast lent,
    But, Lord, the will—there lies our bitter need,
    Give us to build above the deep intent
    The deed, the deed."

Here, too, is the poem *Love* in which he speaks of love as—

" Sole echo of the silver choirs
    Whose dwelling is eternity."

Here too is *A Harvest Thanksgiving*, with the exquisite and perfect imagery of the second of these two lines :

" From down the little lane that wound away
Towards the drooping lashes of the day."

In the same poem we find these lines :

" For surely something to the song he brings
Who cherishes the song the singer sings."

If I have brought something of criticism to my
estimate of Mr. Drinkwater's poems, I do in all
sincerity also bring no little gratitude for poems that
I admire and treasure. In the same volume I find
The Dead Critic, the generosity of which makes one
living and perhaps carping critic feel particularly
small :

" Not of the high heroic line was he
Who wrought the world's deep music, but he knew
The spring pellucid whence rapt poets drew
Brave draughts of Hippocrene ; he held in fee
The songs that woke to immortality,
Trembling from other lips. His loving grew
From loving unto prophecy ; he threw
Untruth from out the fields of poesy.
Yea, though he sang not, he was unto song
A light, a benediction. His desire
Was but to serve his heroes, and we reap
The fruit of his humility. Among
Their names shall his be spoken, and their quire
Shall let him fall upon no barren sleep."

In this early volume, one finds the poems on *Oxford*,
and *London at Night*, already quoted, as well as the
simple but lovely *January Dusk*, which I copy here :

" Austere and clad in sombre robes of grey,
With hands upfolded and with silent wings,
In unimpassioned mystery the day
Passes, a lonely thrush its requiem sings.

The dusk of night is tangled in the boughs
Of leafless lime and lilac, and the pine
Grows blacker, and the star upon the brows
Of sleep is set in heaven for a sign.

s

> Earth's little weary peoples fall on peace
> And dream of breaking buds and blossoming,
> Of primrose airs, of days of large increase,
> And all the coloured retinue of spring."

In the same volume is the poem *At Rottingdean.
To A. N.* No one who has forgathered with Alfred
Noyes at Rottingdean will question who " A. N." is,
for Mr. Drinkwater has with skill and felicity caught
and reproduced the lilting measure which Mr. Noyes
has made so peculiarly his own :

> " The days are sweet at Rottingdean,
> And very sweet at Rottingdean,
> Where leagues of downland travel north and southward leagues
> of sea,
> A sea that flashes blue and green
> With purple shadows thrown between,
> And downs that gather up the song of all the winds that be."

Lastly, in this slender and early volume, *Poems of
Men and Hours,* we find not only *Expectancy,* but
the lovely lines, *The Miracle* :

> " Come, sweetheart, listen, for I have a thing
> Most wonderful to tell you—news of spring.
>
> Albeit winter still is in the air,
> And the earth troubled, and the branches bare,
>
> Yet down the fields to-day I saw her pass—
> The spring—her feet went shining through the grass.
>
> She touched the ragged hedgerows—I have seen
> Her finger-prints, most delicately green ;
>
> And she has whispered to the crocus leaves,
> And to the garrulous sparrows in the eaves.
>
> Swiftly she passed, and shyly, and her fair
> Young face was hidden in her cloudy hair.
>
> She would not stay—her season is not yet ;
> But she has reawakened, and has set

The sap of all the world astir, and rent
Once more the shadows of our discontent.

Triumphant news—a miracle I sing—
The everlasting miracle of spring."

After these instances of simplicity, directness, and beauty, all taken from one volume of Mr. Drinkwater's earlier work, I have neither the heart nor the inclination to say more of the self-conscious blight which has fallen upon some of his later poems. Nor do I wish further to pursue the subject unless it be to say that here, surely, is yet another instance of Portia's saying, in *The Merchant of Venice*, " I can easier teach twenty what were good to be done than be one of the twenty to follow mine own teaching." For it is John Drinkwater, and no other, who warns us, in his fine essay on Thomas Gray, that " Great poetry is never self-conscious."

One other point and I have done with unappreciative criticism, which is never to my liking. *Love's House* is as true, as human, and as beautiful a picture of wedded love, as I can recall. What could be finer than this dispersal—as if they had never been —of the foolish and hasty misunderstandings, the " fallings out " as Tennyson calls them, even between those who love each other truly, or this reference to the " dear reproof " which, if only for love's sake, love must sometimes administer to love?

. . . .

" Dark words, and hasty humours of the blood
  Have come to us and made no longer stay
Than footprints of a bird upon the mud
  That in an hour the tide will take away.

But not March weather over ploughlands blown,
  Nor cresses green upon their gravel bed,
Are beautiful with the clean rigour grown
  Of quiet thought our love has piloted.

. . . .

> When from some dusty corners of my brain
>   Comes limping some ungainly word or deed,
> I know not if my dearest friend's disdain
>   Be durable or brief, spent husk or seed.
>
> But your rebuke and that poor fault of mine
>   Go straitly outcast, and we close the door,
> And I, no promise asking and no sign,
>   Stand blameless in love's presence as before."

These lines do honour to the loved one to whom they are addressed and even greater honour to the lover who can so feel and write. But there is a last quatrain which I must quote :

> " I do not question love, I am a lord
>   High at love's table, and the vigilant king,
> Unquestioned from the hubbub at the board
>   Leans down to me and tells me everything."

My reluctant comment on this must be to regret that the poet and lover should close a beautiful love poem on the note of self. Just as in some of his patriotic poems I miss the service spirit of Maurice Baring, the public-school spirit of Henry Newbolt, the glad forgetfulness—for England's sake and the grandeur of her cause—of self, and all that makes for self, of Rupert Brooke, so in the close of this poem, and in certain other love poems by Mr. Drinkwater, I miss the noble note, which gives all, and forgets self, for love's sake, which marks great love poetry. Perhaps the fault lies in Mr. Drinkwater's conception of love. In *Love's Personality* he writes :

> " If I had never seen
>   Thy sweet grave face,
> If I had never known
>   Thy pride as of a queen,
> Yet would another's grace
> Have led me to her throne.

> I should have loved as well
> Not loving thee,
> My faith had been as strong
> Wrought by another spell ;
> Her love had grown to be
> As thine for fire and song."

It is not so that Stephen Phillips sings of love :

> " His kiss was on her lips ere she was born."

Nor Rossetti :

> " O born with me somewhere that men forget,
> And though in years of sight and sound unmet,
> Known for my soul's birth-partner."

Mr. Drinkwater conveys the impression, not of the inevitability of love, but that, had he and the loved one never met, another might equally well have served his turn, and made him equally happy. Perhaps that is why his noble anthem of love falls at the end upon a shriller note. I remember a recital when a great organist-composer closed on a chord—he was using the *vox humana* stop—which held the soul of his listeners quivering like a thin flame. In the *vox humana*, thus used, we seemed to hear, gathered up into a single strain, the very " still and music of humanity." But the organist who closes his recital by a trumpet-like flourish on the stop of self—even though he be a great composer—leaves us less sure of his greatness as a lover. I hasten to add, for fear of misconception, that self-consciousness by no means implies selfishness, for some of the most self-conscious folk I have met were also the most unselfish. Elsewhere Mr. Drinkwater has written of love as only one who loves nobly and unselfishly could write. In the Dedication of *Poems of Love and Earth* to his wife he says :

> " And you, my Lady, to whose lap I bring
> This little treasure of my voyaging,

> Of you I take how much, of how great worth—
> Of your hands healing, peace of your good care,
> Of your hope strength all perilous things to dare,
> And fellowship with you in Love and Earth."

What woman's heart, as she reads these lines, and those in the poem *Petition*, will not warm to the lover and husband whose first thought is for the one around whom centres all that is meant by the beautiful word, Home, and will not be touched by the prayer that to him may be given to surround her home life with all the joy, the help, and the happiness, that she has given to him ?   Even when he shows us only himself in his own home, we project into the picture out of our own mind, and from our memory of her as drawn by him, the image of Mrs. Drinkwater. And a very lovely picture it is, that of the wisest, sweetest, most womanly, and most comradely of helpmeets and counsellors.   Here is the last verse of the poem, *From London*, in which the poet sees his wife, watching for the hour of his return :

> " The scent of the ploughlands is calling me away,
>   The chatter of the rooks, the open skies,
> And she I know is waiting with the glory of the day
> And the shadow of the night in her eyes."

Loyalties, as the title of one of John Drinkwater's books, is no misnomer, for loyal he is by nature— in friendship as in love.   Every book of his is a record of friendship, and his friends are many. No one who knows Mr. Edmund Gosse, either personally or by his books, can think of him, his seventy odd years notwithstanding, as other than young in heart, in interests and in intellect ; but Mr. Gosse's eternal youthfulness has never been so gracefully indicated as in the second sonnet which forms the dedication, " To E. G.," of *Olton Pools* :

" But there are men who, in the time of age,
  Sometimes remember all that age forgets :
The early hope, the hardly compassed wage,
  The change of corn, and snow, and violets ;
They are glad of praise ; they know this morning brings
  As true a song as any yesterday ;
Their labour still is set to many things,
  They cry their questions out along the way.
They give as who may gladly take again
  Some gift at need ; they move with gallant ease
Among all eager companies of men ;
  And never signed of age are such as these,
They speak with youth, and never speak amiss ;
Of such are you, and what is youth but this ? "

Equally happy is the Dedication of *Tides* to
General Sir Ian Hamilton :

" Because the daring chivalries,
  That light your battle line, belong
To music's heart no less than these,
I bring you my campaigns of song."

To Swinburne, George Meredith, Mr. Thomas
Hardy, Mr. R. C. Lehmann, and Sir William Watson
(whom Mr. Drinkwater hails as " Master, and majestic
maker of majestic song "), song-tribute of homage or
of friendship is offered. To the younger poets, his
contemporaries, Mr. Noyes, Mr. Masefield, Mr.
Siegfried Sassoon, Mr. Robert Garves, the late Francis
Ledwidge, Mr. Nichols, Mr. Ernest Selincourt, and
others, the largest of Mr. Drinkwater's praise is so
generous that when he writes of

" Some heroic hour when I behold
  A friend's long-quested triumph,"

one knows that he feels as felt the great painter who,
in the days of his own obscurity, cried out in exultant
pride, at sight of the work of a master, to whose
eminence the young painter saw small likelihood of
attaining : " And I, too, am an artist ! "

As I interpret the man by his writings, John Drinkwater is, I believe, constitutionally incapable of meaness, envy, or jealousy.   I do not mean that he poses as being other than healthily human.   On the contrary he gives us a delightful and all too rare touch of humour in the glimpse of his own self-conscious self, when he writes :

> " And if a Bishop speaks to me,
> I tremble with propriety."

Nor is he too healthily human not to resent a mean attack, or to protest that he is other than restless under censure, and glad to be greatly praised, but—given honesty and no ill intention in a dispraiser—I question whether there would be a thought of petty rancour in John Drinkwater's mind.   He would not thank you for—

> " Poor profitable smiles upon the face
> Of truth, when smiles are none, nor fear to own
> The bitterness of beauty overthrown,
> But hold in hate the gilded lie's disgrace."

His hatred of insincerity—of smooth falsehood as of foul lies—his invincible determination to be honest of deed and word at every cost, are, as Mr. Drinkwater would word it, " the signature " of his character. I do not say this because he writes fiercely of falsehood and finely of honesty.   Fine sentiments about honesty, love, courage, patriotism, even religion, are written or talked every day, and with all the power, art, or charm, of the born writer, the born orator.   But unless a man have put *himself*, his real self, into what he says or writes, we may admire alike the beauty of his sentiments, or the felicity of his language, but in some strange way we do not feel the man himself behind his words.   A great preacher was indignant and angry when a flatterer expressed admiration for a sermon.   " I do not preach sermons to be admired but to be felt," he said sternly. In the pulpit or on the stage, it may be possible—I do not know—by magnetism of personality, to simulate passion. But words written and printed in cold ink cannot *act*. Where there is no commanding presence, no gesture, no sight of a light in the eye, nor sound of emotion in the voice, to make the spoken word mean more than it really means, but only cold lines of print in a book—simulated feeling carries no conviction. Only when a man breathes into the cold dust of his written words the living breath of his own life, his own soul's true self—then and then only do those who thereafter read his words, hear and feel the soul of the writer speaking to their souls. Never is John Drinkwater more himself than when he not pleads, but commands, his fellows to like honesty to his own:

> " Give me a dozen men whose theme
> Is honesty, and we will set
> On high the banner of dreams . . . and yet
> Thousands will pass us in a stream,
> Nor care a penny what we dream."

None the less, the poet will

> " Create a world for every day,
> And store a dream for every night,"

and so long as he lives no lie shall go unchallenged by him :

> " If one should tell you that in such a spring
> The hawthorns boughs into the blackbird's nest
> Poured poison, or that once at harvesting
> The ears were stony, from so manifest
> Slander of proven faith in tree and corn
> You would turn unheeding, knowing him forsworn.
>
> Yet now, when one whose life has never known
> Corruption, as you know ; whose days have been
> As daily tiding in your heart of lone
> And gentle courage, suffers the word unclean

Of envious tongues, doubting you dare not cry—
'I have been this man's familiar, and you lie.'"

Mark Twain once wittily, if irreverently, said that
a lie is an abomination to the Lord, and a very
present help in time of trouble. Mr. Drinkwater
will have no such help. In a poem only of nine lines
he expresses his own abomination of false speaking
more effectively than some poets could in twice the
space :

" Dawn is up at my window, and in the maytree
The finches gossip, and tits, and beautiful sparrows
With feathers bright and brown as September hazels.

The sunlight is here, filtered through rosy curtains,
Docile and disembodied, a ghost of sunlight,
A gentle light to greet the dreamer returning.

Part the curtains. I give you salutation
Day, clear day ; let us be friendly fellows.
Come . . . I hear the Liars about the city."

Except for one echo of Rossetti to which attention has been drawn, and, in his later work, some
suggestion of the influence of Mr. Hardy, there is
nothing in Mr. Drinkwater's work which can be
called derivative. He is not only, as Sir William
Watson has said of himself, " A tarrying minstrel who
finds, not fashions, his numbers," but he has found,
evolved, or fashioned an instrument of his own. Of
how many in the orchestra of song can this be said ?
Life is a drama on which the curtain never falls, nor
is the auditorium ever empty. The place of a few is
on the stage, the place of most of us is in the body
of the theatre. By and by, whether we be actor, or
one of the audience, the messenger comes to whisper
us away, whither we shall never return. We pass out
silently, often unnoticed ; and, as silently, and sometimes as unnoticed, another steals in, to occupy our
place. So, too, with those who sit in the orchestra,

whose task it is to make music, while others in the
theatre look on and listen. What Mr. Drinkwater
says of Beauty, is equally true of Poetry :

> " For beauty, seen of humble eyes,
> Immortal habitation has
> Though beauty's form may pale and pass."

There comes no break, no moment's pause, in Life's
symphony, which is immortal, and so unending.
This or that musician's hand is failing, his eyes are
dimming ; he has come to the end of his " score,"
but the orchestra may not stop. Ere he has risen
to pass out, another player has stolen in, to take
bow and fiddle from his hand.

It was so that John Drinkwater entered the
immortal orchestra of song, but he would have none
of any other musician's instrument, electing to use
one of his own bringing, and when he lays that
instrument down, no other hand can touch it to like
music.

Were I to vary the simile, and to consider him as
a soloist, not as one of an orchestra, I should be
tempted to speak of his work as Chamber-Music,
as best heard, and appreciated, by reason of its small
volume of sound, in a room, rather than in a hall.
I am not sure that I ought not to say " in a room in
his own home," for in Mr. Drinkwater's work there
is often a happy and homely touch of domesticity.
Best of all, the reader is free of that same domesticity.
If you would be of his company, you must be so as
a friend, as a comradely companion or not at all.

His Cotswold Home
Poems

Turning to his homelier poems from those which
are more ambitious, you feel as one might feel who,
after hearing Mr. Drinkwater's play *Abraham Lincoln*

applauded by an admiring audience, had the good
luck, when passing out, to run into the poet-dramatist
at the stage door, and to be carried off by him to his
own home.

> " It is strange how we travel the wide world over,
>   And see great churches and foreign streets,
> And armies afoot and kings of wonder,
>   And deeds a-doing to fill the sheets
> That grave historians will pen
> To ferment the brains of simple men.
>
> And all the time the heart remembers
>   The quiet habit of one far place,
> The drawings and books, the turn of a passage,
>   The glance of a dear familiar face,
> And there is the true cosmopolis,
> While the throning world a phantom is."

Best of all, he makes you free of that home, free,
even of that " turn of a passage " :

> " High up in the sky there, now, you know,
>   In this May twilight, our cottage is asleep,
> Tenantless, and no creature there to go
>   Near it, but Mrs. Fry's fat cows, and sheep
> Dove-coloured, as is Cotswold. No one hears
>   Under the cherry tree the nightjars yet,
> The windows are uncurtained, on the stairs
>   Silence is but by tip-toe silence met.
> All doors are fast there. It is a dwelling put by
> From use for a little, or long, up there in the sky.
>
> Empty ; a walled-in silence, in this twilight of May—
>   A home for lovers, and friendly withdrawing, and sleep,
> With none to love there, nor laugh, nor climb from the day
>   To the candles and linen. . . . Yet in the silence creep,
> This minute, I know, little ghosts, little virtuous lives,
>   Breathing upon that still, insensible place,
> Touching the latches, sorting the napkins and knives,
>   And such for the comfort of being, and bowls for the grace,
> That roses will brim ; they are creeping from that room to this,
>   One room, and two, till the four are visited . . . they,
> Little ghosts, little lives, are our thoughts in this twilight of
>   May.

Signs that even the curious man would miss,
Of travelling lovers to Cotswold, signs of an hour,
Very soon, when up from the valley in June will ride
Lovers by Lynch to Oakridge up in the wide
Bow of the hill, to a garden of lavender flower. . . .
The doors are locked ; no foot falls ; the hearths are dumb—
But we are there—we are waiting ourselves who come."

As Henry Bishop set the words of *Home Sweet Home* to sweet and simple music that cannot die, so John Drinkwater has brought the four corners of the world within the walls of a cottage home among the Cotswolds, and has made that cottage home loved of us all.

Maurice Baring one would wish to read under the shadow of purple Sicilian hills, lulled by the lapping of waters, and drowsed by the odours of many poppies, till Proserpine should come to cast over us the spell of her dreamless sleep. Henry Newbolt's poems we would carry with us to a Devon combe, or to where great waters dip the white ensign of their spray to some high admiral's flag. For Kipling, one might set up a lectern alike on land or sea, in India, in Africa, or the wide world over ; in drill-yard, in barrack-room, or on battlefield. Alfred Noyes one would steal away to the woods to read, and while blackbird and thrush were fluting, lilting, and trilling to a fairies' dance. But John Drinkwater, true poet and sturdy Englishman every grain of him, one would wish to read in autumn, and somewhere out Avon way, or near by the shelter of a Cotswold copse. Most of all one would wish to read him in his own Cotswold garden, where, haply, an English robin might draw near, to play an accompaniment to our reading, and to sprinkle the crisp autumn air with a blithe and beautiful *obligato* of bird song.

For in some of Mr. Drinkwater's slighter poems there is that which recalls the rare note of the robin. I say " rare " in the sense that it is the very rarification of song, a distillation, into diamond drops of music, of all that was florid and over-toned in the choirs of spring and early summer ; and best read in the autumn because it has the pellucid and marvellous transparency of the clear filtered autumn atmosphere upon which it falls.